THE 2ND TEN COMMANDMENTS

Your Guide to Success In the Consciousness Age

11. FLOW	Maximize your time spent in FLOW and happiness.
12. WHOLENESS	Seek WHOLENESS through ongoing awareness and lifelong education.
13. SELF-ACCEPTANCE	Develop greater SELF-ACCEPTANCE by loving yourself unconditionally.
14. BALANCE	Live with BALANCE, priorities, and moderation in all things.
15. INNER VOICE-MISSION	Act true to your INNER VOICE and fulfill your MISSION.
16. SURRENDER-COURAGE	Exercise mature SURRENDER and unselfish COURAGE.
17. UNCONDITIONAL LOVE	Feel UNCONDITIONAL LOVE and recognize the oneness of humanity.
18. BOTTOM LINES	Base your level of relationship commitments on BOTTOM LINES — what you can't live with and can't live without.
19. SYNERGY	Create SYNERGY by using *win-win* and setting *boundaries*.
20. REPAIR	REPAIR the world by treating others reverently and fairly and doing good deeds.

(Tear out a copy and post it or give it to someone you care about.)

Excerpted from the book:

THE 2ND TEN COMMANDMENTS

Your Guide to Success In the Consciousness Age

Comments and inquiries very welcome.

Published By:

GLOBAL BRAIN™, INC.

555 Bryant St., #369
Palo Alto, CA 94301-1704
USA

Orders: 1-800-U-GO-GLOBAL
    (1-800-846-4562)
    (within the United States)
Tel. 415/327-2012
FAX 415/327-2028
E-mail: GloblBrain@aol.com
http://www.globalbrain.com/global/2ndten

THE 2ND TEN COMMANDMENTS

Your Guide to Success In the Consciousness Age

11. FLOW	Maximize your time spent in FLOW and happiness.
12. WHOLENESS	Seek WHOLENESS through ongoing awareness and lifelong education.
13. SELF-ACCEPTANCE	Develop greater SELF-ACCEPTANCE by loving yourself unconditionally.
14. BALANCE	Live with BALANCE, priorities, and moderation in all things.
15. INNER VOICE-MISSION	Act true to your INNER VOICE and fulfill your MISSION.
16. SURRENDER-COURAGE	Exercise mature SURRENDER and unselfish COURAGE.
17. UNCONDITIONAL LOVE	Feel UNCONDITIONAL LOVE and recognize the oneness of humanity.
18. BOTTOM LINES	Base your level of relationship commitments on BOTTOM LINES — what you can't live with and can't live without.
19. SYNERGY	Create SYNERGY by using *win-win* and setting *boundaries*.
20. REPAIR	REPAIR the world by treating others reverently and fairly and doing good deeds.

(Tear out a copy and post it or give it to someone you care about.)

Excerpted from the book:

THE 2ND TEN COMMANDMENTS
Your Guide to Success In the Consciousness Age

Comments and inquiries very welcome.

Published By:

GLOBAL BRAIN™, INC.

555 Bryant St., #369
Palo Alto, CA 94301-1704
USA

Orders: 1-800-U-GO-GLOBAL
      (1-800-846-4562)
      (within the United States)
Tel. 415/327-2012
FAX 415/327-2028
E-mail: GloblBrain@aol.com
http://www.globalbrain.com/global/2ndten

What People Are Saying About This Book:

". . . Orion Kopelman's book is so valuable. He integrates some of the key concepts of [the] eternal wisdom into a simple set of principles that we can all follow. . . . They are principles that will allow the global brain to function as an integrated, synergetic whole. They are principles that will give the global brain a global heart."

from Foreword by **Peter Russell**, Author of *The Global Brain Awakens, The White Hole in Time*, and five other books

"Orion Kopelman has created a great synthesis between consciousness, technology, evolution and morality. I consider this book to be a signal of the emerging field of conscious evolution. It is a powerful tool for all of us in this time of confusion. I highly recommend it."

Barbara Marx Hubbard, Futurist, Author, *The Revelation, The Hunger of Eve*

"Great book."

Robert Muller, Asst. Secretary-General Emeritus of the United Nations, trusted advisor of three Secretary-Generals, 1948-1993, Recipient of UNESCO Prize for Peace

"*The 2nd Ten Commandments* is an excellent introduction to the new world we're about to enter. It is a wonderful manual based on a broad vision of the human predicament. And what is more, it provides sound directions and practical advice for how to survive and prosper in the next century."

Dr. Mihaly Csikszentmihalyi, author of *Flow: The Psychology of Optimal Experience, The Evolving Self: A Psychology for the Third Millennium*, Professor and former Chairman, Department of Psychology, University of Chicago

"These principles will lead you on a path to total fulfillment and enjoyment."

Ken Keyes, Jr., Author of the million-copy bestseller *Handbook to Higher Consciousness*, Founder of the Science of Happiness and Caring Rapid Counseling

"I was excited and gratified to see you apply your tremendous talent to propagating this critically needed message. I particularly like your harmonizing modern technology with the eternal truths. While these are often seen as being in conflict, a true message of oneness must look, as yours does, for the thread that binds. I wish you every success."
  Martin E. Hellman, Professor of Electrical Engineering, Stanford University, Western Editor of *Breakthrough: Emerging New Thinking*

"A must book for all those who want to live a Happy, Healthy, and Holy life beyond year 2000."
  Siri Singh Sahib (Yogi Bhajan, Ph.D.), Sikh Dharma of the Western Hemisphere, Former President of the World Council of Religions

"This book indeed describes the world we will all be living in—one where you can live anywhere and do your thing thanks to technology. However, unless people adhere to the spiritual principles discussed here, I'm afraid "Big Brother" will be watching us everywhere."
  Thomas L. Brzozowski, Realtor, Maui, Hawaii

". . . A lively, clever presentation of some important observations."
  Willis Harman, President, Institute of Noetic Sciences, Author of *Global Mind Change*

". . . I applaud your efforts and willingness to carry these ideas to a large general audience. . . . I confess that I feel liberated by my belief in the inevitability of the approaching transformations. It is good for people to stay in their seats, as to whether there is anything they should or need to do I am not sure. I feel that we are on an encounter trajectory with a hyper-dimensional object and that human history always responds as it must to the unfoldment of this mystery. . . . Much discussion and soul-searching lies between us and 2012 no matter what the outcome."
  Terence McKenna, Author of *The Archaic Revival*

"This book is not only enlightening, it is exciting and stimulating. Very eloquently written . . . intellectually thought-provoking, it has a way of understanding our purpose on this planet. It offers a way of integration with ourselves for universal betterment."
  Lerma Nagal, Real Estate Agent, Aptos, California

"As our information society accelerates, authors and publishers need new tools. Orion Kopelman has discovered the formula for business success and has provided a road map."

Dan Poynter, Author of *The Self-Publishing Manual* and 70 other books

"Provides an excellent set of guidelines for the individual severed from the security of our familiar ancestral environment and somewhat adrift and inadequately prepared, and to say the least, stressed out by the world in which we now find ourselves. . . . In working with the evolution of culture and with the somewhat new perspective of evolutionary psychology, it seems that people today are especially in need of (such) guidelines of how to do and be in this new world which we have helped to create."

Richard L. Rathbun, Trustee, Foundation for Global Community

"It is meaty! There is a lot to think about and muse about. Your strong assertions and convictions request the reader to *really* try on these ideas. You make a compelling case, weaving the scientific with elemental truths and the empirical. I really love your work."

Jan Reynolds, Vice President, Portal Publications Ltd.

"I rejoice that your message, which I deeply believe in, will at last reach people who need it but might not otherwise hear it: particularly the Four P's (Pale Patriarchal Penis People) in business and government who run our country so greedily and shortsightedly. You make concepts accessible to them and others that have been confined to more enlightened segments of our society until now. And you bring these ideas together in an easy-to-grasp form that everyone, enlightened or not, should appreciate."

Ellen Roddick, Author of *Writing That Means Business*

"This work goes well beyond the self-help, spiritual awakening, and consciousness material I've seen across my desk."

Stanley M. Thiessen, President, Partnership Book Services

THE 2ND TEN COMMANDMENTS

*Your Guide to Success
In the Consciousness Age*

ORION MOSHE KOPELMAN
WITH MARC LEHRER, PH.D.

GLOBAL BRAIN™
PALO ALTO, CALIFORNIA, USA

Published By:

GLOBAL BRAIN™ , INC.

555 Bryant St., #369
Palo Alto, CA 94301-1704, USA

Orders: 1-800-U-GO-GLOBAL
(1-800-846-4562)
(within the United States)
Tel. 415/327-2012
FAX 415/327-2028
e-mail: GloblBrain@aol.com
http://www.globalbrain.com/global/2ndten

"Synergizing Technology and Consciousness"

Global Brain™, Inc.'s purpose is to accelerate the development of appropriate technology and personal evolution to further the formation of a sane Global Brain.

First Printing 1996

Printed in the United States of America

Publisher's Cataloging in Publication
(Prepared by Quality Books, Inc.)
Kopelman, Orion Moshe.
    The 2nd ten commandments: your guide to success in the consciousness age / Orion Moshe Kopelman with Marc Lehrer.
        p. cm.
    Includes bibliographical references and index.
    ISBN: 1-885261-02-0
    1. Self-actualization. 2. Spiritual life. 3. Consciousness. 4. God. 5. New Age movement. 6. Kopelman, Orion Moshe. I. Title. II. Title: Second ten commandments.

BF637.S4K67 1996   158.1
                                    QBI95-20752

Content Editing: Shirli Kopelman, Jerusalem, Israel; Danielle LaPorte, Seattle, Washington; Gloria St. John, El Cerrito, California

Copy Editing: Nancy Capelle, Santa Barbara, California; Joel Friedlander, San Rafael, California; Ellen Roddick, Santa Fe, New Mexico

Cover design by Lightbourne Images, Ashland, Oregon

Layout design by Joel Friedlander, JFBOOKMAN@AOL.COM

Final proofreading by Margaret Dodd

CONTENTS

FOREWORD BY PETER RUSSELL xiii

**PART I: EVOLUTION TO A GLOBAL BRAIN AND
THE CONSCIOUSNESS AGE** 1

  1. An Invitation to the Global Promised Land 3

  2. Your Flight Plan Summary 13

  3. The Map for Success as a Motof 19

  4. From Moses to Motofs: From Slavery to Freedom 45

  5. The Impact of Accelerating Change 69

  6. Humanity and Technology Form the Global Brain 87

  7. Does 2012 A.D. Equal 0 G.B. (Global Brain)? 101

  8. Gev: An Updated, Universal Concept of God 109

  9. Global Spirituality Creates a Heaven-on-Earth 119

  10. The Rewards of Truth and Freedom 133

PART II: THE COMMANDMENTS .137

  11. Commandment No. 11: FLOW 138

  12. Commandment No. 12: WHOLENESS 144

  13. Commandment No. 13: SELF-ACCEPTANCE 154

  14. Commandment No. 14: BALANCE 160

  15. Commandment No. 15: INNER VOICE-MISSION 168

  16. Commandment No. 16: SURRENDER-COURAGE 178

  17. Commandment No. 17: UNCONDITIONAL LOVE 184

  18. Commandment No. 18: BOTTOM LINES 192

  19. Commandment No. 19: SYNERGY 202

  20. Commandment No. 20: REPAIR 212

**PART III: GETTING ON THE PATH TO THE GLOBAL
PROMISED LAND** 221

21. Accepting the Responsibility of Being a Motof 223
22. Nine Great Ideas for Becoming a Motof 231
23. Motofs: The Adapters Survive and Succeed 245
24. One Is All, and All Are One .261

AFTERWORD: DO YOU WANT TO SAVE CHANGES?
[YES, NO, CANCEL, HELP] 267

Appendix A: Orion's Journey of Discovery 273
Appendix B: Religions of the World 293
Appendix C: Recommended Reading 295
Acknowledgments 299
Glossary 303
Notes and References 307
Index 315

FOREWORD

By Peter Russell

THE MOST EXCITING TIMES

We are living through the most exciting times in human history. Since the dawn of civilization, human beings have sought to understand the nature of the universe in which they find themselves; and now, in our lifetimes, we stand on the edge of realizing our ambitions. Mathematicians are getting close to discovering Einstein's long-dreamt-of "Unified Field Theory"—or "Theory of Everything", as it is sometimes called—the synthesis of all the laws of nature into a single set of equations. Astrophysicists are looking out to the edges of the universe and beginning to understand how this universe was born. Molecular biologists are fathoming the code of life, and by the turn of the millennium should have completed the deciphering of our own genetic programs.

At the same time, our burgeoning technologies are fulfilling many of our long-held dreams. We can create virtually any comfort we desire. We can travel round the planet in less than a day—and even step off the planet into space. We can talk to almost anyone, anywhere, and observe events around the world as they happen. We've built computers and robots to do tasks that we could never do. For centuries we have sought to be free from the drudgery of work, and now, at last, our goal is in sight.

Moreover, not only are these some of the most significant times in human history, they may also be some of the most significant in the history of this planet. They are, in some respects, the culmination of a trend that has been developing ever since the dawn of life on Earth. To see why, we need to consider the history of evolution not in terms of the familiar story of the development of structure and form—the evolution of biology—but in terms of a parallel, although less visible, evolution of life's ability to process information.

THE EVOLUTION OF LIFE ON EARTH

At the core of all life on earth is DNA, a highly complex organic molecule containing millions of atoms. These molecules are life's data banks. Encoded within them are programs that specify the structure of the basic building blocks of life. The code itself consists of only four "letters", but, combined in triplets, they form a language of sixty-four "words". Strung together, these words build "sentences", often hundreds of words long, defining complex biological molecules. The numbers and types of molecules produced determine the structure and form of the cells that are created, which in turn determine the structure and form of the organism. From this perspective, the evolution of life is the evolution of the information stored in the DNA molecules.

Approximately halfway through life's evolutionary journey, a major breakthrough occurred in the way this information was handed down from one cell to another. Until then life had reproduced by a process of "asexual reproduction", in which a cell simply divided into two sister cells. The two new cells contained the same genetic information as the original cell: they were genetic clones. With the advent of "sexual reproduction", however, two cells came together and shared their inherited genetic information, and from this combination produced a new cell with a new set of codes. Until this time genetic information had evolved very slowly over time—only as errors crept into the code could the genetic databases change; now a new database was created with every reproductive act. This was a most significant advance in molecular information processing. As a result, the rate of evolution sped up a thousand times.

The development of senses was another major step forward in life's ability to process information. Organisms developed organs such as eyes, ears, and noses that enabled them to take in data from their environment. Some developed senses that were sensitive to heat radiation, to electric fields, or to the planet's magnetic field—whatever information would help the organism survive better.

The more data that organisms took in from their environment, the more processing was required. They needed to make sense of the data, filter out the "signal" from the "noise", extract the information from the data, decide what should be attended to, compare it with past experiences, and so build up a body of knowledge about their environment. To handle these tasks, life developed its own bio-chemical data processing systems—nervous systems.

Over time these systems have grown increasingly complex. This evolution has led to brains such as ours—some of the most complex information processors in the known universe. Brains are not only able to see, hear, taste, smell, and feel the world around and merge all this information into a single, integrated experience of reality, but also to think, reason, count, form concepts, develop theories, consider the future, create fantasies, experience hope, fear, sorrow, and joy, make conscious choices, contemplate the meaning of existence, and, most significant of all, ponder the nature of consciousness itself.

What has made all of this possible? Another evolutionary breakthrough in information processing: speech. Instead of having to build up their picture of the world solely from their own experiences, as for example a dog or cat does, human beings can share their experiences and learn from the experiences of others. As far as the evolution of information processing is concerned, this was as significant a breakthrough as the advent of sexual reproduction. Just as two cells come together to share their genetically inherited information, so two people can come together and share their perceptions and learning. From this came two major changes: the evolution of human culture underwent a very rapid acceleration—all that we call human history has taken place in the last one hundred thousandth of the Earth's history. At the same time, humanity began to form a single, integrated information-processing system, amassing its own collective body of knowledge.

At first the links were very localized. With speech alone, the sharing of ideas was limited largely to one's own tribe. But over time, humanity began making its own breakthroughs in information processing. Five thousand years ago, the advent of writing allowed us to make more permanent records of our experiences and hand them down to others. The development of pen and paper made our writings more transportable, enabling us to share ideas with people in distant lands. Five hundred years ago, the invention of printing made it possible to mass-produce the written word. Later breakthroughs allowed speech itself to travel farther: The telephone allowed us to talk to someone far away, and radio enabled one person to broadcast speech to many others. Television gave us the ability to "see at a distance". Fifty years ago, we created electronic information processors, speeding our development even further.

In the last few years, global telecommunications have taken us another step forward. The interlinking of human beings that began with the emergence of language has now progressed to the point where information can be transmitted to anyone, anywhere, at the speed of light. Billions of messages, continually shuttling back and forth in an ever-growing web of communication, link billions of minds together into a single global brain.

As yet this global telecommunications network is not nearly as complex as the network of cells inside our own brains—many of our billions of neurons are in direct communication with tens of thousands of other neurons. However, if our development continues to accelerate—and there is every reason to suppose that it will—then we could find the global brain's complexity paralleling that of the human brain in the early years of the next millennium.

OVERCOMING INSANITY WITH WISDOM

However, exciting and significant as these times may be, all is not well with humanity. Everywhere we look—at the atmosphere, the land, the rivers, the oceans—we find that human actions are upsetting the delicate fabric of life, threatening to destroy us, and with us, perhaps, life on this planet. Never before, as far as we know, has a species arisen which had such destructive potential.

We like to think of ourselves as the most intelligent species on this planet. But how intelligent is a species that can discover it is destroying the global biosystem upon which its own existence totally depends and then continue with that destruction? The question we are now being forced to consider is whether we are becoming a sane or insane global brain.

The issue is at its core one of values. Western civilization in particular has trapped itself in the belief that to be at peace within we have to adjust the world around. This might be true if we lacked a physical need, food or warmth, for example. But the majority of us in the more developed world have, thanks to our prolific creativity, been able to satisfy our physical needs. What drive us now are deeper psychological needs. But we continue to act as if these inner needs can be satisfied by the world around. If we are not at peace within we try gathering more material possessions or try some new experience. Unfortunately, such approaches provide only passing fulfillment at best, so like a drug addict looking for his or her next fix, we try again and again to extract inner peace from the world around. This is the root cause of our consumption, and the reason we continue to pour more and more waste into our environment.

We know in our hearts that this does not make sense. We know that whether or not we are at peace within depends not on what we have or do, but on our attitude and perceptions. We know that what we really need is not yet greater mastery of the material world, but a greater mastery of our own minds.

This knowing is the perennial wisdom behind all the great spiritual traditions. They have each in their own way sought to show us that it is our attachment to things that lies at the root of our unhappiness, not our lack of things. And they have each in their own way sought to release us from our materialist value system, so that we can live in greater peace, and with greater love for each other and for all living beings.

Unfortunately, however, this wisdom always gets lost. It is absorbed by society and takes on the garments of the material value system it came to replace. In the end, all that remain are various dogmas and doctrines—and a few good intentions.

Realigning oneself with this perennial wisdom has always been important for individual salvation. Today, however, it has also become crucial for our collective salvation. If we continue to think and act from a materialist mind-set—the belief that our inner well-being depends upon our outer well-being—then we will continue to exploit and abuse our surroundings until they are no longer capable of supporting us.

If humanity is to survive these most challenging and critical of times, we must insure that the values that are propagated through our global information matrix are values in accord with this perennial wisdom. But to do this we need to begin to live these values in our lives. This is why Orion Kopelman's book is so valuable. He integrates some of the key concepts of this eternal wisdom into a simple set of principles that we can all follow.

He further shows that those who learn to follow such principles in their lives will have a distinct evolutionary advantage in the times to come. They will be better able to cope with the pressures of accelerating change without burning out, better able to relate to and communicate in an increasingly complex world, and better able to summon the inner resources to guide themselves through what may well be the most turbulent times in human history. They are principles that will allow the global brain to function as an integrated, synergetic whole. They are principles that will give the global brain a global heart.

Peter Russell, author
The Global Brain Awakens,
The White Hole in Time

PART I

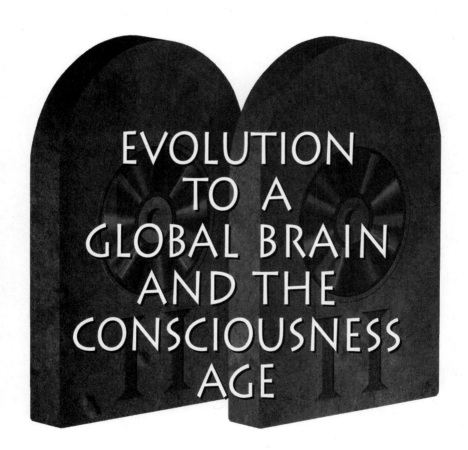

EVOLUTION TO A GLOBAL BRAIN AND THE CONSCIOUSNESS AGE

1

AN INVITATION TO THE GLOBAL PROMISED LAND

Life is not a puzzle to be solved, but a mystery to be lived.

> —John Bradshaw, modern psychologist

The Earth is a sphere, and a sphere has only one side. We are all on the same side.

> —A Peace Corps volunteer[1]

I n the beginning, we humans were put on Earth and had to first figure out how to survive. To do this, we roamed the planet as nomads for hundreds of thousands of years. Then, about 10,000 years ago, our ancestors began to settle down and experiment with various forms of civilization. What resulted is the recorded past of the human tribe, Homo sapiens.

By the years approaching 2000 A.D., the time of this writing, we humans have developed enough technology and know-how to potentially enjoy the abundance of the planet without fear of death from starvation, war, or certain forms of illness. Freedom from basic survival concerns can be assured, if only we all can learn to get along with one another and with ourselves.

However, learning to live in harmony is an achievement that continues to elude our species. Even though for thousands of years the sparks of consciousness have spread through our minds like fire, our essential character has barely changed. Most of us still behave primarily like animals in nature, driven by fears of not having enough, of aggression from the outside, and of lingering illness, infirmity, and death. Despite the profound changes we have forged in the outside world, such as our monumental technological feats, we cannot fully enjoy them. Until all of us change our fundamental natures we will not liberate ourselves from basic survival worries.

And yet, many of us have started to sense that the time has come for the world to evolve toward unity, peace, and a global consciousness that can create a heaven-on-Earth. As a people of the whole planet Earth, we yearn to free ourselves from the "desert" of starvation, poverty, lack of resources, violent conflict, materialistic consumption, and meaninglessness. For the first time in history this appears possible, since we have developed enough technological know-how to meet our collective basic survival needs.

Unfortunately, humanity's self-evolved gifts—this know-how, and the technology capable of transforming the planet so all can survive in abundance—are still being used unconsciously and threaten the very existence of our whole species. Problems have sprouted up all over the globe that ultimately affect all of us: pollution; holes in the ozone layer of the atmosphere; nuclear arms in destructive hands; deadly diseases such as AIDS; and many more. A final ending, like that of many species before us including the dinosaurs and 90 percent of all species that have ever inhabited planet Earth, now seems possible.

Having been here for only the last one-tenth of one percent of the Earth's history, or about four million years out of four billion, evolution has set the stage for a crescendo: humanity will either pass into greater consciousness or descend into extinction holding the solution for our problems—technology with right values—in its hands.

This is where we find ourselves at this moment in time: in a race against time itself. We have, or are capable of developing quickly, the technology required to win evolution's challenge and save ourselves and the planet. But which are the "right" values? Where will they come from?

A UNIVERSAL CODE OF VALUES

About 3,000 years ago, Moses divined the Ten Commandments, and gave them to the Israelites to keep law and order in the harsh desert conditions of the Sinai. He was struggling to deliver one nation from 400 years of slavery in the Egyptian house of bondage, to freedom in their Promised Land, Canaan—modern-day Israel. After 40 long, hard years they got there, and their moral code formed the foundation for Western civilization up until now, the end of the twentieth century.

Moses' code altered his people's slave-mentality ways. They were instructed to live by commandments appropriate for the tribal and clan societies of the time, laws that would keep order and harmony among the tribes. The Commandments formed the basis of Judaism. Later they became part of the development of Christianity, Islam, and the rest of Western culture.

The Ten Commandments have fulfilled their purpose over the numerous generations since Moses' time to the present age. Even though war, hardship, and inequity continue to exist, the Commandments reminded Western civilization that there was an ideal for which to strive.

Other cultures developed their own codes, too: the way of the Tao in China; Buddhism's Noble Truths and Pathways to Right Living; the Hindu *Bhagavad-Gita* in India; and many more. In each case the codes helped to elevate and bring together the culture toward some common purpose and an acceptance of a right way of living in the world as it existed.

We believe humankind has now gone as far as possible with these unicultural guides. They have served us well. They have given humankind a chance to survive thus far. They were developed to speak to people living with common needs, with similar languages and cultural beliefs, in a local geographical region. They were not intended to provide for a multicultural, multi-belief, global society—one in which for the first time in history, all of us now live in the same room with each other.

The struggles we now face require a new universal code to help future generations survive in a global and planetary society, freed from individual or unicultural survival concerns. Too often in history, one group has tried to impose a code upon others who believed in a different code, resulting in tragedy. Enough is enough.

A new universal code of ethics would have to contain those right values that could save our tribe of humanity as a whole from ourselves, and continue our evolution. These guidelines would have to steer us through a transition period, perhaps similar to the 40 year deliverance march led by Moses, toward a *Global* Promised Land. Our march might last from 1988 to 2028.

This code would build upon the original code of ethics of Moses, the Ten Commandments, and also on the other codes developed all over the world throughout history. And yet, this new code should also include the cumulative insight and wisdom developed up until now. These insights have led us to what has been referred to as the upcoming Consciousness Age, or a time when learning and enjoyment supplant survival as the primary reason for our existence.

There are great challenges ahead. As Moses' code altered his people's slave-mentality ways, living by a new code would have to fundamentally change attitudes and behaviors deeply embedded over eons in the human subconscious mind. These are the result of each of us worrying first about our individual or unicultural survival. It's time from now on to also think about the survival of our planet and our species as a whole.

Already, understandably, many individuals are experiencing this massive push by evolution toward a new reality. Until the twentieth century, the constant struggle for survival had provided the purpose for living. But by now, technological improvements have increased standards of living so that even a poor person of today's modern society lives a better life in many ways than the kings of only two centuries ago. We have already begun to take for granted an ever-improving standard of living, and have forgotten how to appreciate the one that we have achieved. The immense impact of change will remain a mystery in our lives until each of us realizes that evolution's course over millions of years has come to a turning point: we no longer need to struggle for survival, but instead are free to pursue learning and leisure. It's time to stop living by the "law of the jungle."

What then are the purposes to live for in a society where there is (or can be) enough for everyone? It is time to begin to live in harmony with our planet and in coordination with all who inhabit it. It is time to adopt a new code right for the needs of today, tomorrow, and as many tomorrows as we can imagine, a global code for all to live by.

YOU NEVER DON'T KNOW WHAT MIGHT HAPPEN[2] (SEE APPENDIX A FOR THE REST OF ORION'S STORY)

I came to realize that, coincidentally or not, I had *assembled* or *synthesized*—not invented—such a code that might reveal a message of value to others. I had learned it from my own pain, exploration, and transformation. Fortunately, much of this wisdom already existed in codes that had been around for centuries, making my task somewhat easier.

I, too, was among those people moving away from the slavery of a survival-oriented mentality. At the age of 26 I had achieved a fair amount of success by society's standards. Yet I faced a life crisis that threatened my continuing existence. As a result, I became aware of a path that differed from many of the beliefs and traditions I had been taught. It dawned on me that the rituals that I and others were brought up with had not advanced or unified the people of the world as a whole. They had just served to protect us from each other, while individuals and/or groups worked at ensuring and propagating their survival and success on the planet.

As a small part of a much bigger whole, I have dedicated my efforts to turning the lessons from my own suffering into a constructive role for helping my fellow human beings, by offering to share the lessons I've gained.

Specifically, I hope to shed some light on the process of *synergizing technology and consciousness* for the purpose of helping to form a way of living in a global society. As Peter Russell discusses in the Foreword, information processing and telecommunications technology have brought us to the most exciting times in our history. We stand on the verge of using our technology to make a leap to planetary consciousness. Through proper personal and societal information management and response in a Global Brain, we can construct a better, beyond-individual-survival-oriented world for ourselves.

We can build and shape a world that merits bringing our children into. An abundance of appropriate technology, technology that improves the human condition, not worsens, endangers, or threatens to destroy it, can help us achieve this. By accelerating the development, progress, and use of appropriate technology, we can liberate ourselves and unify the planet into one harmonious global community.

Using the code presented here, I hope that others will join me in seeking the personal-growth that will propel them into higher consciousness. This might free them, too, from viewing Earth as a prison, and instead allow them to create their happiness and self-actualization on the Earth kindergarten (combination of school and playground).[3]

Clearly, we are living in an age in which the powerful forces of evolution are passing on to all of humanity a new code of living to match its novel realities. Day by day, we learn individually and collectively. Many speakers and books announce similar messages and heighten the general level of awareness. Over half of the books on the bestseller list promise "self-help." These truths, which I have attempted to synthesize and summarize in this book, form the basis of a code that lies deep in the nature of all humans. I offer them as a teaching to anyone who may choose to read it. And I genuinely dream that it will serve as a useful guide to abet in some way your success in life, in these most exciting, and perhaps most difficult, of times to live in.

FEARS AND DREAMS

I acknowledge, even if I don't fully grasp, the arrogance of attempting to develop a universal code of behavior and ethical living and calling it the *2nd* Ten Commandments.

I submit that in these times everyone can become a "second Moses." Every one of us is now capable of contributing to leading us

9

out of today's wilderness, through access to higher consciousness and global communication networks.

I feel that through my own access to higher consciousness I "just knew" that I had to use *The 2nd Ten Commandments* as the title for the book, only used once before on record in the United States Library of Congress, for a pamphlet in 1986. How is it possible that nobody else up until now chose this title for a book, even if just to profit from it commercially?

Throughout the five years I wrote this book, my ambivalence, fear, and reluctance to carry out my mission continued to torment me. I remembered that most people in history who had attempted to undertake this kind of a mission, even if for truly compassionate and altruistic reasons, had risked or even lost their lives—Martin Luther King or Anwar Sadat, for example.

In 1993, as I hesitated to proceed with a nearly finished first draft of the manuscript, my consulting business began to thrive. I helped many high-tech companies bring new products to market much more quickly, using the QRPD™: Quality *Rapid* Product Development management methodology I had developed. Often, my clients amazed me by delivering new products in half the time that it used to take them, substantially increasing their profits as well as mine. At times, this very rewarding and joyous occupation even furthered my temptation to abandon *The 2nd Ten Commandments*, which consumed large amounts of my time and money. And since I believe that neither greed nor ego inspired me as my main motive behind this book—I had already satisfied these in the high technology business world, and could continue to—I often ponder why I, and not someone else, was "chosen" for this task, and if I should publish the book at all.

And yet, the metaphor and material itself seemed to be pressing me to make whatever effort it would take to spread the word. I hope you will share my excitement in the usefulness of the comparison of Moses' exodus to freedom with our own trek. It really seems to fit. Metaphors help to give us a better understanding of new situations we face. As Aristotle, the Greek philosopher, said in 330 B.C., "It is from metaphor that we can best get hold of something fresh."[4] We need to comprehend something different as we are at a time in history when our whole existence as a species seems perilous—ironically not because of our technology, but rather because of our lack of consciousness in using it—and the world seems in jeopardy of becoming an insane Global Brain.

So, moved mainly by conviction, I feel compelled by some greater force to assume the burden and blessing of placing *The 2nd Ten Commandments* on the doorstep of humanity. At times I've wished that the CD-ROMs depicted on the front cover had actually arrived at my doorstep, but then I would not have engaged in the incredible and difficult journey of clarification and self-inquiry that the process of bringing this manuscript to press has mandated. This book, then, is my best effort to explain what I have been inspired to learn combined with my personal commitment to spread its message.

To achieve my own joy and self-actualization, I have accepted my destiny: to offer the truths of the 2nd Ten Commandments, with their ensuing freedom, to the world; to make the best case for all to adopt a code designed for living in a global village.

I have committed myself to hastening the creation of a new, *Global* Promised Land.

Some of us dream about this possibility occurring within our lifetimes. Many of us will help to make it happen. Even more of us just know, deep down inside, that it will. These are the *Motofs*.

I invite you, too, to join those of us who wish, from the bottom of our hearts, to become a conscious <u>M</u>ember <u>O</u>f the <u>T</u>ribe <u>O</u>f the <u>F</u>uture, a *Motof.*

2

YOUR FLIGHT PLAN SUMMARY

To laugh often and much; to win the respect of intelligent people and children; to earn the appreciation of honest critics and endure the betrayal of false friends; to appreciate beauty; to find the best in others; to leave the world a bit better, whether by a healthy child, a garden patch or a redeemed social condition; to know even one life has breathed easier because you have lived: this is to have succeeded.

—Ralph Waldo Emerson

Either lead, follow, or get out of the way.

—Plaque on Ted Turner's desk, founder of CNN and TNT

I n your hands you have a map that will assure your success as a participant in the twenty-first century and beyond. *The 2nd Ten Commandments* contains many new and challenging ideas that you will want to understand thoroughly.

To facilitate your reading, and for future reference, this chapter contains a very short description of each of the Commandments, and a synopsis of the major concepts of the book. In Chapter 3 you will receive an overview of how the rest of the book will help you to blast off on your mission to the Global Promised Land with your flight plan in hand.

The book is carefully structured in a sequence that methodically builds your comprehension of the material. Take your time, have fun, "go with it," and remember your parachute for the happy landing.

THE COMMANDMENTS IN BRIEF

The 2nd Ten Commandments are numbered 11 through 20 in reverence to the first Ten Commandments and augment them rather than supersede them.

Commandment No. 11: FLOW
Maximize your time spent in FLOW and happiness.

Engage in the present moment for all it's worth instead of worrying about the future or replaying the past. Do what makes you happy and challenged whenever possible.

Commandment No. 12: WHOLENESS
Seek WHOLENESS through ongoing awareness and lifelong education.

Integrate your body, mind, and spirit for increasing serenity and satisfaction. Then learn how to become one with everything around you.

Commandment No. 13: SELF-ACCEPTANCE
Develop greater SELF-ACCEPTANCE by loving yourself unconditionally.

Embrace yourself and your life without blame, guilt, or excuses. Make peace with yourself and your past, and follow the path that allows you to reach your full potential.

Commandment No. 14: BALANCE
Live with BALANCE, priorities, and moderation in all things.

Keep your perspective and set your priorities so that you devote as much of your valuable time as possible to realizing your own highest goals and dearest dreams, in all areas of your life.

Commandment No. 15: INNER VOICE-MISSION
Act true to your INNER VOICE and fulfill your MISSION.

Your INNER VOICE aligns you with a greater intelligence within you that brings out the best in you and weaves us all together. This voice, which you may have been aware of only rarely until now, will also divulge your MISSION as a participant in the Global Brain.

Commandment No. 16: SURRENDER-COURAGE
Exercise mature SURRENDER and unselfish COURAGE.

COURAGE and SURRENDER are key tools to help you contribute, learn, and grow. Knowing when to take a courageous leap of faith and when to surrender to the will of your higher intelligence can make miracles happen.

Commandment No. 17: UNCONDITIONAL LOVE
Feel UNCONDITIONAL LOVE and recognize the oneness of humanity.

Recognize all members of the human family as your relatives. Discover how compassion and forgiveness can bring out the best in you and in others.

Commandment No. 18: BOTTOM LINES

Base your level of relationship commitments on BOTTOM LINES—what you can't live with and can't live without.

Define and live by your BOTTOM LINES. Base your commitments on a clear understanding of your minimum requirements for all of your relationships.

Commandment No. 19: SYNERGY

Create SYNERGY by using *win-win* and setting *boundaries*.

Synchronize the energy and effort you expend to maximize results. Follow *win-win* strategies that allow everyone to win, prevent anyone from losing, and produce results that exceed your expectations.

Commandment No. 20: REPAIR

REPAIR the world by treating others reverently and fairly and doing good deeds.

Be of service by treating people, other species, and the planet reverently and fairly. Do good deeds whenever possible to make the world a better place to live, for yourself and for everyone else.

WHY WE NEED TO LIVE BY THE 2ND TEN COMMANDMENTS NOW

Humanity, with the aid of technology, is swiftly forming a network that will serve as a Global Brain to provide responsible management of Gaia (Earth as a living superorganism).

Each one of us has a role to play as a cell in the newly forming Global Brain. If we don't all participate in this adventure—perhaps the modern equivalent of being with Moses 3,000 years ago on the way to the unknown, but Promised, Land, with continued slavery as our only option if we turn back—then current planetary problems will grow beyond our capacity to address and solve them.

We've already reached "condition red": the rapid depletion and destruction of our vital natural resources now threatens our survival; and the violent use of cheap, powerful technology for wars, terrorism, and crime now endanger our safety.

The year 2012, or thereabouts, will be a crucial turning point. We don't have much time left to avert an unacceptable future for humanity. Wake up and get the message. Please.

Today's technology *is capable* of solving all our most urgent problems, and it can provide a decent and sustainable standard of living for every citizen of our planet. But to achieve this goal, we must harness and redirect technology. We must radically revise our priorities through our own goodwill and the adoption of appropriate values that will allow us to live in harmony with each other and with the Earth.

By exercising goodwill and appropriate values on a global scale, we will create a heaven-on-Earth that has no historical precedent. We can achieve this within a few decades.

We need to replace materialism and selfishness, which stem from an individual survival- and security-oriented mind-set, with a spirituality that focuses on the welfare of humanity as a family and of Earth as the family home. It's time for a mass exodus from being enslaved in the old ways to finding the freedom of enjoying the newfound abundance, communal caretaking, and joy afforded by our technology.

A grass roots movement is growing around the globe. It is a Gevolution (Global Evolution). Participants are Motofs—Members Of the Tribe Of the Future. If you're not one of them now, you can join.

Motofs are ushering in a new era for humanity, the Consciousness Age. Learning and innovative pleasures will replace consumerism and violence. The deep satisfaction of community will replace the pursuit of self-interest at the expense of others. We will live on Gaia and contribute to a planetary society that is as benign as it is exciting.

We are lucky to live in a time of revolutionary, evolutionary change. But we need a universal code to live by that is based on spiritual principles. To succeed as individuals and as group participants in the Global Brain, we need the 2nd Ten Commandments. Based on the timeless and time-proven wisdom of spiritual masters throughout the ages and around the world, the new Commandments are presented in contemporary language for contemporary readers. When enough Motofs follow them, these principles will give the Global Brain a Global Heart, and Gaia will finally have a Global Soul.

3

THE MAP
FOR SUCCESS
AS A MOTOF

The trouble with the rat race is that even if you win, you're still a rat.

—Lily Tomlin, comedian/actress

Success is when you get what you want.
Happiness is when you want what you get.

—Anonymous

*T*he *2nd Ten Commandments*, if you stick with it to the end, and follow its recommendations afterwards, will serve you as a guide to true success in your life in the twenty-first century and beyond. True success provides gratification which endures.

This book is for people seeking to understand how to be successful in a world that is undergoing unprecedented changes, especially the incredible technological and political changes that are transforming our current world of individual nations into a global society. It facilitates a great exodus, already occurring every day in all of our lives, from the ways that have characterized human existence for thousands of years to a new frontier of as-yet-uncharted territory. *Ultimately, everyone on the planet will need a guiding set of principles dealing with how to lead their lives in connection with the way global society is developing.*

For now, in the last decade of the twentieth century, there are a sufficient number of us who yearn to know how to cope with life in the next millennium. We are willing to invest time and energy to adapt to and keep pace with the times. We seek the most gratifying and enduring form of success, relating to and enjoying life as it is and as it will become. We are motivated toward self-development and self-growth by the opportunity to live a maximally fulfilling life. We are receptive to and are learning to thrive on the futuristic aspects of today, and want to avoid *future shock* tomorrow. *We are interested in achieving individual success in all domains, including health, happiness, career, relationships, family, and prosperity, yet not at the expense of ourselves or the survival of humanity.*

For us *The 2nd Ten Commandments* comes at just the right time to offer guidelines for success. It is not the ultimate get-rich-quick manual, or a guide for picking the right stock or date or selling things in the swiftest and most efficient way. Instead, it is the plan for success in an ever-changing world, a way of living by synergizing technology and consciousness in a way that is necessary for the individuals of today's world to become the citizens of tomorrow's global society.

AN OVERVIEW OF THE REST OF PART I

Since change races on so rapidly on our planet, to comprehend how to become successful in the future first requires a full understanding of the new environment we will live in. To succeed, we have to know what is happening now; what is likely to happen in the next few years; and how ways of living that we have taken for granted are changing. Life as we know it resembles many sports: once we figure out the game, we can begin honing our skills to master it. We already explained that the rules of the "Game of Life" on Earth have changed for good. There's no going back. Business as usual is out the window. Learn the new rules of the environment so you can begin to adapt to it.

Chapter 4 metaphorically compares Moses, and his people's exodus from slavery, to our planetary departure from an individual survival-based mentality. Now we can each choose to view life on Earth as a "prison" or as a "playground."

Chapter 5 outlines the changes that have brought about this new epoch. The many "factoids" presented will give headaches to numerophobics, leave number-junkies hungry for more, and perhaps suffice for most. The facts paint a scene aimed to convince you that we have arrived at an unprecedented time in history.

Chapter 6 then speculates on how these changes set the stage for the formation of the Global Brain. It suggests that technology is linking humanity into a single intercommunicating entity, with each individual functioning like a cell in a Global Brain.

Chapter 7 may jolt you into realizing the imminence of these predicted worldwide realignments of technology and consciousness. When will they happen? Within most of our lifetimes—very, very soon!

Chapters 8 and 9 suggest a practical spirituality that combines a scientific outlook with all of the current religious wisdom of the world into a world view that allows us to live successfully in a global society. Please consider its positive potential. *If we, the inhabitants of the planet, could all agree on a minimum set of world views, it might provide the common ground that would allow us to weave the future together and guarantee the survival of our species as a whole.*

Chapter 10 explores the rewards that the adventurers who embrace this new set of world views will receive: living in truth and freedom, without fear.

Like them, Christopher Columbus didn't expect an easy journey when he set sail to the west. Many people warned him that he might fall off the edge of the earth. Clearly he and (most of) his crew believed and thought otherwise. But imagine what it might be like sailing for weeks on end on one of his ships, waiting for the moment when your vessel may plunge you to your doom, as you had been taught your whole life would definitely happen. We can only speculate that many sailors would have volunteered to climb the masts to watch for the drop-off, rather than sleep in their cabins in mortal fear.

Happily for them, the European explorers who discovered the "New World" found a land of plenty, and gold mines galore. Their adventurousness and bravery gained them everything but the Fountain of Youth.

Five hundred years later, our courage to face the unknown might even show us the secret of eternal youth and, better yet, how to live in harmony in a heaven-on-Earth. But this will not happen if we dismiss new possibilities out of ignorance, stubbornness, or impatience, and stay on safe shores. Try to keep your mind open to new ideas and concepts, as alien or initially unacceptable as they may seem to you. Our world's whole future depends on you—and many thousands and then millions like you—choosing to journey to the Global Promised Land, because, unlike Columbus, we no longer have an "Old World" to go back to.

> **Be willing to lose sight of the continent so you can embark on the discovery of a new world.**

NEW REALITIES DEMAND NEW WORDS AND DIFFERENT WAYS OF THINKING

In *The 2nd Ten Commandments*, we introduce a number of new words designed to help you comprehend the vast changes occurring in this new world. Dictionaries keep adding new words every year, so this shouldn't seem too outlandish. As innovation and management expert Peter F. Drucker says, "New realities often demand new words."[1] Otherwise, old, outdated terms take on different meanings to different people. This creates discrepancies that forestall both our own ability to grasp meaningful new concepts and our ability to communicate them clearly to each other.

As a simple example of how progress in science requires that we change the terms we use to communicate with others, think of not having the word "volt," and having to discuss this concept both with people who understand how electricity works and with those who don't. The *American Heritage Dictionary* defines *volt* as:

> the unit of electric potential and electromotive force equal to the difference of electric potential between two points on a conducting wire carrying a constant current of one ampere when the power dissipated between the points is one watt.

Replacing all this with one word, "volt," in common usage is less confusing and lets us more quickly integrate our knowledge to higher levels.

Every science has its own terminology, its own shortcuts for communicating complex concepts with simple and easy-to-use terms. Of course, "volts" existed (for example in lightning) long before we started explaining how they work, or created a word to describe the experience. So a new reality often means that we simply now have a new understanding of something that has always been present in one form or another.

As another example, consider the evolution in the meaning and connotations of the word "Indian." Soon after Columbus' sailing, settlers named these indigenous peoples on the "new" American continent. Initially, the colonists saw them as savages with little or no cultural values, and the word "Indian" described this new race of people discovered by the "white man." It has taken centuries for the white man to recognize and to begin to appreciate what the "red men" knew and practiced long before they were discovered. We are only now updating our concept of "Indian" to include an appreciation of their code of protecting the environment in which they lived, and learning to respect their use of the Great Spirit as their concept of God.

Similarly, people who have attempted to live by a greater, yet perennial or timeless wisdom, have always existed all over the world. Relatively few throughout history, but now rapidly increasing, they have adeptly used the ancient and proven wisdoms of the past, while learning to master the best their society had to offer. They have catalyzed humanity toward its further evolution. They have been called monks, mystics, geniuses, philosophers, leading-edge scientists, or brilliant artists. There have also been many who simply led their lives, but who were greatly valued by those who knew them, never attaining fame beyond their immediate cave, farm, village, town, or city.

Recently, we have discovered enough about these people to warrant the creation of a new word: Motofs. We can now attempt to generalize the traits that make Motofs successful, and share them with as many people as possible. We hope that this will speed up the processes of self identification and action that need to be done by this select group of people. It is incredibly exciting to have come to a time in humanity's evolution when there are so many people alive at one time who have a common understanding of the way society is evolving, and have both the desire and the means to help in the process. You don't have to label yourself with the new word to understand whether you can identify with the tribe. That's your choice.

Each time a new key word or concept is introduced in this book a clearly marked box provides the definition for how to use the word throughout the rest of the book. The Glossary near the end of the book contains a list of all these terms. Here's the one for Motof.

Motof, (mot' uf) noun

Member Of the Tribe Of the Future. A conscious human who chooses to live by the principles of the 2nd Ten Commandments—whether named such or not—and thereby participates in evolution's creation of a Global Brain in the Consciousness Age.

The words people use, especially in regard to spiritual or religious concepts, can all too often cause those with different, strongly held spiritual concepts to misinterpret or distrust each other. Throughout *The 2nd Ten Commandments,* new concepts and ideas are meant to resolve such difficulties so that persons holding a very wide range of spiritual beliefs have the possibility of sharing spirit in the same way that, from ancient times, sharing bread came to mean acceptance and trust even amongst strangers. Saving our planet and our species depends on this.

Think of how much separation and alienation words in use today cause amongst people. For example, consider your reaction to the following two statements, and as you read them, notice which one you relate to better:

I have to pray to God, and see what He would like me to do about . . . (a decision, for example).	I need time to close my eyes, take a deep breath, and listen to my innermost wisdom to carefully decide about . . . .

In practice, either person would more or less do the same thing. And yet, these two people might easily find themselves on opposite sides of the fence. The person quoted on the left side might call the other person a "heathen," or "atheist who lacks faith in and gratitude to the Creator." The person quoted on the right side might call the other person a "religious fanatic who leaves it all up to God, instead of taking charge of their own life." But don't these two people actually have a lot in common?

Eventually, perhaps, you will find that the new words introduced actually help you to think and to act differently. They may assist you in recognizing many others who will share your appreciation of a global perspective on getting along with others. After all, that is what living by the 2nd Ten Commandments is meant to do.

OVERVIEW OF PART II: THE COMMANDMENTS

In Part II, we attempt to thoroughly explain the 2nd Ten Commandments, a set of guidelines based upon spiritual and psychobiological principles applicable to all human beings. Spiritual guidelines serve to keep us within the bounds of the morals in which we believe, when our baser impulses arise, especially in times of confusion and stress. For thousands of years, up to and into the beginning of the Information Age, following the Ten Commandments has helped people lead better lives and develop their moral strength and spiritual selves in the world. Similarly, the 2nd Ten Commandments are meant to help us lead better lives in the modern age of technology and consciousness. When adhered to, they will lead to the most lasting form of success possible in our times.

You can comprehend these laws at many levels. To properly appreciate how to learn to follow them to achieve your full potential, you really have to first understand the new paradigms presented in Part I. Then the 2nd Ten Commandments can prove useful to devout believers, agnostics, and atheists alike. They apply to many different situations. Try them. Their magic lies in their pragmatism.

The Commandments follow a logical sequence, which takes an individual along the personal continuum of maturity from *dependent*, to *independent*, to *interdependent*. Stephen Covey, in one of the best-selling books of the 1990s, *The 7 Habits of Highly Effective People*, defines the paradigms used in each of these modes of operation. Table 3-1 shows those definitions.

Table 3-1
Covey's Maturity Levels[2]

Dependent	"Paradigm of you—you take care of me; you come through for me; you didn't come through; I blame you for the results."
Independent	"Paradigm of I—I can do it; I am responsible; I am self-reliant; I can choose."
Interdependent	"Paradigm of we—we can do it; we can cooperate; we can combine our talents and abilities and create something greater together."

Covey goes on to explain that ". . . dependent people need others to get what they want. Independent people can get what they want through their own effort. Interdependent people combine their own efforts with the efforts of others to achieve their greatest success." Success is what this book is about. It will address it at the most fundamental level, that of the principles that underlie all of human behavior.

To move from the dependent to the independent level, an individual will have achieved a certain degree of mastery of Commandments No. 11 through No. 16. This includes: finding a quality of experience that delivers happiness (11); a way of being that moves toward self-actualization (12); and a healthy way of acting toward oneself (13 through 16). Then, to advance to the interdependent level and thus start to become a Motof, an individual must also have mastered all of Commandments No. 15 through No. 20. This includes serving others while growing individually (15, 16), and relating to others in a way that demonstrates global consciousness and responsibility (17 through 20).

To help you begin to imagine the lifestyle of an interdependent person who lives by the 2nd Ten Commandments, the section below describes in general terms how the Commandments may govern one's actions. The words in SMALL CAPITALS represent the names of each of the commandments, discussed in numerical order. (It may help to refer to the first page of this book.) This brief sojourn in the life of an imaginary and exemplary Motof is intended to point out to you the general direction in which this book suggests you head, and to show you the benefits toward which the personal-growth and development it recommends may lead.

> Motofs will experience life, much of the time, from a happy, optimal, challenged, and timeless state of mind called FLOW. They will be aware of, and become more and more attuned to, their oneness with all other people and with nature, so that they can grow towards even greater WHOLENESS. This will include integrating the various parts within themselves that constitute a human being. Once accomplished, this leads to truly having SELF-ACCEPTANCE for who they are right now, and accepting the part of the whole they represent as an individual, but con-nected, entity. They will have achieved a reasonable BALANCE in their lives, including choosing amongst their many roles and types of activities, and prioritizing them on an ongoing basis. As a participant in the Consciousness Age, they will tap into their higher mind, intuition, or INNER VOICE, and use it to pre-serve their integrity, honesty, loyalty, and self-esteem, and thereby others' sense of trust in them. This will also tell them their life purpose, or personal MISSION—the contribution that they can make to the whole. This new sense of meaning will transform their work into a fun endeavor which at the same time provides them with sufficient income to live comfortably.

> In doing their work, or going about any of their activities, they will know when to SURRENDER to watch and experience what's

occurring, either within themselves or out in the world, and when to jump in and exercise COURAGE to affect the outcome. Their relationships with others will be principle-based, and will rely on having UNCONDITIONAL LOVE in their hearts for all their fellow human beings. By being open to everyone, emotionally accepting them, forgiving them, and feeling compassion for their predicaments, they will experience the higher state of consciousness that Jesus talked about, with its inherent rewards. That means that out of consideration for the well-being of others and themselves, they will only engage in relationships if their BOTTOM LINES are met: their requirements for what they can't live with, and what they can't live without, given how much they are putting into, and expect to get out of a relationship. This includes the most fulfilling and difficult of all relationships, the romantic or significant-other ones. They will use *boundaries* to choose to spend their time with anybody else strictly on the basis of an interaction that produces SYNERGY; that is, a *win-win* situation that produces a harmonious and more advantageous outcome for both parties involved, thereby helping the whole. Finally, they will apply the principles of reverence for life and fairness in every situation, and voluntarily do good deeds. This helps to REPAIR the world and to make it a better place to live in for everyone, including themselves. They have now proven to be highly successful, interdependent Motofs.

If this sounds idealistic and difficult to achieve, remember that such people already exist, and many more join the ranks each day. These highly evolved individuals are moving toward what psychologist Abraham Maslow called *self-actualization,* or a state of reaching more of one's potential. At the same time, they participate in and serve the whole—the Global Brain. They will also usher in the Global Promised Land and a heaven-on-Earth.

OVERVIEW OF PART III: GETTING ON THE PATH TO THE GLOBAL PROMISED LAND

What should you do after reading this book? How do you start becoming a Motof?

Chapter 21 discusses how becoming a Motof requires first and foremost accepting the responsibility for being one, and living your life accordingly. This is a difficult path to follow. In the history of humanity it has indeed been difficult to live by the Ten Commandments, even for persons who accepted the rightness of those ways of living. It is equally difficult and challenging to live your life in accordance with the 2nd Ten Commandments. However, this chapter strongly suggests that you embark on a heroic journey to explore this new frontier.

Chapter 22 puts forth nine great ideas to propel you forward on your trip toward becoming a Motof. With will and determination, and by following these suggestions (and your own ideas, too), you will be well on your way. Don't expect it to happen overnight. But if you persevere, the rewards will be everlasting and could easily keep you young, healthy, and happy well beyond what we currently think of as a normal life-span, and give greater purpose and meaning to your life.

Chapter 23 describes how evolution's natural selection process will work in relation to Motofs and which traits characterize these global citizens, so you can see how to adapt to life in the Global Brain.

You are on this planet for a reason. You don't have to go to the top of a mountain to find all the answers. You are here to be part of *this* world, here and now. You are here to participate in, and are called to help weave, a world dream that will usher in a new era, a global civilization. And, as Chapter 24 shows, ultimately to create greater oneness in the universe. We will use the words "grok" and "ikorgant" throughout the book to remind us of this oneness.

Grok, verb

The simultaneous comprehension of fully knowing with the head or rational brain, feeling with the heart, and clearly and completely experiencing through all our senses and physical instincts. Really "getting it," not just intellectually knowing it. Coined by Robert Heinlein in his classic science fiction book of the 1960s, *Stranger in a Strange Land.*

Ikorgant, adjective

Having knowledge without yet grokking.

We human beings are a tribe of animals, possessing much knowledge, which we have not yet grokked. We are attempting to pass into higher consciousness in a period of half a century, a mission infinitely more difficult than putting a person on the moon in a decade. We must accomplish this new endeavor as well. It will require each and every one of us to do our share. *It will require each and every one of us to move from ignorance, to knowledge with ikorgance, and finally to grokking their part in the mission.*

PARABLES AND ONE-PARAGRAPH SUMMARIES OF EACH COMMANDMENT

Humans have told stories to motivate others from the earliest times that they huddled around fires and gazed at the stars. For thousands of years, wisdom was passed on from generation to generation through the oral tradition of storytelling. People only recorded in writing the tale of Moses and how he received the Ten Commandments 200 to 300 years after his epic journey. Jesus' parables, stories from which moral or religious lessons may be drawn, constitute much of the New Testament and were written down many years after Jesus' lifetime.

In this subsection you will find a parable and one-paragraph summary for each Commandment as "food for thought" as you read through the remaining chapters in Part I. Contemplate the multiple levels of meaning that they convey. Enjoy.

There is an old story of a wise Sufi Dervish (a Muslim mystic) taking a hike down a narrow mountain path, who comes to the end of the trail—a cliff overhang. He starts to turn back, only to see a tiger about to pounce on him and devour him. Undaunted, he quickly jumps down the precipice and grabs hold of a tree branch several feet below. He then looks down, and sees yet another tiger with open jaws, waiting for him to fall. Hanging on for dear life, he becomes aware of one small, red, ripe berry on the tree, just within reach. Upon tasting it he remarks, "My, this is the sweetest berry I have ever had."

Maximize your time spent in FLOW and happiness.

Commandment No. 11 summary

FLOW means letting go. You allow yourself to be completely engaged in the moment. In this optimal psychological mode of experience, time seems to move both slowly and rapidly simultaneously. You're challenged and yet completely absorbed by what you're doing. You feel strong, alert, in effortless control, unselfconscious, emotionally calm, and at the peak of your abilities. With the right attitude *all* activities can be experienced in FLOW. Look around you. Some people do it, usually the ones who "have their act together," the "winners" in life. Through discipline and perseverance we can maximize the time we spend in FLOW and enjoy all of our activities in a state of happiness.

(See Chapter 11 for a complete discussion of this Commandment.)

"To be conscious of what you do and why you do it," said Rabbi Ahakum, "makes all the difference. Just last night I saw Shela on her knees, crawling about in the dim light shining from the window of Atzlan's shop. She did this for over an hour! She had lost the key to her home. I questioned her. Where had she lost it? She replied, 'In the dark, way over there, by that tree.' 'Why then, poor woman, are you looking here rather than there,' I asked. 'Because I see light here, and none over there,' she said."

> ## Seek WHOLENESS through ongoing awareness and lifelong education.

Commandment No. 12 summary

WHOLENESS means becoming successful by knowing more about yourself and the world, so that you can participate more effectively with everything around you. You can achieve this by exercising your *free* choice to integrate your body, mind, and spirit in a way that enhances your life and all of life. The more you become aware of your inner world, and thus become more WHOLE within yourself, the more you become ready to join with and contribute to the outer world. If you harm life, you violate WHOLENESS and deprive yourself of feeling better and healthier, mentally and physically. If you add to life, everything becomes an exhilarating educational experience that further advances your spirit. It is a lifelong process, one in which we get closer to our goal but never totally arrive. We gain consciousness as we try to transform into greater WHOLENESS, and someday, holiness.

(See Chapter 12 for a complete discussion of this Commandment.)

A nd God said unto Moses, "Go bring my people out of Egypt, and take them to the Promised Land." "But who should I tell them sent me?" asked the doubting Moses. "Tell them that I AM THAT I AM sent you." And thus Moses accepted himself, his freedom, his destiny, and his responsibility to be the best he could be. For all of us as well, we are that we are.

> ## Develop greater SELF-ACCEPTANCE by loving yourself unconditionally.

Commandment No. 13 summary

SELF-ACCEPTANCE means to feel good about yourself just the way you are right now. You're not perfect yet, and you won't be for a very long time. But you're perfect for right now. So have complete SELF-ACCEPTANCE. Come to terms with your present self and with all of your past. Can you not only accept, but even be thankful to the point of saying that you would not have changed a thing in your life to get to where you are now? As a responsible, conscious person, really do the best you can, and take full responsibility for everything manifesting in your life. Recognize your mistakes, rectify them where possible, learn from them, and get better and better each time new situations present themselves. Your essence, the soul, the best of who you really are, will come out and express itself more fully. You will contribute your unique abilities to help create a Global Promised Land, and increasingly love yourself unconditionally as you are now, as you develop greater SELF-ACCEPTANCE.

(See Chapter 13 for a complete discussion of this Commandment.)

King Solomon, the wisest judge in history, sat on his throne and heard a case of two women fighting over their claims to a newborn baby. He weighed the merits of Hagzama's and Shakula's arguments, and sent for a sword with which to cut the infant in half and seemingly to quickly resolve the conflicting claims. "Stop!" the real mother Shakula yelled, "Give *her* my baby! The world needs this precious soul to live!" Shakula knew her limits and priorities. The King recognized that only the natural mother could balance the conflicting emotions of giving away her baby, and saving her loved one's life. He rewarded her by returning the baby to her. The other women was beheaded for not knowing how far to go with a particular behavior.

Live with BALANCE, priorities, and moderation in all things.

Commandment No. 14 summary

BALANCE means keeping all your activities in perspective to everything in your life, at any given time, and over your lifetime. Chose very carefully what to do with your time, your most valuable resource, ever ticking away. Set goals for all the roles in your life, and consider what results you wish to attain. The recent spiraling acceleration of technology increases the significance of prioritizing your time as we evolve to an interdependent world. We get bombarded with interruptions and demands for our time, money, and energy. Make the optimal choices that take both your own good and that of the global system's into account, by using moderation. Ensure your maximum health and success by serving your highest good. Contain yourself within proper limits, and act with an appropriate BALANCE of your individual strengths and weaknesses.

(See Chapter 14 for a complete discussion of this Commandment.)

The great philosopher Plato, speaking to a group gathered around a campfire in a cave near the Parthenon in Athens, explained how the soul guides our life. "You see," he said, "normally our senses perceive only the shadows, that the flickers of this fire's flames project on that wall. They fool us to call those shadows a tree. Our soul, however, knows of another more true reality, which rises above the darkness of the cave, outside to the light, and sees the tree itself. If you would but listen and heed this wiser voice within, it will point you in the right direction. Use it as your compass, to navigate from your port of entry to your final destination, to steer your ship along the journey of life in the safest, surest and most meaningful way possible."

Act true to your INNER VOICE and fulfill your MISSION

Commandment No. 15 summary

INNER VOICE-MISSION means awakening your higher mind within and acting in accordance with a greater intelligence that connects all of us. The INNER VOICE is what you know you know, deep down inside. You may have had a "gut feeling" or intuition which has paid off for you in the past. Your ultimate success comes from constantly doing what this true self or INNER VOICE really urges you to do. Adhering to it honors not only what's best for you, but for others, too. By heeding it you maintain the highest level of *integrity, honesty,* and *loyalty,* which promotes *self-esteem* and *trust.* It also divulges to you your role or MISSION as a neuron in the Global Brain. Fulfilling your MISSION brings to your life meaning, lessons you need to evolve further, authentic power, sufficient money to survive and thrive on, and lasting happiness. Every cell in your body experiences harmony with a powerful energy, and senses an unparalleled vitality. Follow your bliss, follow your song, follow your INNER VOICE-MISSION.

(See Chapter 15 for a complete discussion of this Commandment.)

Wei-Chei Ho, while in his Zen Buddhist meditation at dawn, suddenly heard his horse break through the fence. He opened his eyes just in time to catch a last glimpse of it on the horizon. "Who knows if it's a crisis or an opportunity," he contemplated, as he returned to his practice. Later that day, while he was plowing in the fields, who should arrive but his son Buck Ho, proudly mounted on the thought-to-be-lost beast. "Who knows if it's a crisis or an opportunity," he remarked, and kept tilling. Not an hour later, a shriek! His son, fallen off the horse, with a broken leg. "Who knows if it's a crisis or an opportunity," he exclaimed. As the sun slowly descended on this eventful day, soldiers rounded up all the village's young men to go to war, but spared Buck Ho as unsuitable. "Who knows if it's a crisis or an opportunity," he thought. When the soldiers left, he climbed on his horse and rode off to meet with the other freedom fighters and warn them about the army's new offensive.

> ### Exercise mature SURRENDER and unselfish COURAGE.

Commandment No. 16 summary

SURRENDER-COURAGE means to realize when to have the peace of mind to accept the things you cannot change, and when to have the fearlessness to act boldly and impact the things that you can change. Every action you take influences both global evolution and everyone else. Take all consequences into consideration, and bear responsibility for them. With each free action that stems from love, not fear, you make a contribution to the world, perceive new truths, and grow yourself. *Mature* SURRENDER occurs when evolved individuals, who can clearly perceive reality, know and choose to accept their powerlessness to change a situation. *Unselfish* COURAGE means exerting power and influence for the sake of all, rather than only for oneself. Listen to your INNER VOICE to decide when to passively observe, and when to take a leap of faith using SURRENDER-COURAGE to make miracles happen.

(See Chapter 16 for a complete discussion of this Commandment.)

Brah Harris, from a family of the most courageous Hawaiian warriors, when asked about the Aloha spirit of UNCONDITIONAL LOVE said, "T'ree little words Brah: Look at me! Look at me! What do you see? If you call me at two in the morning and ask me to come over and help, I'll be there. When I want to sell my bike for $700, but the neighbor's child wants it for distributing newspapers, I geev um. The spirit of Aloha is in everything I do. It's here, right here, in my heart, always."

> ## Feel UNCONDITIONAL LOVE and recognize the oneness of humanity.

Commandment No. 17 summary

UNCONDITIONAL LOVE means treating every human being as though they are members of the same tribe, whom you care about as deeply as you should care about your own spirit or soul. You see beyond their immediate behavior to the positive beneficial intention behind it. Love manifests in many different forms, only one of which, UNCONDITIONAL LOVE, you can feel for all people. It is the most pure form, and substantially enriches your life. In the Global Brain your well-being vitally depends on everyone else's, so stay *open to* and *emotionally accept* each person. Coupled with Jesus' attitude of "Love thy neighbor as thyself," this enables you to act rationally and appropriately toward your fellow human beings. Be and let be, and don't judge others. Perceive and act with *compassion* and *forgiveness*, open your gateway to the planes of higher consciousness, and feel ecstatic states of at-one-ment with all of humanity. Ultimately, UNCONDITIONAL LOVE defies a written and intellectual explanation: it must be felt and experienced through your heart.

(See Chapter 17 for a complete discussion of this Commandment.)

Prince Profitus, a business executive in the Valley of the Silicon, one moon ago had been told by his wife Devota, "Even though I love you with all my heart, I can only be happy living near my family, in the Land Beyond the Sea, far, far, away. Let's journey there together and live happily ever after." Having wondered long enough if indeed love conquers all, Profitus awoke from a dream in which he was in Devota's Land seven years later, lying in bed at night, glimpsing *his* Valley on the horizon, in the sunlight. He realized that he loved her with all his heart, but couldn't live in her Land. Profitus sadly bid her farewell and gave her many worthy gifts for her long journey. Just at this time, his company, Empire Computus, decided to re-assign his management position in a way that didn't recognize his essential contribution. Remembering that his dream had taught him to follow his bliss, he knew that he couldn't live without appreciation. After he resigned, and the judge awarded him a pair of golden wings, he felt freer and more joyous than ever before. He flew off to live with Princess Satisfyus in the Ocean of his Dreams, adjacent to his Valley, and consulted to many grateful companies.

> ## Base your level of relationship commitments on BOTTOM LINES—what you can't live with and can't live without.

Commandment No. 18 summary

BOTTOM LINES means *really* understanding what your minimum requirements are for each of your relationships, given how much you put into and expect to get out of them. You commit to and create different levels of significance in your relationships with: your spouse or partner and children, other family, best friends, friends, associates and community, state/nation, world, and universe. Depending on the level of relationship you wish to form, and what you hope to receive in return, you invest only in a manner that assures your own joy and well-being. BOTTOM LINES further your growth at a satisfactory pace, with a tolerable level of pain, while guaranteeing your greatest success in the long run.

(See Chapter 18 for a complete discussion of this Commandment.)

"Listen, all my children," said the Siddhu, (a Hindu mystic) "as I tell you an old Hindu story. There was once a sparrow, his life an endless motion, his needs taken care of with but a fraction of his flitter. One day he spotted a beach from above that had once been a dinosaur. Moved by this sign of the power of heaven and earth, he knew that he had to make a mountain. 'Folly,' cried the rest of his flock. But then they watched him painstakingly progress, a few grains of sand at a time. When Lord Vishnu arrived, one bird after another joined in, and the sand began to fly in the beaks of the many. 'Till lo and behold, the beach disappeared and the mountain arose from the actions of these tiny little birds. And thanks to this miracle, we are sitting on this hilltop today."

Create SYNERGY by using win-win and setting boundaries.

Commandment No. 19 summary

SYNERGY means synchronizing energy and effort expended so that in all of your interactions the outcome produced by the participants in concert exceeds that which would be produced by the sum of the participants by themselves. *Win-win* strategies for thinking and doing means that you always interact in a way that is mutually satisfactory; no one loses and everyone gains. *Boundaries* are psychological semipermeable membranes or limits which you establish in order to communicate the terms under which you will or will not participate with others—within your own and others' BOTTOM LINES and societal laws. When as individuals we set our boundaries and opt for win-win strategies, we manifest a marvelous characteristic of our higher mind, as we consciously create SYNERGY, accelerate evolution, and form the higher-complexity Global Brain superorganism. Clear intention with common vision, executed responsibly, leads to a world order with a SYNERGY that benefits everyone, since it creates harmony between the goals of its individuals and those of the system as a whole.

(See Chapter 19 for a complete discussion of this Commandment.)

In the market one day, Outasync, a cursing, big, muscled drunk lashed out, sending a woman holding a baby to the ground, reeling from the blow. As an Aikido master sprung into position to counter the next impact of Outasync's waving fists, at the last second a quiet, wizened old Samaritan shouted an earsplitting "Hey!" Everyone froze. "C'mon over," he beckoned to the lost soul, "What have you been drinking?" "Wine! Step back!" threatened Outasync. Unfazed, the good Samaritan continued, "Oh, I love to have my glass of wine, under my favorite tree, as my wife and I sit and watch the quiet sky. Do you like that too?" Outasync began to sob, "My wife left me, I lost my job, I'm no good to anyone." "Yes," the Samaritan acknowledged, "everyone needs someone to talk with. I will listen. Strong men like you can save our world." As Outasync laid his head on this elder's shoulder, the Aikido master learned his greatest lesson.[3]

REPAIR the world by treating others reverently and fairly and doing good deeds.

Commandment No. 20 summary

REPAIR means that you act consciously to effect an ever-renewing heaven-on-Earth society by believing that everything you do either hurts or helps you and everybody else, too. It is really a paraphrasing for modern times of Jesus Christ's Golden Rule: "Do unto others as you would have done unto you." It asks that for the Consciousness Age you take initiative and responsibility to search for opportunities to be of service to others. At a minimum, don't do to others what you would hate to have done to you. Use *reverence* to avoid bringing harm to others, even more than that, let *fairness* guide your actions, and at a maximum, voluntarily do *good deeds* for other people. Eastern traditions use the concept of "Karma" to enforce this principle. When we continuously REPAIR the Global Brain, the nervous control system, we ensure the proper caretaking of the planet, its environment, its people, its other living beings, and its longevity.

(See Chapter 20 for a complete discussion of this Commandment.)

ONE STORY

There is only one story: humanity going from lower to higher consciousness, from ape to human being; and the story continues to unfold. Generation after generation, our brief time on Earth motivates each of us to reach toward our ultimate potential.

Have courage. Be strong. Keep the faith. Be responsible. Struggle for freedom. If we keep these admonitions always in mind and live in accordance with them, they will help us to move ahead and to withstand the ever-present temptation to regress. Any way you look at it, one force pulls humanity forward and another force pulls humanity back. Guess which one will eventually win?

4

FROM MOSES TO MOTOFS: FROM SLAVERY TO FREEDOM

Security is mostly superstition. It does not exist in nature, nor do the children of men as a whole experience it. Avoiding danger is no safer in the long run than outright exposure. Life is either a daring adventure, or nothing. To keep our faces toward change and behave like free spirits in the presence of fate is strength undefeatable.

—Helen Keller (1880-1968)

A ship in a harbor is safe, but that is not what ships are built for.

—William Shedd

What made Pharaoh Ramses II, around 1270 B.C., agree to lose his cheap work force which was building monumental creations like the great Temples of Luxor and Karnak? Can you imagine Moses going to the great ruler of ancient Egypt and saying, "I want you to release from bondage your 600,000 Israelite slaves and let me take them to the land of Canaan. Let my people go!" Why, in the end, did the Pharaoh actually give his consent? How did Moses pull it off? Did he convince the king that these were in fact "the chosen people"? Or was Ramses II an enlightened leader who recognized he had to accept Moses' demands, since Moses had been raised in the Egyptian court and had reached the highest grade of priesthood?

UNTHINKABLE EXODUS FROM PRISON TO PLAYGROUND

The Bible states that God inflicted ten plagues upon Egypt that so demoralized Pharaoh that he finally let the Hebrews go—only to shortly thereafter change his mind and chase them across the desert. The Hebrews escaped as Moses parted the Red Sea, drowning the pursuing Egyptian armies.

Moses managed to free his nation and pull off the greatest, most unthinkable exodus in history. Following the directions of his God, whom the Old Testament calls "Yahweh," he led the chosen people to the Promised Land of milk and honey. Yet the journey to the Promised Land was almost as difficult as being a slave for Pharaoh had been. The freed slaves struggled through the desert for 40 years, and faced many life-threatening situations. According to the Bible, God often came to their rescue, through Moses, and miraculously provided water, food, and other necessities.

It was during one of these times, when the chance of survival seemed bleak and desperate at best, that Moses answered the call by coming down from Mount Sinai with the Ten Commandments. This code of laws was inspired by Yahweh and was meant to guide the Israelites to live in greater peace, harmony, and freedom according to God's rules. They differed substantially from ways in which the former slaves had grown accustomed to living.

46

For example, in Pharaoh's time, who dared to ask if yet another temple or monument was really needed? The decision was made by one person or, at most, a very few people who ruled based upon their own needs and desires. Pharaoh ruled supreme; his law was divine, and his actions could not be questioned. The best a person could do was to survive as well as possible. Moses led his people from that Egyptian world to develop a society where the Ten Commandments would guide the way that people lived and treated each other. The Commandments helped the Israelites survive and taught them how to treat each other with far more respect than had been possible in Pharaoh's world of slavery. They indeed began to experience a brand new world of freedom.

Indeed, this freedom smacked many of them with greater responsibility than they could handle. This helps us to understand why God decreed that a generation of slave-mentality people—including Moses—would have to die en route, at the very entrance to Canaan, modern-day Israel.

Joshua took command of the new generation, seeking the land where they could live in freedom. He toppled the walls of Jericho, at the entrance to Canaan, and proceeded to conquer the rest of the Holy Land. Finally released from bondage in the prisons of Egypt, and from the desolation of the desert, the Israelites settled down in their new homeland.

Now truly free, the Hebrews went on to build the magnificent Kingdom of David with Jerusalem as its capital. Only in the twentieth century have archaeologists unearthed the veritable splendor that these people constructed. This included the first gigantic Temple of God, whose remains today constitute the famous Wailing, or Western, Wall in Jerusalem. The federation of 13 tribes peaked soon thereafter, during the reign of King Solomon. Under his leadership, the Israelite empire spread far and wide, perhaps as far south as modern-day Ethiopia, as it amassed riches of gold and other trading goods. Yet it remained a moralistic and just society, a society based upon the founding principles learned in the desert during the long struggle to find freedom.

Today we face a mission as daunting as Moses': can we fathom <u>freeing</u> the whole world from survival concerns within a generation, ending all suffering and wars, and creating a utopian heaven-on-Earth? If we can't, we too may become slaves in a modern society building temples to the "Pharaoh" of technology, and using up our planet while not caring for the long-term needs of all of its people. The mission seems almost impossible. And yet, over and over again in history, people have proven that what was previously thought to be inconceivable ended up happening only a short time later. Whether the story is of Moses' unthinkable exodus, or of putting a man on the moon within a decade of the 1961 declaration by President Kennedy of the United States that we would do so—when space travel had only been pioneered in the prior decade—history records many heroic accomplishments of humankind.

The challenge we face today is just as difficult as that faced by the Israelite slaves of long ago, because we have become accustomed to seeking more and more creature comforts, and in the process have become slaves to the material benefits of our technological society. Yet it is becoming clear that at some point, greater material benefits alone do not satisfy us, make life more enjoyable, or give us the ability to respect and co-exist with each other. Why doesn't extra wealth insure greater satisfaction? Because the very idea of greater wealth comes from a basis of the individual needing to dominate others to insure individual survival, a behavior that has persisted throughout the history of civilization. In a world where there is enough for all to survive, a new and different basis of living becomes necessary. In fact, a planetary society needs all of its members to behave in ways that will insure the survival of all. All need to become conscious of their actions, and of the consequences of their actions for the planet as a whole. The poverty of ghettos, the hideousness of crime, the atrocities that societies' discontents can wreak with powerful homemade firearms, terrorists on the bandwagon of a cause, or dictators on a warring rampage, will eventually affect even those materially well-off. So what can we all do about it, before we fall victim to another Holocaust, in whatever form it manifests itself?

All of us can make the transition from a survival-oriented society to a consciousness-dominated one, but it requires a lot of changes. Many people will experience these changes as stressful and very painful. Ultimately, some will adapt, and some won't. This has already happened many times in the past. For example, when some tribes began to use fire, others resisted it because they considered it dangerous. Or later, when certain societies discovered the survival advantages of using language, some people chose to continue to grunt. The *grunters* didn't fare too well in evolution. In each of these cases, the adapters learned to enjoy their increased sense of control over their environment. They subsequently passed on their genes, and the non-adapters became extinct.

Those who adapt to the consciousness-oriented community will gradually begin to view Earth as a playground, not a prison. In a prison—whether in bondage in Egypt or in jail—people do their best to pass the time, just trying to survive from day to day. Unfortunately, most people alive today live in this constricted way. However, a new generation of people all over the world will leave this way behind to live in a beyond-individual-survival-oriented world. Like the brave people who triumphed in the Promised Land in biblical times, they will establish an idealistic and model society, but this time a global one.

Even adapters take time to adjust to higher and higher levels of freedom, because it involves more responsibility. In this world, everyone will have far more choices for work, education, health, and happiness than ever before, thus building a freely creating and synergistic society. Is this hard to get used to? Who knows? It will seem like being back in kindergarten, on the playground, taking everything as a serious, but fun, learning experience. The only exception is that the "children" will also have to take responsibility for meeting each other's collective needs.

Which of us "chosen people" will make this new reality happen? What kind of a moral code will we follow? Will the original Ten Commandments suffice?

COMPARING THE 2ND TEN COMMANDMENTS TO THE ORIGINAL TEN COMMANDMENTS

Whenever a major shift in society occurs, reactionary factions form to object to the change. They argue for a return to the "comforts" of Egypt and "the good old days," often nothing more than a mythical, nostalgic attachment to the past. The Israelites trekked for 40 years in the harsh desert conditions. God and Moses had decreed that one whole generation had to die there as a punishment for lacking faith in the search for the Promised Land. Undoubtedly many of them rebelled, wished to return to Egypt, and probably even wanted to kill Moses. They couldn't understand why he took them from a life of total security, albeit in slavery, to one of complete uncertainty, starvation, and peril. Moses responded by going up on the mountain for 40 days. He returned with God's word, the Ten Commandments. These provided an answer to the nation, established law and order, and saved Moses from the anger of his own people.

Today we face a similar transition. Once again, evolution has presented us with a chance to move toward more freedom. Whether we do or not depends on the choices we make, individually and collectively, and who chooses to follow the 2nd Ten Commandments. Let's briefly explore how they relate to the original ones. The Ten Commandments from Moses' times have continued to serve us to the present day, will continue to, and thus merit reviewing.

For easy reference, here's the wisdom from about 1270 B.C., the Ten Commandments (EXODUS 20:3-17):[1]

THE TEN COMMANDMENTS

1. Thou shalt have no other gods before me.

2. Thou shalt not make unto thee any graven image, . . .

3. Thou shalt not take the name of the Lord thy God in vain; . . .

4. Remember the sabbath day, to keep it holy. . . .

5. Honour thy father and thy mother: . . .

6. Thou shalt not murder.

7. Thou shalt not commit adultery.

8. Thou shalt not steal.

9. Thou shalt not bear false witness against thy neighbor.

10. Thou shalt not covet thy neighbor's house, . . . , nor any thing that is thy neighbor's.

These decrees represent one of civilization's first giant, formalized steps: moving human beings beyond the law of survival, of each primarily looking out for his or her own, and toward responsible behavior on a societal level. Moses gets credit for receiving, interpreting, and enforcing this significant codification of laws of consciousness (although, arguably, Hammurabi and others had done it before him). The Israelites, and many subsequent generations in the Western World, have tried to live by them.

The first Ten Commandments encourage the use of the rational mind to rule impulses and determine right actions. This differentiates humans from animals who rely only on brutal self-interest. In the state of nature, each individual engages in a war against all, and even "man is a wolf toward man."[2] So the Ten Commandments protect individuals, each of whom is attempting to survive, from one another, while also maintaining law and order in society. They have served as precursors for many of today's legal systems.

The first Ten Commandments as they were divined and written are stated in the **negative** voice to play on human fears. Even the two commandments that don't start with "Thou shalt *not,*" numbers three and four, imply what not to do: *don't* do work on the Sabbath day, and *don't* act disrespectfully toward your parents. In the days of Moses the consequences for violating any of these commandments was nothing less than capital punishment.

The object of God's covenant with Moses was to enable people to live in peace, prosperity, and stability. Yet the Mosaic laws are not presented as utilitarian rules to ensure the greatest happiness of the greatest number of individuals. According to noted biblical scholars, God guarantees happiness to the community, rather than to the individual, that obeys them.[3]

The 2nd Ten Commandments promise to deliver happiness to both the individual and the society, by stating laws of human nature in the **positive** rather than the negative. This allows the creation of a synergistic community, one in which the happiness of each of the individuals adds up to a community that functions even better than the sum of its parts.

While the threat of retribution for transgression scared many of Moses' followers, he never explicitly mentioned the rewards of adherence. Let's look at each of the Ten Commandments and their unstated or missing promises, which we can now manifest for ourselves in the Consciousness Age.[4]

1. Thou shalt have no other gods before me.

2. Thou shalt not make unto thee any graven image, . . .

The first two Commandments, when looked at affirmatively, could mean that you have the security of knowing that there is just one Almighty God to follow, or that as a human you should pay attention to your Higher Self and the consciousness God gave you. By not worshipping false sources of power, you can find inner peace and establish dominion over the Earth.

3. Thou shalt not take the name of the Lord thy God in vain; . . .

The third Commandment promises that by not denigrating God you won't put yourself down either. Respect all of creation, and you respect yourself.

4. Remember the sabbath day, to keep it holy. . . .

The fourth Commandment grants you peace and rest, as you occasionally get to sit back and enjoy both the fruits of your labor and the rest of creation.

5. Honour thy father and thy mother: . . .

The fifth Commandment guarantees that you have a perfect identity and can accept yourself, as you positively value everything that your parents passed on to you.

6. Thou shalt not murder.

If you—and everyone else—follow the sixth Commandment, you yourself will not get murdered.

7. Thou shalt not commit adultery.

Again, if you—and everyone else—follow the seventh Commandment, you will feel pure, and will not have to worry about somebody else having sex with *your* husband or wife.

8. Thou shalt not steal.

If we all adhered to the eighth Commandment, we'd never have to worry about keeping what belongs to us.

9. Thou shalt not bear false witness against thy neighbor.

Tell the truth by following the ninth Commandment, and you will earn the ability to witness the marvel of creation in all its truth.

10. Thou shalt not covet thy neighbor's house, . . . nor anything that is thy neighbor's.

Be content with what the universe gives you by living by the tenth Commandment, and all the goods you could possibly need will come to you.

The 2nd Ten Commandments include the missing promises of the Ten Commandments. Yet they go further and include messages necessary for living in a society never envisioned by Moses—a Global Society. They are meant to help lead to the creation of a heaven-on-Earth, where we all live together as one tribe—humanity—with many unique ways of expressing what is important to us.

The 2nd Ten Commandments do this by presenting laws and wisdom in an evolutionary manner which appeals to today's individuals and leads us into higher consciousness. Over the last 3,000 years, the outside world we live in has changed significantly. With all due credit to Moses' inspired leadership of thousands of years ago, so has our perception of the rules of behavior humans should follow. The actual laws never change; we just come to understand them with increasing clarity as we evolve. For example, imagine Moses walking with sandals and a robe into your house.[5] He couldn't operate your microwave oven. He couldn't possibly have heard of the *Big Bang* theory and its implications, or conceive of airplanes, other than as objects that must belong to aliens or other gods (and try showing him your frequent flier mileage statement . . .). No matter how sincerely he would try to communicate with you, you'd be reluctant to accept his wisdom as the last word for the world of today. We need wisdom stated in modern terms, wisdom with which we can more easily relate.

The first Ten Commandments worked for the generations of humanity who were embodiments of what today we would call the Inner Child, who lacked the security of a strong and rational Inner Parent, and whose behavior could be controlled by fear. The Ten Commandments—and many religions throughout history—have provided a strong, parental guiding force, while promising a practical reward of protection and personal salvation. The need for such guidelines in illiterate, poor, and undeveloped societies, with ongoing fear and distrust, makes perfect sense.

However, as humanity develops, we incorporate elements of both the Inner Child and rational Inner Parent. As we enter the Consciousness Age when, at some point soon, most of humanity will be sufficiently literate and connected by technology to want a say in what happens to our planet, isn't it time for all of us to grow up and act in concert, to insure our planetary survival, as well as our own personal security and happiness?

The 2nd Ten Commandments encourage everyone to tap into their higher mind and act out of love. They urge us to heed our INNER VOICEs, or Higher Selves, and integrate the parts of us that belong to a greater consciousness into our daily lives. They offer a set of strong guidelines, based upon self-interest and love rather than fear, to allow us to accept ways of behaving that will be effective both for us and for all with whom we come in contact. They differ from the original Ten Commandments by allowing some mistakes without societal punishment. They ask you as a responsible, conscious person, to do the best you can, recognize and apologize for your mistakes, and strive to get better and better. This attitude represents evolution toward a higher order of mind and consciousness.

Whether you comply with the 2nd Ten Commandments, and to what degree, only you and your INNER VOICE will really know. Others may observe improvements in your corresponding level of overall health, a direct result of increasingly living by these laws. Perhaps these Commandments will form the basis for societal laws of the future, to be applied to all tiers of society, and interpreted by the highest courts of the world. And if a disagreement should arise about how to apply the wisdom of the first versus the 2nd Ten Commandments, the more modern, *affirmative* Commandment should take precedence.

OUR BRAINS EVOLVE TOWARD PARTICIPATING IN A GLOBAL BRAIN

As we saw, the Israelites fled from a pagan land of many gods and subsequently embraced a monotheistic belief system. According to the law of Moses, each person was responsible and accountable directly to God for their own conduct. This constituted a major shift toward personal responsibility and away from seeing oneself as a victim of the environment. We now stand on the verge of making another such leap, moving, as co-creators, toward an interconnected world.

Our first glimpse of the planet as a whole *superorganism* (a system containing many organisms) came only in the second half of the twentieth century, when we marveled at pictures of our home taken from outer space.

In order to understand the concept of the Earth as a superorganism, it is helpful to consider the most popular conceptualization of how our brain is structured, and how it evolved. (There are competing models amongst neuroscientists today.) Around 1950 Paul MacLean introduced the *triune* model of the brain.[6] According to this model, the human brain is composed of at least three different parts, each of which developed at a different time in our evolution, and each of which reflects a different quality of consciousness.

The first and oldest part of the brain, the *medulla,* is usually said to include our brain stem. It is most closely related to a reptilian, survival-oriented, "basic instinct and needs" consciousness. Originally, we used it as "first alerts" for survival.

As we developed further, but still millions of years ago, we evolved the second part of the triune model, called the *limbic,* or *paleomammalian,* brain, identified by scientists as an egg-shaped area in the center of our skull enclosure. It enhanced our fight-or-flight response, and thus our individual survival, even further. This part of our brain is most reflective of mammalian consciousness. Many psychologists today refer to some combination of the medulla and limbic system as the subconscious mind.

Later still, perhaps only two to three million years ago, the third part of the triune model, our *neomammalian* brain, called the *cortex,* a cap-like covering of the two older parts of our brain commonly referred to as the "gray matter," began to develop. This reasoning ability led our distant ancestors to group together and form hunting and gathering societies which would one day allow the dawning of cradles of civilization, where ever-larger groups of individuals would help each other to survive more securely. Over the course of the most recent hundred thousand—and especially the last ten thousand or so—years of humanity's existence, the outermost layers and the frontal areas of the cortex developed and/or began to be used increasingly. Most psychologists today refer to this faculty of our brain as the conscious or rational mind.

We are still very much products of that recent, by the evolutionary time clock, wave of improvement. Unfortunately, at this point in our evolutionary history, we are also much like young adolescents who have gone out of control with this newfound power. We play with matches (factories that pollute our atmosphere), sticks (bulldozers that rip apart our ground and uproot forests), and arrows (chemical and nuclear weapons). We are capable of learning and following rules designed for safety and mutual enrichment, yet have not done so to the extent that is needed to insure our survival. Because of the powers we have already discovered while using only a part of our brain's potential, we have come to endanger our entire planet.

Fortunately, evolution, with its self-preserving characteristics, has now made available to us another, higher, part of the brain. It seems that alternative states of mind, which have existed throughout history and have typically been associated with creativity and religion, result from certain combinations of the limbic system and the cortex. In 1985, neurologists found evidence that the analytic processes of the cortex depend on how it receives information: "In determining salience and valence, what we might call *qualitatively significant information*, the emotional (limbic) brain acts like a valve, regulating the flow of nervous information throughout the body, integrating both the direct wiring and volume of transmission."[7] In the right emotional states a higher wisdom, a combination of emotion and reason, seems to emerge.

Many people around the world, many more than ever before, have started to tap into this higher mind. You can call it intuition, divine guidance, or your INNER VOICE. When we grok something, rather than just thinking about it and comprehending it analytically, or just feeling it, we "get it" at a deeper level. Grokking is one example of utilizing the supraconscious, higher mind. Moments of creativity, inspiration, "ah-ha's," are some other examples.

At this point in our maturation as a species, we have only just begun to use the tremendous potential inherent in our higher mind, and will undoubtedly discover much more about it in the years to come. It seems to make us more concerned with the good of the whole, and to begin to connect us into a collective consciousness or mind. With its use, perhaps our species can learn to survive.

We can make a case for the evolutionary development of humanity based on three stages of the mind's evolution: the subconscious mind assisted our species to survive as individual animals, our rational mind to survive as groups of animals, and now our higher mind has the potential to allow us to survive and coexist peacefully in the whole biosphere, Earth.

This can only occur if we live by a set of societal guidelines that let us use more of our abilities in coordination with all others on our planet for our mutual survival and well-being.

This is also the first time in humanity's evolutionary history that there is no geographical frontier anywhere on Earth. We are all very quickly becoming more and more intermingled, and we are affecting each other by our actions. One car that breaks down on a metropolitan freeway can make tens of thousands of people late for work; cause millions of dollars of loss to society; untold stress to the people who sit and wait it out; sickness due to exposure to exhaust fumes; and who knows what else?

Yet frontiers have always existed and always will exist. The formation of the Global Brain is the current challenge for human life as we know it. This frontier involves both "inner space"—the expansion of our individual consciousness—and coordinated, interconnected activity—the expansion of group consciousness on a global level. Only by responsibly venturing into this frontier, and by learning how to wield our power, can we stop the havoc and madness that we cause every day to ourselves and to each other.

In a Global Brain, each person functions as a nerve cell of the larger system, the entire human race. As in our individual brains, the Global Brain consists of billions of cells. In the Global Brain these cells are connected and organized through technology and consciousness. Our telecommunication systems, for example—telephones, fax machines, and cable TV—are now increasingly serving a similar role to our brain's nerve cells in our vast developing global information network. These systems are similar to the large number of fibers linking the individual nerve cells and "ganglia" (clusters of nerve cells) in our brain's extensive personal information network.

An emergence of this kind of new techno-biological fabric is moving the Earth to a new, higher order of evolutionary complexity, and heralding the dawning of a new age for its people. As we courageously face this challenge, we must persevere in a deliverance march, as we free ourselves from survival concerns.

WHAT IS SUCCESS IN THE CONSCIOUSNESS AGE?

Spiritual principles govern human behavior, and are as real, unchanging, and universal as the laws of physics are in the physical dimension. In the hard sciences we come to new understandings of the laws of the physical world as we discover new models that better explain our observations. We assume that the laws themselves have held true since the beginning of time, and will continue to. (Imagine how interesting—and confusing—our universe would be if this wasn't the case, and if, for example, the law of gravity worked one day, but not the next.) Similarly, in the spiritual dimension the laws also remain constant, but our understanding of them improves with time, as we refine our models. As with natural, physical laws, spiritual principles are objective, inviolate, and apply at all times, everywhere.

The *spiritual principles* proposed here as the 2nd Ten Commandments are our best model, at this time in our evolution, of the laws that pertain to human behavior, relationships, and organizations. They can also be viewed as "Ten Evolutionary Laws of Human Nature" that can help each of us, and all of us, to advance.

Dr. Stephen Covey, who has extensively studied historical success literature, defines *effectiveness* based on spiritual principles as bringing "the maximum long-term beneficial results possible."[8] He goes on to say that a life based on principles creates "an empowering center of correct maps from which an individual can effectively solve problems, maximize opportunities, and continually learn and integrate other principles in an upward spiral of growth."

Unlike the rest of physical nature, however, the human mind and "soul," or spark of divinity, give humans free will to choose to follow, or to attempt to violate, these laws. But as Cecil B. deMille, creator of the movie *The Ten Commandments,* observed, "It is impossible for us to break the law. We can only break ourselves against the law."[9] To live wisely and succeed, we must choose to adhere to these evolutionary laws. Knowing that spiritual principles have always pointed the way to individual success, we can now put forth these two definitions:

Spiritual Principles
Fundamental underlying laws that govern human nature, that we can use our free will to choose to follow.

Success
Exercising our free will to choose to evolve toward higher consciousness and eventually enlightenment, by increasingly following spiritual principles.

Our definition of success encompasses all the more common ones. Most people, when they think about success, think of achieving happiness, having a lot of money, doing well in their career, and looking good. Some people also include having satisfying relationships with their families, an intimate partner, friends, and other community members. Those who have had health problems, and eventually everyone as they age, figure out that a prerequisite to any of these accomplishments is to get up every morning and feel good, and to have few or no physical problems. Spiritual evolution provides physical health and growth as well as these other achievements. Since it increases your use of your infinite potential as a human being, you open more and more doors as you grow. Suddenly you realize that your personal evolution expands your horizons, allowing you to realize your truly important and worthwhile goals.

Living in a state of higher consciousness is like putting yourself in a continuously better stream of life. What comes your way keeps improving. At the extreme, if you ascend as far as one can (as far as we know), you might reach a state of enlightenment. Experiencing this extraordinary feeling all the time, you would view life very differently, and perhaps not really care as much about the things that seem so important to you now.

Nothing matters. Everything is important.

Up until now the path to true success (as defined here) has often been obscured by the "noise" and barriers erected by each of us in our attempt to win the physical, individual survival game of life on Earth. As we have discussed, like all other mammals, our brain first automatically and instinctively pursues self-preservation of the organism. As our species evolves, we awaken to the capabilities of the higher mind and seek the preservation of all, rather than just of the individual member. We will achieve success, allowing us to evolve spiritually as well as to survive, individually and collectively, by following the 2nd Ten Commandments.

In order to understand how we evolved to a place where the 2nd Ten Commandments could guide us to an imminent Global Promised Land, let's briefly survey the major time periods our species has undergone. Our first ancestors spent several million years in the prehistoric Stone Age, learning how to survive by the "law of the jungle" (See Table 4-1). As recently as 12,000 years ago, many of them discovered the benefits of organizing into agrarian civilizations, giving rise to the Agricultural Age. Only then did writing and "history" begin. The third stage, the Industrial Age, commenced in the 1700s. Innovators in England and the newly formed United States of America began to mechanize many manual tasks, such as food production, textile fabrication, and even wax candle manufacturing. Later, mass production techniques delivered large quantities of goods for less work. These machines operated with minimal built-in intelligence, primarily repeating the same function over and over again. This age lasted about 200 years. Finally, in the decades since World War II, the explosion of communications, computing, and information processing technology has fueled the growth of the Information Age.

The major advances of each age lead to the significant changes for life in the next. People in the Agricultural Age used stone tools developed in the prehistoric era for grinding metal, thereby turning metal into tools used to farm. The Industrial Age refined the use of metal by assembling it into more complex machinery, mostly steam- and petroleum-driven, used for mass production. Today, global corporations utilize mass production methods to spread technological innovation through silicon-based commodity consumer products, as the Information Age proliferates. Each new age has had to wait for a critical mass of discovery and knowledge to form, before building upon the previous one, as progress then takes its next major step.

Table 4-1

The Accelerating Ages of Humanity

AGE	PERIOD	DEFINITION
I. Prehistoric (stone)	3 - 4 million years? $[3 - 4 \times 10^6 \text{ years}]$	Little or no written records; "law of the jungle" survival; nomadic tribes; food gathering.
II. Agricultural (metal)	12,000 years (10,000 B.C. - 1700s A.D.) $[1.2 \times 10^4 \text{ years}]$	Beginning of written history and urban, agrarian civilization.
III. Industrial (steam and oil)	200 years (1700s A.D. - 1940s A.D.) $[2 \times 10^2 \text{ years}]$	Mechanization of most manual tasks; mass production with minimal built-in intelligence.
IV. Information (silicon)	40 years (1940s - 1980s) $[4 \times 10^1 \text{ years}]$	Creation of computing and communication technologies to the point of mass, commodity-like, worldwide availability.

But notice the incredible acceleration in evolution's pace. We go from an era lasting millions of years (10^6, Prehistoric), to succeeding eras lasting tens of thousands of years (10^4, Agricultural), then hundreds (10^2, Industrial), then mere decades (10^1, Information). Let's assume that the ubiquitous use of computers today has already made an impact, especially in the first, or economically and technologically developed, world. If indeed we have come to the end of the Information Age, what's next? Could this quickening bring us an era lasting less than 10 years, or only a year or so (10^0)? Or are we at the gateway to a whole new epoch in humanity's development?

We clearly need new guidance to cope with this quickening. Human life-span has increased dramatically in the twentieth century. People in the first world now live, on average, over twice as long as humans in any other recorded time in history. In this century we have also experienced unprecedented technological acceleration and accomplishment, which has resulted in the changes discussed in the next chapter. Interestingly enough, during this time period world population, which was under 1 billion throughout all previous history, also began growing exponentially, and will continue to grow to a possible 10 billion people within the next 40 years. Indeed we face a "brave new world" never before imagined! What is happening, and why?

This acceleration means that the discoveries and products of each new era will spread more rapidly than they did in the previous era. As a whole, the human race moves gradually into each new age. Today we can expect this hastening to reach all the corners of the Earth. Many parts of the world have not yet even become industrialized. Nonetheless, the world turns with each step toward a place of no return. For example, in 1988 Cable News Network (CNN) television became available globally, at about the same time as personal computers. People everywhere could now tap into a common picture of the news on the planet. Leaders of the world rely on networks such as CNN and computers to collect and disseminate information. Pervasive changes such as this have allowed countries like South Korea to migrate from an agriculturally based society to a technologically based one, fully immersed in the Information Age, in only 25 years! All the other countries will soon follow, expeditiously achieving this transition, or the even easier one from an industrially based society, in an estimated 10 to 15 years.

Furthermore, information is now used to influence people's mind-sets worldwide. As one example, during the Russian

Revolution of 1991, Boris Yeltsin used a computer link to determine if NATO would support him. Upon receiving this assurance electronically, he summoned the courage to step up on the tank, a scene that many people all over the world remember seeing on CNN.

Another example is the electronic town hall meeting concept. In the near future, people may vote on their home computers on political issues or candidates, bringing about a truer form of democracy than most representative democratic systems. The founding fathers of the United States would roll over in their graves if they heard this—they didn't trust the common folk to make decisions of such importance. But the future will see villagers in the most remote places on the planet linked in to a bigger, global vision. They probably already drink Coca Cola or Pepsi, listen to popular music stars like Madonna and Enya, wear Levi's and Casio watches, and watch the International Olympic Games on television. And yes, they all want to grow up and "be like Mike" (Michael Jordan—the globally renowned NBA professional basketball star of the 1990s), or whomever else is receiving worldwide attention and media coverage at any given time.

So what will a member of the world connected into this new global mind-set seek in the twenty-first century? Consciousness. They will attempt to grasp the very essence of being human, and to transcend viewing life as just a creature trying to survive.

Consciousness will come to mean knowing what we're all about individually and collectively. In the Consciousness Age, society will value learning as the primary reason for existence. The Information Age provided us with the means to generate reams of data. The next age will be one of information management via interactive monitoring and control. All entities, individual and collective (corporations, communities, countries, and others) will find that to survive they must learn to know themselves, understand how they work, and then continuously use this knowledge to develop as a part of the whole, the Global Brain. This necessary transition will require a new genre of people, thinking and living with new guidelines.

Consciousness

Knowing what we're all about individually and collectively.

Consciousness Age

An era in which personal growth, learning, and pleasurable enjoyment supplant individual survival as the primary reason for existence.

A NEW TYPE OF HUMAN

Between about 1988 and 2028 people will adapt to the reality of the Consciousness Age and create and enjoy a newfound freedom that will profoundly affect humanity's destiny. We use 1988 as a marker for the beginning of the transition since the Global Brain's ability to deliver information throughout the planet, instantaneously, was born at this time via CNN and Internet, and became accessible in a significant way to people everywhere. Forty years from then, the same time span as Moses' exodus, a majority of people will be Motofs. This will be 2028.

We hope you will choose to empower the word "tribe," the "t" in Motof, with its positive associations, and leave its negative ones behind. To some people "tribe" has negative connotations based on images of warlords and warriors wielding spears, hunting and killing everything in sight. True, many tribes engaged in a myriad of what we now consider primitive and barbaric practices, including cannibalism. Perhaps we can forgive them on the grounds of their ignorance; they were doing the best they could to survive. But at the same time they held sacred, and managed over centuries to pass on, a heritage of oneness and commonality amongst their clan members.

They took care of each other, and felt a strong sense of connection to Mother Earth.

Today we romanticize tribal people's close sense of family, community, and earthiness precisely because we recognize these features as missing from many of our somewhat insulated and lonely lives. There's no going back to the days of living in the bushes and hunting for our food. But it is our hope that the favorable connotations of "tribe" will spark a feeling of unity among all spirits here on our beloved planet, and will help us to remember, as we forge our future, that we depend very intimately upon one another and our planet for our survival, as do the members of any other tribe.

To comprehend the tribal metaphor a little better, imagine having lived on a secluded island, such as Hawaii, hundreds of years ago, with 2,500 miles of ocean separating you in every direction from the nearest land mass and other peoples. You would have felt a kinship with all the tribes-people on your island, and the island itself, as you knew you depended on them. Similarly, Motofs will come to see all of humanity as living on "Island Earth," secluded in vast amounts of space, separated by who knows how many millions of light-years from the nearest living population. Perhaps, as was the case for the Hawaiian islands, someday ships of some sort will also land on our secluded Island Earth, bringing missionaries and alien goods from other parts of the universe. Will we see them as a threat, or greet them as another part of our tribe?

Recognizing their own membership in the planetary tribe of Island Earth, Motofs will transcend the "me and mine only" survival mentality, and make a quantum shift to a new species of humanity, while those who do not have this world view will suffer and may die off quicker. Motofs will realize that people's fears and concerns for physical survival, based on animal-like responses lodged in the subconscious mind, now only rarely apply in our lives today. Consequently, they will transcend the fear-based emotions that result from inaccurately perceiving situations based on past realities of scarcity. This mental shift will afford them with vastly better health and longer life-spans than any human species has had until now.

The attachment to materialism, based on false programming of what we need to make us happy, results in addictions and subsequent pain. Its remedy is realizing, actually grokking, that technology has already provided the basics. In modern society, starving or freezing to death has become a choice, and no longer a real threat. This is true in most of the developed nations. There's no reason why we couldn't provide 90 percent of what the median person in a developed nation has today to all members of the planet. That would certainly provide a sufficient standard of living for all.

Freed from individual survival concerns, Motofs can choose to create whatever they want in their lives, as long as they align themselves with the physical and spiritual laws of nature. Motofs are the self-chosen people who will adapt to and succeed in the Consciousness Age and someday be the only people left on Earth.

How does one become a Motof? By starting to live by the 2nd Ten Commandments. But the first step is to acknowledge the significance of the changes that have taken place in our recent history. Without this recognition, none of us would have the impetus to adapt to the new reality that's already happening. The next chapter will further explore some of the specifics of these changes.

5

THE IMPACT OF
ACCELERATING
CHANGE

*Western society for the past 300 years has been
caught up in a fire storm of change . . . with waves
of ever accelerating speed and unprecedented
impact. We are (now) living through the greatest
wave of change on the planet since the
Enlightenment and the Industrial Revolution.*
                        — Alvin Tofler, *Future Shock* (1970)[1]
                    and in a speech in San Francisco in 1993

*In our society at present, the "natural course of
events" is precisely that the rate of change should
continue to accelerate up to the as-yet-unreached
limits of human and institutional adaptability.*
                        — Psychoanalyst Erik Erikson,
                        The Challenge of Youth (1963)[2]

I n 1970, in his best-selling book *Future Shock*, Alvin Tofler was among the first to dazzle us with his insights about how fast the world was changing. Until then, people had dismissed Aldous Huxley's *Brave New World* and George Orwell's *1984* as interesting but implausible descriptions of futuristic totalitarian societies. They viewed Robert Heinlein's *Stranger in a Strange Land*, which portrayed a new model of living meant for all people (quite similar in some ways to the 2nd Ten Commandments), as science fiction. Very few of us expected that these "futuristic" fictional works of yesteryear would become tomorrow's realities within a few brief decades, or what consequences this might have for society.

"FUTURE SHOCK" ON A DAY BY DAY BASIS

In *Future Shock*, Tofler argued convincingly that the accelerated pace of technological change would create one or more generations of lives wholly unprepared to contend with it. He also showed the undeniable and far-reaching negative effects that rapidly occurring change has on the lives of those who are unprepared or unable to cope with it. He defined *future shock* as "the shattering stress and disorientation that we induce in individuals by subjecting them to too much change in too short a time."[3]

In previous centuries, stress had resulted from the physical hardships of security-related concerns such as inadequate food, shelter, and lawlessness. Now, Tofler claimed, we would see stress induced by a society in constant upheaval resulting from fast-paced, technologically-driven innovations.

In the past several decades, all evidence has pointed to faster and faster change, perhaps even faster than Tofler believed would occur. Finally, the population of the planet Earth is awakening to the realization that it must not only adapt to an ongoing wave of accelerating change, but also develop the personal skills to cope with continuous change and avoid *daily* future shock.

Why will the adapting population want to live by the 2nd Ten Commandments? Let's briefly review several major areas of change and their impact on us and on our society. These changes have brought humanity to a condition totally unprecedented in its several-million-year history. They are of such magnitude that in speaking about them exact numbers lose their significance. Please bear with any minor contradictions that may arise from the use of different sources of data.

THE MAJOR CHANGES IN SUMMARY

The following dozen major changes are discussed in more detail in the next section, with their potential impacts explored in brief here:

1. The exponential growth of the Earth's population will level off at about 10 to 12 billion inhabitants early in the twenty-first century.

2. The average life-span has almost doubled in the twentieth century, to over 80 years.

3. The number of scientific and technological advances is doubling every year and a half; if this rate of increase continues, it will approach infinite change by 2012.

4. In the developed world, only 2 to 3 percent of the population produce basic sustenance, compared with almost 90 percent 200 years ago.

5. We have the technological ability to meet the basic survival needs of the whole planet within six years by using money now spent for defense.

6. Communication networks have grown exponentially and can now interlink people all over the world at the touch of a button.

7. One hundred of the world's 160 countries now have some form of democratic government.

8. Traveling the globe now takes hours, compared to months only 100 years ago.

9. English has emerged as a global language.

10. Computers, an invention of the last 50 years, now affect most people's daily lives, and almost everyone will have some form of a computer in the next century.

11. Developments in medicine in the second half of the twentieth century have given doctors the ability to prevent or promote procreation, using effective contraception, abortion, and fertilization techniques.

12. Recent medical advances now enable doctors to cure many previously terminal diseases, and genetic research may even alter life-span expectations.

What is the sum total, or ultimate significance, of these changes?

FACING THE FACTOIDS

1. **The exponential growth of the Earth's population will level off at about 10 to 12 billion inhabitants early in the twenty-first century.**

The world's total population has exploded, from under 1 billion from the dawn of humanity up to 1900, to 5.4 billion in 1992 (see Figure 5-1[4]). The greatest rate of change of population ever on the planet in the past, and most likely in the future, is occurring in our lifetime. This is shown in the vertical dashed-line "blip" in Figure 5-2.[5]

Scientists project that further growth will follow the solid line in the S-shaped curve shown in Figure 5-2. An S-shaped curve rises slowly at first, then accelerates rapidly until it reaches half of the maximum value, and then increases at a slower rate again until it reaches the maximum value. The population S-curve will attain a maximum of about 10 to 12 billion people early next century, where it is expected to remain for centuries to come.

Figure 5-1
World Population Growth

Billions of people

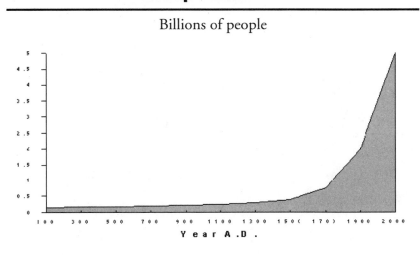

Figure 5-2
Population Changes S-Curve

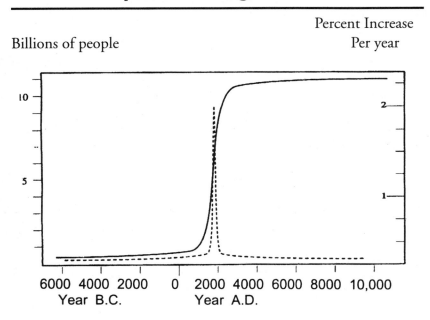

Various sources, including United Nations agencies, have reported that the Earth cannot sustain more than 10 to 12 billion humans. It's as though someone has monitored us and decided to "beam down all the rest"[6] and send 10 billion people in a 100-year period. Perhaps this will prepare us for our next evolutionary phase. (More on this later.)

How will we be able to cope, and not lose ourselves, with so many people around?

2.   **The average life-span has almost doubled in the twentieth century, to over 80 years.**

In the developed countries of the world, we have seen life-span increase from under 50 to over 80 years in less than a century.[7] In the next century, centenarians (people who are at least 100 years old) will abound and amaze us with their good health. Further advances in medicine could easily boost this number even further, especially with genetic alteration. Table 5-1 shows how average life-spans have progressively increased throughout history.

Table 5-1
Average Human Life-spans

Time Period (Eras)	Average Life-span (Years)
Cave man period	**19**
B.C. until the 1800s	**29**
1900 (United States)	**47**
1995 (United States)	**78**
2095 (Motofs worldwide)	**120 (estimated)**

Realize also that even the current life-span estimates derive from past data. Thirty or 40 years ago, many people alive today didn't expect to live this long. When they were children, people 60 years old were considered rare specimens. Likewise, life-spans of over 100 years in the next century may surprise many of today's young.

As an example of the impact of a change like this, consider the concept of marriage, which involves the vow, "until death do us part." With a life-span of 40 to 50 years, this used to mean around 20 to 30 years together, a little longer than the time it takes to raise several children to adulthood. This made good sense from the standpoint of nature procreating responsibly. With today's expected lifespan, the traditional marriage could easily result in 70 years of partnership. Is this too long? What norms will future societies establish?

The concept of work also requires rethinking. On average, people today will change careers seven times in their lives; prior to this century, most people expected to stay in their chosen career for a lifetime.

How will we cope with this type of change?

3. **The number of scientific and technological advances is doubling every year and a half; if this rate of increase continues, it will approach infinite change by 2012.**

The collective amount of scientific and technological human knowledge has increased to a point at which it doubles every year and a half. Table 5-2 shows data[8] normalized to the year 0 A.D. This means we assume that all know-how humanity had acquired by the time of Jesus Christ was one unit. It then took 1,500 years to double to two units, and finally reached 32 units in 1962. Since then, notice how the doubling times shrink. Knowledge has increased 256 or 512 times during the lifetime of people alive today. We could reach a million units by the end of the millennium, another increase of more than a hundredfold.

The pace has become so staggering that we can now chart *tenfold times* (the number of years it takes for our knowledge to increase by a factor of ten). By the year 2000, every three years we'll know ten times as much, clearly rendering obsolete a significant amount of our knowledge in a very short period of time. Extrapolating from its current course—and no one has reported a slowdown or limiting factor—this rate of change will theoretically reach infinity on December 21, 2012 (see Figures 5-3 and 5-4).[9]

Significantly, creativity indices such as the number of patents issued per day, have also increased rapidly. In 1991, the United States issued 488 patents per day, a record number. Here we see evidence of a global scientific community at work, since only 54 percent of the patents were issued to American inventors.[10]

What can help us cope with and accept the numerous and unpredictable ways our lives will be affected by rapid technological change?

Table 5-2

Collective Human Scientific Knowledge

Year	Units of Knowledge	Doubling Time (years)	Tenfold Time (years)
0 AD	1	50,000	500,000?
1500	2	1500	
1750	4	250	
1900	8	150	1900
1950	16	50	1200
1960	32	10	335
1967	64	7	142
1973	128	6	48
1978	256	5	23
1982	512	4	17
1985	1024	3.5	12
1988	2048	2.5	10
1990	4096	2	9
1992	8192	1.5	6
1994	16384	1.?	5?
1996	100,000	?	4?
1999	1,000,000	?	3?

Figure 5-3
Collective Human Scientific Knowledge

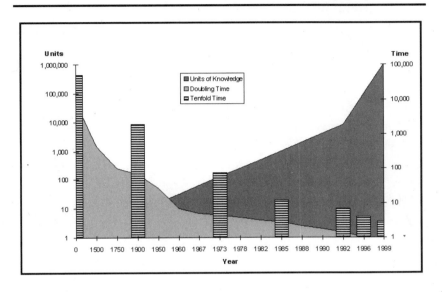

Figure 5-4
Ingression of Novelty Spiral

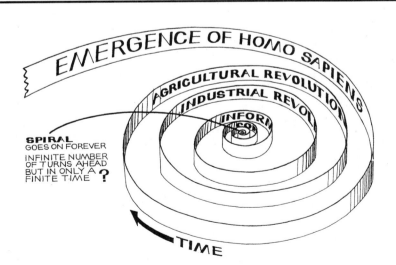

4. **In the developed world, only 2 to 3 percent of the population produce basic sustenance, compared with almost 90 percent 200 years ago.**

In the "first world," or about 20 percent of the world's inhabitants, only 2 to 3 percent of the population produce survival-level goods and products like food, compared with 50 percent in 1900 and over 90 percent in 1800. This has enabled the creation of an ever-improving standard of living based on many conveniences and comforts. Most people buy their basics with money earned in higher-level jobs. This trend will continue, and extend to all nations and geographic areas in the near future, as technology from the "first world" spreads.

How will people learn to lead meaningful lives with so much leisure time available?

5. **We have the technological ability to meet the basic survival needs of the whole planet within six years by using money now spent for defense.**

For the first time in history, all of humanity could transcend basic animal survival needs. As a world, we could invest our aggregate annual defense budgets ($750 billion) for six years and develop the technology that could meet the basic survival needs of the planet's entire population.[11] The Information Age has facilitated the creation of a technological infrastructure able to cooperate in this kind of a mission.

What will motivate us to allocate our resources so as to allow us all to live in a world of plenty?

6. **Communication networks have grown exponentially and can now interlink people all over the world at the touch of a button.**

Communication and information exchange, especially through all forms of electronic media, have exploded and are becoming available at a proportionately decreasing cost.[12] These include exponentially increasing numbers of telephone lines, fax machines, cable television hookups, overnight mail delivery services, and more. For example:

☎ The average number of telephone conversations per day per person in the United States has increased over 50 percent per decade for the last four decades. Meanwhile, the miles of telephone wire per person almost doubled in each of those decades (in 1992 about ten miles per person, or ten times the one mile per person in place in 1960).

☎ AT&T transmitted one billion faxes to Japan alone in 1992.

☎ In 1995, 20 million people chatted on cellular phones in the United States (about one in every 15 adults), and over 11,500 new customers signed up every day. Portable telephones are growing in favor in most developed countries. Recent loosening of United States regulation has led to predictions that every home will own a portable telephone by the year 2000. Also by then, many people will have a "world phone": a pocket telephone with their own personal, global telephone number that will work from anywhere on the planet.

☎ Cable TV reaches more viewers with more channels and programs every day. Many predict widespread availability of 500 channels, requiring new types of devices for channel selection and for previewing what to watch. Some companies are already testing such systems in limited areas in California.

☎ The United States Postal Service delivers 550 million pieces of mail per day, and increasing numbers of packages and letters are shipped by a multitude of rapid delivery and overnight air services. These fast-turnaround brokers track and route parcels using sophisticated in-and-out data processing systems that didn't exist a decade ago.

Everybody wants more information, sooner, and most can get it. But what principles will show us the way to transact our business with trust and fairness as we come into electronic contact with ever-increasing numbers of people all over the world?

7. **One hundred of the world's 160 countries now have some form of democratic government.**

The trend to democracy seems to be continuing. Between 1988 and 1992 alone, 40 countries "converted." As the bells of freedom ring louder, and communication technology spreads the news, individuals in every corner of the Earth will demand their inalienable right to participate in sovereign self-rule.

Every day, current events seem to indicate the coming about of a new political order. For example, in an article called "Catalyst of Change," the *San Jose Mercury News* reported that the Middle-East peace agreement signed by Israeli Prime Minister Rabin and Palestine Liberation Organization Chairman Arafat on the White House lawn on September 13, 1993 would put tremendous pressure on all countries in the twenty-first century to participate in a peaceful, world economic system. "From Baghdad to Beijing, the accord is almost certain to accelerate patterns of global change that began with the fall of the Berlin Wall in 1989."

With this incredible new freedom, how will individuals find a common set of principles to help them succeed, and at the same time avoid one nation's ideas from dominating another's and eradicating the uniqueness of each society?

8. **Traveling the globe now takes hours, compared to months only 100 years ago.**

Travel on our sphere can deliver materials or people almost anywhere within a day. Transportation giants help companies set up warehouses in Alaska so that their parts can be airfreighted anywhere on the planet within 24 hours. Only a century ago, we didn't even have automobiles. Just 40 years ago, it took eight days by boat to cross the Atlantic; now it takes eight hours by jet.

Given these staggering advances, one can only speculate on what the next century will hold. By 2001, airlines will carry 1.8 billion passengers per year, roughly double the number in 1990, and ten times as many as in 1970.[13] The United States National Aeronautics and Space Administration (NASA) predicts that by the year 2012 many of those passengers will zoom along on a fleet of 500 to 1000 supersonic planes flying at over twice the speed of sound, over two and a half times current average velocities.[14] The High Speed Civil Transport Program, as currently funded, will spend over $1 billion by the end of the century on basic research to facilitate the new designs required.

NASA is also studying "hypersonic" aeronautics, which covers speeds from three to 20 times the speed of sound. In fact, in 1992 the United States military tested a spy plane, no doubt to be commercially available within a few decades, that flies at "Mach" 8, or eight times the speed of sound.[15] This means crossing the Atlantic in less than an hour, and getting from any point on Earth to any other within 3 hours!

In a world where you can be virtually anywhere with anyone and doing anything, what will help you enjoy life and remain "centered" without being overwhelmed by the possibilities that are available?

9. English has emerged as a global language.

A single language has emerged as a planetary standard for business and politics: English. Over ten percent of the world speaks it as a first language,[16] and possibly up to 50% as a second language. Today's schoolchildren will need it for business or any other profession, and are learning it worldwide.

How can we enjoy the convenience of a primary communication language, such as English, without denigrating the importance of other languages, losing the nuances that other languages provide in a multicultural world experience?

10. Computers, an invention of the last 50 years, now affect most people's daily lives, and almost everyone will have some form of a computer in the next century.

Computers have become communication and processing tools for both individuals and corporations. In 1992, a little more than a decade after their inception, over 150 million personal computers constituted the global installed base. In 1993, one in every three homes in the United States possessed one. At the same time, 100,000 to 150,000 new ones roll off the assembly lines each day, progressively shrinking in size and cost while expanding in power!

The availability of ever-greater computing power at ever-decreasing cost will make computers ubiquitous, or universally present, in the near future. Today's supercomputer will fit into a portable notebook in the next few years. The cost for a million instructions per second (MIP) of personal computing potency decreased by half every two years in the last 12 years to $600 in 1993.[17] A new generation of microprocessors threatens to decrease this figure to well under $100 per MIP by the twenty-first century.

Among other things, this kind of computing power will allow personal virtual reality systems that will enable us to play simulation games in "virtual worlds" that feel real. With the accelerating growth rate of well over 30 to 40 million new computers each year, there could easily be an average of one per person in the world in the next 30 to 40 years.

Together with the explosion in the number of communication lines, computer networks offer a global, instantaneous sharing of information. Sophisticated presses simultaneously pump out the same daily newspaper in New York, Paris, Hong Kong, London, and elsewhere. The Internet, the rapidly growing global computer network, may supersede and overtake all other forms of data exchange. Figures 5-5 and 5-6 show that at the current rate of growth of new users, by the year 2001 every person on Earth may have access to the network. Already most of the world's map is blanketed by hosts and users tapping into this vast source of information, products, services, and more.

How can we retain our individual rights in such an interlinked society? How can we assure ourselves that the people who are responsible for making the decisions that so profoundly affect our lives will take into account our best interests?

Figure 5-5
International Connectivity

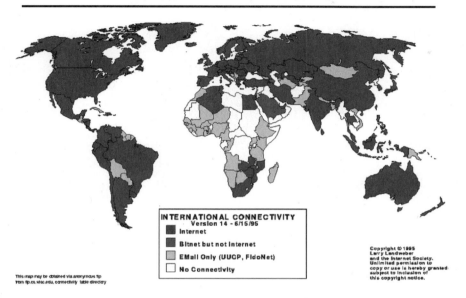

Figure 5-6
2001: Users = Human Population?

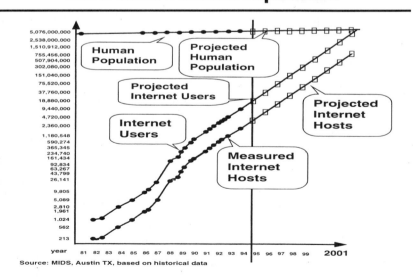

Source: MIDS, Austin TX, based on historical data

11. **Developments in medicine in the second half of the twentieth century have given doctors the ability to prevent or promote procreation, using effective contraception, abortion, and fertilization techniques.**

Contraception, successful experimentation with test-tube babies, and the abortion pill, demonstrate humanity's newfound power to help create or prevent new life, almost at will. In the last 30 years medicine has given women a nearly fail-safe contraceptive, the birth control pill. Its high efficacy liberated women from the unpredictability of pregnancy by chance and enabled them to achieve equality with men in all realms of life. Until this time, the dilemma couples faced was to either abstain from intercourse or acquire more mouths to feed. Even other forms of contraception, like condoms, only became widely available in this century.

We have also developed ways to help give each wanted baby, while still in the womb, a chance to maximize his or her intellectual and physical potential prior to birth.[18]

But what can we do to insure that each baby, once born, will be wanted, loved, and appreciated as a needed and contributing new member of humanity?

12. **Recent medical advances now enable doctors to cure many previously terminal diseases, and genetic research may even alter life-span expectations.**

Medical advances have cured a tremendous number of illnesses. Antibiotics and vaccines have eliminated maladies and plagues that used to kill millions. Doctors routinely cure many cancers that were until recently considered terminal. They extend the lives of heart disease patients through open heart surgery and other techniques, first performed in the 1960s. Of course, the doubled life-span also allows more time for diseases to surface. Nonetheless, in the next hundred years we can expect an accelerated pace of medical breakthroughs—including, hopefully, a cure for AIDS—as we continue to mold the bionic human.

Medical science can now achieve what used to be attributed only to various forms of magic or miracles. One such miraculous advance, gall bladder surgery, today involves only four tiny quarter-inch incisions in the abdomen, versus a six-to-eight-inch major incision just a few years ago. Furthermore, the hospital stay for this procedure has been reduced from a week to a day, and recovery at home from six weeks to one.

As another example, researchers recently discovered that in some circumstances the adult nervous system can regenerate. In 1992, Barth Green, director of the Miami Project on spinal cord injuries, said, "What we've done is made more progress in the last 12 months than the 3,000 years before."[19] These and other repairs and alterations of the very gray cells that make us conscious beings could profoundly affect future humans. Add to that the planned mapping of the genome sequence by the year 2000, including the possible use of genetic engineering to stall or inhibit aging, and one can only speculate on what the humanoid will look like in the future.

As we live longer and longer lives, and become more and more connected to the rest of humanity, what will help to keep us healthy and feeling good and give meaning to our extended lives?

CAN WE GO BACK? IF NOT, WHAT'S NEXT?

For those of you who are skeptical about the permanence of these changes and their influence, we concur. We know that many times in our history evolution has taken two steps forward and one or two steps back. Even if this type of regression were to occur now, it would happen within less than a lifetime, due to the accelerating pace of change. In a very short period of time, some changes will prove themselves to be enduring, and will continue to produce daily future shock.

Many changes have already established themselves and are here to stay. It would be hard to imagine a world without many of the discoveries (and the attendant new terminology) just in the last half of the twentieth century: calculators, computers, lasers, optical fibers, networks, atomic weapons capability, space shuttles, space walks, robots, genes, nuclear energy, photocopiers, and many, many more. What new words will we create over the next 40 years for discoveries and inventions of which we cannot yet even conceive?

If the facts and figures discussed above don't convince you how dramatically technology has influenced our external world, please consider the following humorous but true examples:

1. In 1992, a patent was issued for "Aquashoes," which are similar to snowshoes, but people can use them to walk on water. Do you wonder what that might feel like?

2. The Israeli phone company has introduced a service whereby anybody, from anywhere in the world, can send a fax to Jerusalem, and a messenger will run over and insert it in the Wailing Wall. (Many Jews believe that pieces of paper wedged between the ancient blocks of stone will rise to God as prayers that will be answered.) So you can now send a fax directly to God.

The miracles of the past are indeed turning into today's realities.

Few would deny that in our times, in the world we live in, we find ourselves living twice as long; there are ten times as many of us in the world as there were a mere 100 years ago, and the incredible advances in technology can potentially free most of us from working simply to sustain ourselves, while greatly improving our physical well-being and longevity. What's happening? How can we explain it? Where will it lead?

What's next?

6

HUMANITY AND TECHNOLOGY FORM THE GLOBAL BRAIN

It does indeed seem possible that we alive today could witness the beginnings of the emergence of a high-synergy society, a healthy, social superorganism. If so, we could be among the most privileged generations ever to have lived.
> —Peter Russell, *The Global Brain Awakens*, 1995[1]

*All are but parts of one stupendous Whole,
Whose body Nature is, and God the soul.*
> —Alexander Pope, *An Essay on Man* (1733-34)[2]

n recent years scientists have put forth the "Gaia Hypothesis"—that the round sphere we live on is a living organism.[3] In ancient Greek, *Gaia* means "Earth Mother." Gaia would include the entire biosphere of our planet: its atmosphere, oceans, mountains, rivers, lakes, soil, and all its more than 140 million species.

GROUNDING OURSELVES IN THE "GAIA HYPOTHESIS"

The Gaia Hypothesis resulted in large part from the space program. It would have been hard even to conceive of ourselves as a single living organism before we saw pictures of the whole planet, just as a flea on an elephant would have to leave the surface—the elephant's skin—to gain a better perspective of the organism—the elephant—as a whole.

Gaia, noun
The living organism Mother Earth, including all of its geophysical components and life forms.

Dr. James Lovelock, working in the 1960s at the California Institute of Technology on how to look for life on Mars, amassed a fascinating set of data to propose the Gaia Hypothesis. His book, *Gaia: A New Look at Life on Earth,* summarizes his findings.

To see how it might prove plausible to view the Earth as a living organism, let's briefly compare it to other organisms that we already know to be alive. First, Gaia appears to maintain a *homeostatic,* or constant, condition, a characteristic common to all living systems.

For example, the temperature of the human body remains close to 98 degrees Fahrenheit, regardless of the external temperature. It continuously adjusts to maintain this temperature, depending upon outside conditions and internal activity, using temperature-regulating systems highly dependent upon evaporation of sweat, movement of warm blood, burning of stored and processed energy sources, and insulating properties of the skin and other body tissues. Like our bodies, the Earth's average surface temperature has remained within a small range (60 to 100 degrees Fahrenheit), for hundreds of millions of years, despite drastic changes in atmospheric composition and a large increase in heat received from the sun. Temperature fluctuations are controlled by evaporation, climatic changes, seasonal variations, and protective layering of gases such as ozone. From this perspective, the planet Earth's and the human body's methods of temperature regulation seem quite similar. And both keep temperature in the range that proves most suitable to the existence of life.

The Earth also has regulatory methods for keeping many other parameters constant and optimal for life. It maintains the salt content in the oceans at 3.4 percent and the oxygen concentration in the atmosphere at 21 percent. Any significant variations in these percentages would not have allowed life as we know it to exist on the planet.

Beyond exhibiting homeostatic behavior, Earth also meets the criteria for the subsystems found within a living system. Dr. James Miller found that all living systems exhibit 19 characteristic and critical subsystems.[4] An example of a subsystem would be an *ingestor*, one that brings matter and energy across the boundary from the outside. In our bodies the ingestors are the mouth, nose, and lungs. For Gaia this might be the atmosphere and volcanoes. Gaia can be shown to display all 19 of the subsystems required for living systems to function.

Good planets are hard to find.

Lastly, only living systems behave in self-organizing ways: machines don't. They wear out and get run down. Since Gaia is self-organizing, displays homeostatic characteristics, and meets all of Miller's 19 criteria, we have excellent support for the Gaia Hypothesis. We may in fact consider the Earth to be a living system.

But if the Earth is a living organism, what interactive role might human beings play in connection with the planet as a whole?

HUMANITY'S ROLE AS AN EVOLVING SUPERORGANISM

One of the first people to speculate on humanity's possible role in a Gaian world view, and still perhaps the best authority on the subject, is the futurist/philosopher Peter Russell. In 1983 his book, *The Global Brain: Speculations on the Evolutionary Leap to Planetary Consciousness* (completely revised and reprinted in 1995 as *The Global Brain Awakens: Our Next Evolutionary Leap*), postulated what might be humankind's function in relationship to Gaia:

> One possible response to this question suggests that humanity is like some vast nervous system, a global brain in which each of us is an individual nerve cell. Human society can be seen as one enormous data-collection, data-communication, and data-memory system. We have grouped ourselves into clusters of cities and towns rather like nerve cells clustered into ganglia on a vast nervous system. Linking the "ganglia" and individual "nerve cells" are vast information networks.
>
> Society's slower systems of communication, such as the postal service, are like the relatively slow chemical communication networks of the body, such as the hormonal system. Our faster, electronically based telecommunication networks (telephones, radio, computer networks) are like the billions of tiny fibers linking the nerve cells in the brain.
>
> At any instant there are millions of messages flashing through the global network, just as in the human brain countless messages are continually flashing back and forth. Our various libraries of books, tapes, and other records can be seen as part of the collective memory of Gaia. Through language and sci-

ence we have been able to understand much of what happens around us, monitoring the planet's behavior much as the brain monitors the body's. And humanity's search for knowledge could be Gaia's way of knowing more about herself and the universe in which she lives.

Many of the above parallels relate to the higher mental functions, to thinking, knowing, perceiving, and understanding. These are functions associated with the cortex of the human brain, the thin layer of nerve cells wrapped around the outside of the brain; so it might be more accurate to liken humanity to the cortex of the planet. In evolutionary terms, the cortex is a relatively late addition, most of its development occurring with the mammals. It is not necessary for the maintenance of life. The cortex of an animal can be removed, yet the circulation, breathing, digestion, and metabolism continue. In a similar way, the planet Earth survived perfectly well without humanity for over 4,000 million years and possibly could continue very well without it.

There is, however, a second, very different response to the question of humanity's role in Gaia. We might be some form of recently erupted, malignant growth, which the planet would be better off without. . . . Technological civilization looks like a rampant malignant growth blindly devouring its own ancestral host in a selfish act of consumption.

But perhaps these two views of humanity's role in Gaia are not opposing. Perhaps we *are* some kind of embryonic global brain, *and*, at a very critical stage in its development, this planetary nervous system is getting out of control, threatening to destroy the very body that supports its existence.[5]

According to Russell, if humanity survives, it is on the threshold of emerging as a *social superorganism*, a collection of multiple organisms, that will serve as a Global Brain.[6] A superorganism must consist of a quantity of diverse or unique organisms, highly organized, connected, and acting synergetically. In this kind of a more complex, synergistic system, the goal of each individual part harmonizes with the overall system's needs. For example, in the South Pacific, 150 million shearwater birds can turn synchronously in fractions of a second, with no apparent leader: ". . .the flock is integrated into a functional whole."[7]

Such a superorganism would represent an evolutionary leap in complexity. Nature, obsessed with wholeness, seems to organize systems in increasing levels of complexity by favoring a magic number of about 10 to the power of 10, or 10 billion.[8] It takes about that number of molecules to make a single-cell organism and roughly that number of cells to form a single human brain.

What does it take to create a Global Brain?

First, we already have a population of the order of magnitude of 10 billion (the next order of magnitude down being 1 billion, the next one up being 100 billion). The cells exist.

Second, the products and processes of the Information Age provide the necessary technology to connect and allow organization of these "cells." For example, one estimate suggests that the number of telecommunications lines on Earth will rival the number of synapses connecting neurons in the human brain by the year 2000.[9]

And third, fair market competition, in concert with a world view that supports responsible business—business practices that ensure our planet's long-term well-being—can supply the vehicle for the natural selection of products and services that facilitate the most rapid and efficient formation of the Global Brain. Evidence already points to the fact that cells (people) are being connected with technology that is selected by a "survival-of-the-fittest" competition amongst computer- and telecommunication-related types of companies.

Evolution has presented us with the opportunity, within one lifetime, to form this Global Brain as the planet's nervous and control system. In the 1930s, the French priest Pierre Teilhard de

Chardin coined the term *noosphere*[10] (from the Greek *noos*, or "mind") to refer to the cumulative effects of all the human minds on the planet. This helps us to define the *Global Brain* officially as: a superorganism consisting of all the people on Earth, functioning as a *noosphere*, or single, inter-thinking group consciousness, and Gaia's nervous and control system.

Global Brain

A superorganism consisting of all the people on Earth, functioning as a *noosphere*, or single, inter-thinking group consciousness, and Gaia's nervous and control system.

Humanity has advanced far enough to develop the technology that will enable the Global Brain to function. Isn't it time we caught up with the rest of the plan, by adapting psychologically?

USING APPROPRIATE TECHNOLOGY RESPONSIBLY TO EFFECT THE TRANSITION TO A TRULY NEW WORLD ORDER

Our transcendence of basic survival needs resulted from several thousand years of technological innovation, and now requires us to change our point of view from a fear of scarcity to a confidence in abundance. The former assumes an uncertain supply of adequate water, food, shelter, and clothing for everyone; the latter assumes that there's enough—even plenty—for everybody, if we all share fairly. This change, once internalized, liberates individuals to pursue self-actualization and to contribute to the system as a whole. We have called this the coming era of beyond-individual-survival-oriented living.

But it takes time for the population to adapt to living by this new paradigm. Paradigm shifts—like accepting Copernicus' model that the Earth does not lie at the center of the universe—at first encounter a lot of resistance. However, as time goes by, they prove themselves, as the paradigm explains further observations and predicts new findings. Sufficient evidence mounts, and objectors eventually bow to a new scientific consensus. Fortunately, due to the present rate of acceleration, we may reap the benefits of the current fundamental shift within a lifetime.

Willis Harman, a futurist and President of the Institute of Noetic Sciences, has referred to this shift in consciousness as the "*new* Copernican revolution."[11] Copernicus showed that the Earth is not at the center of the universe but rather revolves around the sun. Similarly, we now seem to be discovering that the "only-me," egocentric individual is not at the center of our inner universe, but rather that we participate in a greater collective consciousness. Just as the Earth maintains its autonomy and yet orbits within a solar system, so we each keep our own identity and yet interact within the Global Brain.

The period of the 1980s to the 2020s will feature a showdown between the fear-based reactionaries caught in the past and the adapting Motofs, who embrace innovation and change. People often initially resist the liberation that technology offers. Therefore, stress in non-adapters will cause disease and death, and continue to root out the last of the physically, mentally, and spiritually unfit to adapt to technology and the Global Brain. The adapters *and* the technological innovations will prevail.

Once introduced, innovations—whether fire, computers, or TV—tend to remain a part of the fabric of humanity. History proves that all such novelty eventually gets used either for the destruction or betterment of civilization. Fire (or nuclear know-how) can either incinerate or provide warmth, energy, and vitality. *The technology itself is neutral; it can be either bad or good, depending upon the degree of responsibility with which it is used.*

As we surpass the survival-orientated era of existence, physical wars will subside or, hopefully, even come to an end. In the future, rather than focusing on physical survival-of-the-fittest, conflicts will center around the selection of *memes,* or mental thought patterns and ideas that best further evolution and the advance of civilization. Memes were first described in 1976, when Oxford University zoologist Richard Dawkins published *The Selfish Gene,* in which he compared *genes* to *memes.*[12] Dawkins defined a *gene* as a self-replicating *molecular* pattern that competes "selfishly" for available physical or *material* resources. Likewise, a meme is a self-replicating *thought* pattern that competes selfishly for available *mental* resources. Just as genes contain physical and chemical information, memes represent information that may create something new, through ideas and thoughts.

Meme, noun

A self-replicating thought pattern that competes selfishly for available mental resources. Similar to *gene,* which is a self-replicating molecular pattern which competes selfishly for available physical or materials resources.

Dawkins asserts that the laws that govern genes and genetic evolution appear to apply to memes as well. Both try to replicate themselves and multiply, while competing with other genes or memes attempting to do the same. In the last few decades, a trend has already begun toward global competition and "mind wars" which focus on economics, productivity, and creativity, a trend essentially toward finding the fittest memes to help solve the planet's problems.

During the next several decades, evolution will continue to select memes that produce the technology for "sustainable planetary survival." This means providing human physical essentials and supportive surroundings for all inhabitants of the planet, in a way that doesn't degrade the environment. It includes all productivity, connectivity, and information gains resulting from technological development, that can free Motofs to engage in learning, personal growth, and pleasure activities. We define this kind of technology, which facilitates the formation of the Global Brain, as "appropriate." It is then up to all of us to use it responsibly.

Appropriate Technology

Technology developed for accelerating the formation of the Global Brain. It includes freeing us from survival-oriented concerns, and subsequently liberating us to engage in learning, personal growth, and pleasure activities.

As discussed earlier, in first-world societies relatively few people produce sustenance for all. As more productive memes emerge they will wrestle control away from old ways of "survivalist" thinking and assure meeting the survival needs for all peoples of all countries, through technological automation.

The Global Brain paradigm, assisted in its creation by such new memes, makes sense of many of the significant changes already occurring on our planet. Like any other new hypothesis or model, further observation and confirmation of predictions will bear out its accuracy, or perhaps modify it somewhat. But it already explains many of the changes we discussed in Chapter 5.

For example, much like a human brain or computer, all the subsystems of the planet are beginning to interface more and more via a common language, English. Much like the human brain, each subgroup (country, area) may still choose to communicate in its own particular primary language. But most, if not all, will have to have at least a functional knowledge of English. Linguists can debate its merits, but when one looks at the world today, English provides evolution with its best or most immediate hope for establishing a globally interlinking language.

What might a Global Brain do? Similar to the way the human brain manages the human system, it will manage Gaia's subsystems that take in, process, and put out matter, energy, information, or combinations of these.[13] For example, a human body gathers and ingests food and water, uses some of it for nourishment and energy, stores some of it as reserves for later, creates waste in some of its parts, and continuously detoxifies itself by getting rid of the garbage. A Global Brain managing Gaia may also do this by assembling and molding raw materials into necessary products (cars, housing, etc.), collecting the leftovers worldwide, and properly disposing of them.

Of course, the Global Brain will have many more responsibilities, analogous to those of our brain as it manages our body. It may keep the oceans, rivers, and air clean, much as our own body purifies its blood and oxygen supply. It may prevent floods (hemorrhaging) and holes in the ozone layer (skin cancer). Of course, it will always provide sufficient nourishment for all of the species in the ecosystem, including humans, just as our brain furnishes all of our internal organs and cells with nutrients. The computer networks of the world will store information on hard disks and other storage media that will be accessible to the rest of the brain, just like our own memory cells. This will facilitate more intelligent decision-making.

Appropriate Technology, used consciously and responsibly, will unlock the door to the formation of this amazingly well-functioning Global Brain. It will connect the people of the world, and meet their basic needs. Already in the twentieth century, it has created common global customs across cultural, geographical, and national boundaries. Strange as it may seem, drivers all around the world now honk their horns on their way to a wedding in a cacophony similar to the ritual itself. New jokes seem to travel around the world, perhaps by computer bulletin boards. A person may hear the same new joke on two sides of the Pacific Ocean, two days apart, from unrelated people. Messages such as pop singer Michael Jackson's hit song of the early 1990s, "Heal the World," travel far and wide by music TV (MTV), radio, and various personal entertainment players (CD, cassette, Walkman, etc.).

Conscious and responsible technological development has already begun. In California, for example, half of 500 company presidents surveyed reported that they had chosen to implement some kind of "consciousness-raising" techniques.[14] Many corporations have begun to use environmentally correct materials and to recycle them (including the paper and ink used for this book). Some mutual funds now invest only in organizations that are also concerned about the long-term well-being of the planet.

After technology unlocks the door to the formation of the Global Brain, only the inhabitants of the planet can actually decide whether to open, and walk through, the door. In 1776, a phenomenal group pronounced the prerogative of all the citizens of the United States of America to enjoy freedom. The Founding Fathers' vision accomplished this by valuing, and granting to all citizens, the inalienable rights of life, liberty, and the pursuit of happiness. The Declaration of Independence, a monumental achievement in the history of consciousness, led to the building of one of today's most powerful, productive, democratic, and prosperous countries (although partly at the expense of other countries and peoples). Many other countries have followed in its footsteps and achieved great success.

Now it is time to replace this "American Dream" and its increasing standard of living with a *World Dream* of greater responsibility, oneness, and meaning.

As Motofs discover themselves and identify each other, they will unite and lead this evolutionary process with a quiet, gradual revolution. The ensuing tussle will result in an opportunity for success for one and for all. When they have achieved sufficient awareness and critical mass, the Motofs can implement and enforce a "Global Declaration of Planetary Independence," to usher in prosperity for everyone, as the Global Brain starts managing Mother Earth effectively and efficiently. This will create a truly new world order.

When will we awaken to this new, utopian-sounding reality? One thousand years from now, 100, or 10? The next chapter provides some insights into this question.

7

DOES 2012 A.D. EQUAL 0 G.B. (GLOBAL BRAIN)?

At each epoch of history the world was in a hope-less state, and at each epoch of history the world muddled through; at each epoch the world was lost, and at each epoch it was saved.
        — Jacques Maritain, *Reflections on America* (1958)[1]

The Global Brain Awakens *is a fascinating vision of how the information revolution is shifting con-sciousness. A much-needed, optimistic perspective on humanity's future.*
                —Ted Turner, founder, CNN television[2]

Where are we in time? Let's go back to the beginning and then march forward to the present. Modern science claims the universe literally banged itself into existence 10 to 20 billion years ago. The little planet we call home emerged four billion years ago. Humans only arrived on the scene during the last several million of those years.

THE END OF TIME (AS WE KNOW IT)

The Judeo-Christian tradition, however, based on the ancient Hebrew lunar calendar, maintains that the world "began" in about 3700 B.C. and that Adam and Eve fled paradise soon thereafter. This date concurs rather well with calculations made by another ancient civilization, the Mayans of Central America. Almost two thousand years ago, they invented a "Calendar Round,"[3] a large block of stone only unearthed early in this century. The Mayans studied time and cycles extensively. The first date in their calendar, in what they call the current "long cycle count," is 3100 B.C. Further, the first well-documented historical civilization that we know about is the Pharaoh Menes' First Dynasty in Egypt, which also dates back to around 3100 B.C. Many of the teachings of the dynasties of the Egyptian priests were passed on to Moses, who proceeded to deliver the original Ten Commandments sometime around 1270 B.C.

That was about 3,300 years ago. We have a fairly good written record of civilization's history since then.

Now let's look at the present. Remarkably, the current cycle of the Mayan calendar, number 13 and the only one they calculated on their "Calendar Round," simply ends on December 22, 2012! As mentioned in Chapter 5, McKenna, author of *The Archaic Revival* and several other books, arrived at this very same date, December 22, 2012, as a time of infinite change, based on current trends (please review Figure 5-4, the Ingression of Novelty Spiral).[4] He analyzed the "King Wen sequence" of the "I Ching" using state-of-the-art computer modeling techniques, based on the recently discovered mathematical theory of fractal geometry. We obviously have no idea what primitive techniques the Mayans may have used to come to the same conclusion, so long ago. Nonetheless, it seems that ancient society's timekeepers and an ultra-modern (although not proven) scientific model agree that a cycle may be coming to an end.

What started this cycle? Could it be that an event in the third millennium B.C. sparked the beginning of human consciousness as we know it, and this current cycle will be completed in 2012? Perhaps Homo sapiens, our species, did evolve from apes and the animal kingdom, and only around 3100 B.C. did we emerge as human beings, who we have called the descendants of Adam and Eve. Could this possibly solve the creation versus evolution debate, by suggesting that some inner quality of what we now consider "being human" came into being five to six thousand years ago? Might this not also suggest that by around 2012 another leap of consciousness will occur? Could this turn out to be the ability to tap into our higher mind?

Tapping into the higher mind might signal an end to a fight between "good" and "evil." From the standpoint of evolution, "good" might mean people progressively heading toward higher consciousness. "Evil" might refer to those choosing to live in ways that threaten others and prevent themselves and others from achieving their greatest potential, especially by inflicting physical harm. Increasingly, that "evil" part in humans will tend to disappear. The battle will have selected the survivors best suited for more advanced, beyond-individual-survival-oriented civilization. (Unfortunately, however, evil may take on new forms, such as denying people access to information.) A long-standing battle will have finally come to an end.

Time itself may take on a different meaning, as well. Not having to fear for our physical survival may allow our internal "death clocks" to slow down. Earlier in the twentieth century, Einstein brought to light the relativity of time and space and proved that time is just another spatial dimension. If 2012 brings to an end a cycle of our species, maybe it will also change our notion of time and our longevity. 2012 may then herald what many people outrageously call "the end of time," or at least the end of time as we now know it.

THE TIME HAS COME FOR A SHIFT IN CONSCIOUSNESS

Whether some dramatic, or even apocalyptic event occurs in 2012 or not, the evidence points to a turning point, a major shift in consciousness, somewhere within the next 40 years. The complete shift may take the whole 40 years and will follow the characteristics of the S-curve in Figure 7-1. But future historians will observe that one of those years signaled a significant and irreversible turning point in the evolution of our species and the world. At the inflection in this curve, or turning point (denoted by a "II" in Figure 7-1), the trend will have assumed sufficient critical mass to go beyond the point of no return. It really doesn't matter if it has already occurred or if it happens in the year 2000, 2012, 2028, or even 2043. What does matter is that by virtue of youth, over half the population alive today will live to witness this monumental changeover.

Figure 7-1
S-Curve Shift in Consciousness

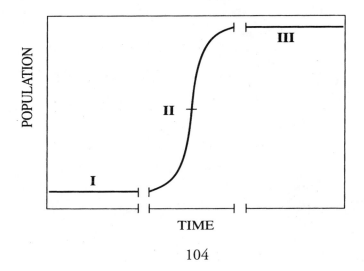

To help us better understand the significance of dramatic turning points in history, let us look at society's attitude toward slavery in the United States in the 1800s.

Society's tolerance of slavery followed the characteristics of an S-curve. While most agreed with it until about 1800 (period "I" in Figure 7-1), hardly anyone supported it in 1900 (period "III" in Figure 7-1). Sometime during that century, perhaps during the American Civil War, a shift occurred (period "II" in Figure 7-1). Historians can argue about the particular year or event after which the outcome could no longer go either way and a turning point was reached. After this point of no return, enough people had adopted a new moral code about slavery to steer the course of events toward emancipation; whether it was 1863 or another year really doesn't matter. The transition became unstoppable, and since it has endured until now, the change seems to have become irreversible.

The entire population of the planet is now undergoing a similar adoption process. The new ideas have until now been labeled (and mislabeled) as "New Age" thinking.

This cultural/spiritual/personal-growth movement began somewhere between the 1960s and the 1980s. According to sociologists at the University of California at Santa Barbara, the number of people in the United States identifying themselves as "New Agers" by 1992 would make it the third largest religion in the country.[5]

New Age thinking is characterized by a belief that a new era is dawning for humanity, with a shift in consciousness similar to that previously discussed. Recurring themes in the movement include: "We all have potentials beyond those we are now using and perhaps others of which we are even unaware; humanity and the environment are a single system; we can improve how we treat ourselves and our surroundings; humanity *can* change for the better."[6] These beliefs don't necessarily contradict the teachings of most of the world's religions.

The New Age movement, however, has no central organization unifying it, but rather constitutes a loose and diverse network of groups united principally by their common attitudes and values. Many of its members put an emphasis on spirituality and various practices that advance them into higher consciousness. These include: meditation, Yoga, esoteric practices such as astrology, techniques that improve health and physiological well-being, and many unconventional forms of healing.[7]

Parts of New Age thinking have increasingly found their way into the mainstream, primarily through self-help books and self-help groups and a genre of serene music. Over half the bestsellers on *The New York Times* nonfiction list consistently belong to the New Age/self-help category. New Age recording artists often have *gold* compact discs—those with over 500,000 copies sold.

New movements and ways of thinking always take time to develop, and go through many mutations before becoming a part of the collective consciousness, if they do at all. One could look at the "rationalist" movement of the seventeenth century to see how long it took for its ideas to impregnate society. It took almost 100 years for the ideas of philosophers like John Locke—that all of us are created equal and deserve to be free to pursue our lives and happiness—to be written into a socio-political document, the United States Declaration of Independence. Even so, many of the Founding Fathers of the United States owned slaves even as they signed this document. Then, as we know, slavery was abolished in 1865, after the American Civil War. After that it took almost 100 years for blacks no longer to have to sit in the back of the bus in some parts of the country. It therefore took several hundred years for the rationalist arguments to reach full implementation, and some may question whether they are, even now, complete.

Fortunately, the acceleration in our times speeds the espousal of any useful new memes as we begin to process ideas globally and quickly. The current phenomenon of New Age sprouted as an offshoot of the love and flower children of the 1960s, fueled by rock groups such as the Beatles and by "hippies" and others. But those ideas and tunes later caught on in larger parts of society, too. By the 1980s one no longer had to be a fringe member of society, like a "hippie" was, to admit they were New Age. In less than a generation, many of the New Age ideas have permeated mainstream society.

Calling a movement New Age seems humorous when looked at in historical perspective. Hasn't there always been a "New Age" dawning? How about the age after the Europeans discovered the New World? Examples in history abound. Arguably, the beginning of the coming new epoch may be as substantial a shift as has ever occurred, and justifies the name "New Age" more than any previous one. Undoubtedly, as more and more of it gets absorbed as part of the primary culture, the movement will undergo several further mutations. In some form, however, its ideas will become globally pervasive in the next millennium.

The New Age social movement, with the impending shift in consciousness, allows us to begin to speak of the formation of an unprecedented, worldwide "supra-religion." "Religion," in its Latin root, means to bind back to the source, or coming back together again. "Supra-religion" denotes one that encompasses, and allows continuing practice of, all others, so that all citizens of the planet can participate in it and it can be a common ground for a global society. Isn't it time?

Supra-religion

A set of spiritual beliefs and practices that encompasses, and allows continuing practice of, all others, so that all citizens of the planet can participate in it.

Jesus Christ may have had this goal in mind when he spread the message of love in an attempt to unite all earth-bound souls. We subsequently reset our calendars to 0 A.D., the year he was born. It will soon be time again to reset our calendar, this time to 0 G.B. This stands for the first instant of a fully functioning Global Brain ("GB") and creation of a heaven-on-Earth. This may turn out to be 2012 A.D.

The era of Jesus' impact on the world will have reached fruition, as we live harmoniously as parts of the Global Brain. Could this possibly be what so many people refer to as the "Second Coming of Christ"? In other words, in the beginning of the third millennium, his central message will have finally swept the whole planet as a new wave of love-consciousness.

As this happens, somewhere around 2012 A.D. (or 0 G.B.), the idea that we are all one people, of one supra-religion, will be familiar to everyone. We will explore these and other basic tenets of the supra-religion of "Global Spirituality" in the next two chapters. But remember, today's major religions, practiced by virtually everyone on the planet (including atheism and agnosticism), have existed for less than 6,000 years. Moses (Judaism), Zoroaster (Zoroastrianism), Krishna (Hinduism), Buddha (Buddhism), Lao Tzu (Taoism), Kung Futzu (Confucius), Jesus Christ (Christianity), Mohammed (Islam), Nanak (Sikhism), and others have founded our current major world religions (roughly in the order stated) only since 1270 B.C.

Isn't it time for a new supra-religion in which we can all participate, and an updated, universal concept of God, which unifies rather than separates us? This will be the topic of the next chapter.

8

GEV: AN UPDATED, UNIVERSAL CONCEPT OF GOD

We should find God in what we do know, not in what we don't; not in outstanding problems, but in those we have already solved.

—Dietrich Bonhoeffer,
Letters and Papers from Prison, May 25, 1944[1]

Science and religion, religion and science, put it as I may, they are two sides of the same glass, through which we see darkly until these two, focusing together, reveal the truth.

— Pearl Buck, *A Bridge for Passing* (1962)[2]

Throughout history humanity has attempted to find meaning and purpose in what otherwise can seem a short and insignificant life. We've attempted to explain the puzzling phenomenon of life by creating world views ranging from existentialism and atheism (no gods), to polytheism (many gods), to monotheism (one God). God or gods have appeared to humans with many different faces, based on our abilities to comprehend and interpret the unknowable. Understandably, as we explore the world and learn more and more about it, our concepts continue to evolve.

Today we have the knowledge to think in terms that were impossible only a century ago. For example, our current thinking, based upon the Big Bang theory, is that we live in an expanding universe. Einstein's Theory of Relativity changed our whole notion of time and space, and introduced the speed of light as the limit of the speed at which matter can travel. Centuries ago, Copernicus altered our view when he stated that the Earth does not lie at the center of the universe. Even before that, explorers discovered that the Earth is not flat, and we don't live on a two-dimensional surface, but rather on a three-dimensional sphere. When, and how soon in the future, will somebody show us that we are living in a four-or-more-dimensional environment? Every day we broaden our horizons pertaining to the universe and our origins as scientific exploration continues.

Until now, the concept of a divine being has continually evolved during humanity's history. Primitive cultures used to worship the sun as a god, and believed that gods made it rain. For us today that seems a little implausible, because we are more inclined to believe that the sun is a scientifically explainable fusion reaction, and that rain comes from clouds (that we can even seed and cause to drop rain). The "gene" concept, now the foundation for much of biology, only came into being less than 50 years ago, and clarified age-old mysteries of birth characteristics previously attributed to a divine being.

Mankind's scientific discoveries have always forced the best and the brightest to question and requestion the mystery we call God. With the incredible acceleration in knowledge about the physical world, we need a new idea of what "God" is all about, one that will endure as we continue to make new scientific discoveries. This new concept would take into account the fact that in five years, humanity collectively will know ten times as much as it does now. This requires forming a construct that can adapt over time and survive ongoing changes. Our new faith must give us a useful framework to live by and believe in, as science continues to provide more answers that help explain things currently unknown.

As science settles disagreements within its own community about currently controversial questions, and continues to offer completely new ways of understanding our world, we want to have a concept of the divine that unifies all of us and endures over time. What can we put faith in, in a world where science and technology keep pushing the limits of the unknowable? What can we put faith in, that doesn't separate one worshiper from another, and doesn't alienate non-believers from people who believe in God?

WHY WE NEED A NEW WORD FOR "GOD"

One of the problems with the concept and word "God" is that it has different meanings to different people. Some of these stem from ignorance and outdated interpretations of the universe that no longer satisfy many of us; others from our tendency to anthropomorphize, or assign human qualities to God. Throughout recorded history, we've made the arrogant error of thinking of God as being human-like, instead of thinking of humans as being God-like.

This anthropomorphization, while bringing the idea of God closer to some, has put off many others. After all, if we humans can create our own "miracles," why should we need God? People who believe this find themselves at some point in their lives, often after having been successful in the material world, in a "crisis" of meaning. They wonder, "Why am I here? What is my purpose on Earth?"

For many people, growing up in these times of accelerated scientific change and technological miracles, the word "God" has earned a bad name. For example, some religions teach that if you don't adhere to certain behaviors (rituals), you will provoke God's wrath. But we see that this doesn't seem to occur, at least not in the sense of immediate retribution for bad behaviors. What do we see instead? A society with jails overflowing with criminals, and courts backed up with cases. A world in which terrorism can and does strike anywhere, anytime. The more we become aware of the myriad problems that beset our world—many of which are of our own making—the more such notions of God lose adherents faster than new converts can replace them.

Many wonder how God can allow such a world to exist. The result of these examples and countless others that we hear of in the news or see with our own eyes is less belief in "God" as a meaningful concept. For many people, God has become an archaic notion not relevant to today's world.

There is also a deep split between those who believe that holy scriptures such as the Bible or Koran are God's word and need to be followed explicitly, and those who react against this by thinking God and religious beliefs are outdated concepts. Many people have also had to contend with, and find ways to reduce, conflict between the religious practices they were taught, and how they live their everyday lives today. As a result, some have found a personal spiritual path by modifying the religious training they were exposed to as children. Unfortunately, there are few guidelines which help people be deeply committed to a spiritual path and, at the same time, relate to the way society is evolving.

It doesn't have to be that way.

As we discover more and more about both the physical and spiritual natural laws of the universe, we continue to search for a clearer vision of Truth, or the powers that govern creation. After all, every one of us has some kind of "religion": an implicit or explicit set of ideas and beliefs about the essential nature of the world.[3]

The time has come to use a new term for God. A new term can allow us a fresh basis for thinking about something that we are still as far away from grokking, or fully knowing and truly understanding, as a spider is from comprehending a human being. A new, globally agreed to concept of God could provide the common ground for a worldwide supra-religion, given our current knowledge. Of course, God itself will not have changed, only the word for God and, hopefully, as a result our notion of what God can mean for us. Using a new word can put behind us all the associations with previous traditions and religions (without losing their basic truth). New words always help us to think in different ways. The time has come to have a concept of God, based on a new word, that makes us think in ways that unify us, rather than separating us.

Our concept and language for the divine being has evolved throughout history. The word "God" itself, "G," "O," "D," only came into use in about A.D. 725. Linguists believe it originated in Old English, and was previously derived from Germanic languages, and before that probably from Armenian.[4] The underlying etymology of "God" is from the Sanskrit *havate*, and the Indo-European base *ghut*, which could be "that which is invoked," or "one to whom libations are poured, one worshipped with libations." Moses used some form of *Yahweh*. Jesus spoke ancient Hebrew, and his disciples subsequently wrote the New Testament in Greek. So we don't really know how he pronounced "The Father's" name in his preaching. Muhammed or his followers began using the word *Allah*. The Eastern religions have also used various names over time, often different names for different aspects of God. With each of these names followers have associated a whole set of beliefs. Often these unified the worshippers within a faith, but also separated them from other groups of humanity.

Here's the word we have selected and its definition:

Gev, noun

Global **EV**olution's intelligent life-force purposefully propelling all matter and energy forward.

HOW THE WORD GEV WAS CHOSEN

The word "Gev" was originally chosen because it abbreviates global evolution. Regardless of individual beliefs, most people agree that evolution happens. We may not have the power to predict its direction or speed, but we cannot deny that the universe moves and changes. Its intelligence has a purpose that remains unknown to us. Evolution is a basic truth of the reality that we can perceive. Matter and life do move on. Whether designed or random, some kind of grander cosmic picture seems to be unfolding.

We—human beings—seem to be participating in an apparently infinite force that is propelling everything forward toward higher orders of complexity. We can choose, with our free will, to what degree to go along with it. We do not need to judge the resulting outcome as better or worse, but just to accept it as real. Each of us can tap directly into this force and derive great energy and power from it. It is a part of us, and we are a part of it.

Many features of the word "Gev" link us to ancient references to the divinity. Its first letter and length remind us of the word "God." It also includes in it an allusion to the number seven, nature's cycle of completion and a holy number in ancient Mesopotamian cultures, including the story of Genesis. Gev begins with the seventh letter of the English alphabet, "G." So do God, good, goodwill, galactic, great, giant, gigantic, grand, gain and grace, all words that refer to benevolence and grandeur.

Gev carries a linguistic connection to the original source of the monotheistic concept of God, ushered in by Moses. According to the Old Testament, Moses was told by God to tell the Israelite slaves in Egypt that he had been sent to lead them out of bondage by "I AM THAT I AM." When translated and transposed in Hebrew, this could become *Yahweh asher yihweh*, meaning "He causes to be what Comes into Existence."[5] This is most likely how the Hebrew name for God came about, YHWH, spelled Yahweh, and pronounced yah-way.

While connecting us to the past, both the concept and the word Gev can catapult us into a more sophisticated future. Interestingly enough, in modern physics, *GeV* stands for "Giga Electron Volts," or the unit of measurement for high energy particles, especially for light! Perhaps Gev can form the basis for a view that balances the observations of pure scientists and the beliefs of righteous clergymen.

THE REUNION OF SCIENCE AND RELIGION

Our new composite concept, Gev, has the potential to reunite science and religion. These two fields had a serious falling out during the seventeenth century Renaissance. Ironically, the spiritual philosopher/mathematician Rene Descartes' conclusions about "mind-body dualism" in the 1600s led to the departure of the so-called rationalists from spirituality.

Barry M. Katz, a Senior Lecturer in Values, Technology, Science and Society at Stanford University in the 1980s, aptly describes the prevailing mood of a new age that dawned in the seventeenth century, in his book, *Technology and Culture: A Historical Romance*.[6]

> God, once grandly depicted as the divine engineer-architect of the universe was reduced to a humble watchmaker who wound his cosmic mechanism but then stepped backward to let it run according to its own mathematical laws. Anatomists failed to find the seat of the soul, but discovered instead a circulatory system with disturbing affinities to hydraulic pumps. And the new physics projected a world of cold, lifeless quantities, inconceivably vast, unresponsive to human prayers and indifferent to their complaints. For the first time in history, science depicted a universe that was ultimately and essentially meaningless.

While perhaps meaningless, since Descartes' time human knowledge and human power have increased hand in hand, as we have applied science to technology and seemingly become god-like ourselves. At times, our power has even begun to endanger our own existence as a species.

Yet all the wondrous science and technology of the last 300 years have only caused us to realize even more strongly that Gev is something we are all a part of, with which we must align ourselves, and to which we must surrender. Science has still not found the seat of the soul. Nor can it completely explain phenomena like "Near-Death-Experiences," reportedly an other-worldly "syndrome" about which up to eight million Americans can testify. Some greater intelligence and life-force remains a distinct possibility even to the majority of scientists, and a certainty to spiritualists. Renaming this primary life-force from the standpoint of an updated world view, which takes into account the modern body of scientific knowledge, may heal the rift between science and religion.

Consider three stages of belief in divinity: the first, a fear-based, angry God, that rewards or punishes; the second, a lack of belief, one that suggests that "We no longer need God, because we can take care of ourselves;" and the third, a sense of awe at the sheer magnitude of all of creation, the beauty, orderliness, and simplicity of the universe, and our place in it. Einstein and many others reached this third stage, and it is this view, in contrast to the first two, that we have named Gev.

Our empirical observations and deductions about physical phenomena don't preclude hypothesizing about spiritual truths and evolutionary laws of human nature. No scientific discoveries contradict the spiritual laws that form the basis for conscious life. They may upstage some of the beliefs of current religions, but this occurs as we learn more about the universe. As Oscar Wilde, the nineteenth century author, said, "Religions die when they are proved to be true. Science is the record of dead religions."[7]

The foundation of all religion is faith, an aspect of human thought, emotion and awareness that transcends observation and verification. Given the way the world is changing, we must be willing on a global level to place our faith in the fundamental connection of all humanity with all of the planet. This faith is necessary to help steer our future into an acceptable, sustainable outcome for Gaia.

This faith will by no means prevent us from continuing to hold other religious beliefs. The belief in Gev allows us to share, on the spiritual level, with all other members of the human race, no matter what other religious beliefs they may hold and practice.

Faith in Gev, in global evolution's life-force purposefully propelling all matter and energy forward, belongs to all. For Gaia to survive, we must all grok Gev, now.

Every religion can only do its best in its time to interpret truth and codify ways to live, based on what's known at that point in the evolutionary process. The American civil rights leader Martin Luther King realized in 1963 that, while "Science investigates; religion interprets. Science gives man knowledge which is power; religion gives man wisdom which is control."[8]

We aspire now to take the advances of science and technology and combine them with the perennial wisdom, to take control and assure ourselves of a successful destiny on planet Earth. The ". . . 'perennial wisdom' has been distilled from inquiry persisting over a far greater span of time than the duration of modern science, . . . (and) can hardly be simply set aside."[9] To reunify science and spirituality, as we near the end of the current cycle (about 2012), we will need to update our scientific methods;[10] and update our religious and spiritual concepts in such a way that all humans can participate in them and which honors our ever-expanding body of scientific knowledge.

It is time for the emergence of a Global Spirituality.

9

GLOBAL SPIRITUALITY CREATES A HEAVEN-ON-EARTH

Science without religion is lame, religion without science is blind.
> — Albert Einstein, "Science and Religion,"
> *Out of My Later Years* (1950)[1]

The next stage will be our entry into a moral global age . . . a global spiritual age. . . . We are now moving fast towards the fulfillment of the visions of the great prophets who through cosmic enlightenment saw the world as one unit, the human race as one family, sentiment as the cement of that family, and the soul as our link with the universe, eternity, and God. [The religions of the world should] get together and define the principles they have in common.
> —Robert Muller, as Assistant Secretary General to the
> United Nations, author of *New Genesis: Shaping a
> Global Spirituality* (1984)[2]

119

To understand this chapter try to keep an open mind and dispose of preconceived and archaic notions you have developed about the word "religion." Spirituality and religion are meant to refer to the same area of human experience: an inner connection with something greater than ourselves, something that can only be accepted by faith. In modern times, "religion," like politics, has become a loaded word.

A NEW PERSPECTIVE THAT UNIFIES

Some readers will resist the idea of needing a new religious understanding. They already have theirs, and they may claim that it is sufficient for their religious needs. Some may even feel that their religion already holds a monopoly on the "absolute truth."

And yet, as a global society develops, as we have suggested that it will, might we not need a global vision of the spirit? A supra-religion that we all buy into could facilitate and even accelerate the formation of a sane Global Brain. We have already laid the groundwork for this shift in perception with the term Gev, discussed in the last chapter. The more each of us can accept having a common concept of the divine entity and life-force energy, the more easily we can start highlighting the similarities amongst all humankind.

You don't necessarily have to believe in the existence of a soul or eternity to accept this teaching—just in the human spirit. Feeling, thinking, and acting in accordance with what serves long lasting value facilitates an alignment with your spirituality and human nature. Aligning with spiritual principles allows detached, carefree—yet meaningful—living, and results in a fulfilling and successful life. It allows you to experience an unparalleled richness in your quality of life.

We define *spirituality* as being able to discern in each moment the enduring from the ephemeral or fleeting, and aligning with the lasting rather than the temporary. We can do this individually and collectively, thus choosing success and well being.

Spirituality

Being able to discern in each moment the enduring from the ephemeral or fleeting, and aligning with the lasting rather than the temporary.

Spirituality may also be seen as relating to our own chemical and genetic makeup: if we adhere to spiritual principles, we'll experience comfort on a physical and emotional level as a result of chemical reactions in the brain and the body.[3] This makes us feel fulfilled and successful in life. On the other hand, if we don't live by spiritual principles, our bodies will experience discomfort, and we'll feel as though we're failing in life. All the religions of the world until now have attempted to help us succeed in life. (See Appendix B for a table of the current memberships in the major religions of the world.)

As we saw, the word "religion" originates from the Latin word meaning "to reunite." As we become more and more interconnected as part of the formation of the Global Brain, how will we experience our connections to each and to every person on the planet with whom we come in contact? Does becoming more connected with every person on the planet merely involve a more sophisticated form of appointment-making, networking, and efficiency, or does something deeper within us occur as we experience the Global Brain forming and growing?

The 2nd Ten Commandments are based upon the premise that our connection of spirit with each and every person on the planet will become obvious as the Global Brain develops. For the first time in humanity's history of religion and spiritual experience we can see that our thoughts and actions can affect the entire planet and can determine how others feel and behave. To re-unite our connection with our inner human spirit and with our mother Earth brings all the people of the planet together as one.

This new, immediately apparent oneness allows us to adopt this world supra-religion of Global Spirituality. We call it Global Spirituality based on a conviction that it applies to all conscious human spirits here on Earth. (One can only speculate whether these truths are merely "Global," or perhaps are part of a "Universal" Spirituality. In that case "Gev" becomes "Uev.") The basic tenets of Global Spirituality do not conflict with most of the teachings of the major world religions, but rather resonate with them.

Global Spirituality

A supra-religion that provides a common ground for all inhabitants of planet Earth to participate in and become a part of the Global Brain.

How do the concepts of "soul" and "spirit" relate to Global Spirituality? Many best-selling books now speak, interchangeably and inconsistently, about these age-old concepts that seem to defy a simple definition or even differentiation. We wish to avoid the quagmire that again will separate some readers from others; there are almost as many opinions on this as there are readers. And to reiterate, one can benefit from the majority of the teachings of *The 2nd Ten Commandments* without believing in the concepts of soul and spirit. And yet, we maintain that holding the belief that there is some part of each of us that transcends our animal part, is eternal in some way, and is connected to Gev, greatly facilitates the adoption of Global Spirituality and its ways of living, and leads to success in the Consciousness Age.

Soul or Spirit

The higher consciousness that transcends our animal nature and bodies, is eternal in some way, and is connected to Gev.

DOES THE SOUL OR SPIRIT EXIST?

Some of history's wisest people have believed unshakably in the existence of a human soul. Philosophers ranging from Plato to Descartes, to modern writers such as Covey, based their doctrines on spirituality. Ingenious scientists like Einstein, and the greatest religious leaders of the world from Buddha to Jesus Christ have all professed the immortality of a non-material soul. They have also affirmed their belief in some kind of a God. The semantics may differ but the ideas bear great resemblance to each other.

Mahatma Gandhi, father of modern day India, wrote eloquently about our spirituality in a letter to one of his disciples:

> It is nature's kindness that we do not remember past births. . . .
> Life would be a burden if we carried such a tremendous load of
> memories. . . . The form ever changes, ever perishes, the
> informing spirit neither changes nor perishes. True love con-
> sists in transferring itself from the body to the dweller within
> and then necessarily realizing the oneness of all life inhabiting
> numberless bodies. . . . Both birth and death are great myster-
> ies. If death is not a prelude to another life, the intermediate
> period is a cruel mockery.[4]

History also recounts notable exceptions who doubted the existence of a soul, including Nietzsche, Sartre and Confucius. Events like World War II and the genocides of this century have shaken even the most devout believers to the core. While these killings should never be condoned, humanity's story tells many a tale of mortal bodies (not souls) paying a heavy price for our further evolution. This urges all of us to adopt the practices and principles of Global Spirituality sooner and faster. Amazingly, some survivors of catastrophes like the Holocaust or the Vietnam war have emerged with an even greater faith in the perfection and oneness of all of creation, including the everlasting nature of our souls.

A modern way to think of the soul and Gev is to liken them to an ultraviolet light composed of photon particles and a wave at a certain frequency. In quantum physics we know that we can observe the same ray of light in these two ways. Similar to the ray, which is invisible to our naked eye, the soul and Gev might exist unseen to us.

THE FOUR CORNERSTONES OF A SECULAR SUPRA-RELIGION

The four cornerstones of Global Spirituality, introduced in Table 9-1, attempt to explain the mystery of human life. They answer the questions: Who are we really? What are we? And why are we here? All religions, spiritual practices, or world views provide acceptable solutions to these dilemmas, at least for their time. The "belief that life has purpose is the beginning and essence of religion."[5] We all seek to find the purpose of life.

Table 9-1

The Four Cornerstones of Global Spirituality

1. All human beings on Earth share in the great human spirit and Gev.
2. We are all connected as one people, one tribe, to one planet.
3. We have the freedom to create experiences of JKLM: *J*oy, *K*nowledge, *L*ev (Unconditional Love), and *M*ission.
4. Individually and collectively, we have free will to choose how to grow and evolve.

These four cornerstones promise all of us an enlightened future, by uniting the people of the globe in a common, ancient, and long-embedded view. They represent a confluence of the messages that the religions of the world have always tried to convey to their followers. At the core of all the major religions is the experience of oneness with creation—what Aldous Huxley called the perennial philosophy. Wise people all over the world have espoused these four cornerstones, or just lived by them—perhaps explained in different words—for thousands of years. And many of them have prophesied a far better world for all, if all of us would decide to live by them.

In Global Spirituality every human finds meaning in their own one-to-one relationship with Gev. No one can tell anyone else how to experience this relationship or how to worship. Each of us decides what to believe and how to feel and behave based upon our spirituality. Each of us decides how to celebrate, and what spontaneously formed rituals, if any, to perform. Practicing Global Spirituality requires no special places of assembly, such as churches, temples, or shrines, and no formal displays of worship. Every building, place in nature, or any spot anywhere can serve as a place of individual worship of our fundamental connection with our planet and all that exists. It truly is a secular, worldwide supra-religion.

Any belief system not yet proven by science, such as the four cornerstones of Global Spirituality, requires a leap of faith until we can collectively agree on concrete conclusions derived from sufficient data. We cannot ascertain the truth of these hypotheses until we learn more precise information and can interpret and express them more generally. For example, in the physical world, Newton's laws made predictions that seemed true and helpful for several centuries but have since been subsumed through further generalization. Newer theories, like relativity and quantum mechanics, refined some of Newton's original and still useful findings.

The apple that fell on Newton's head and awakened him to his discoveries must fall on our collective heads, so we don't, as a planet, self-destruct. We must bite a chunk out of the tree of knowledge that Eve tempted Adam with in the Garden of Eden, to unearth the deeper inner knowledge of these four cornerstones.

Won't you join us in taking this leap of faith into higher wisdom, and in rediscovering paradise?

LOKELANI

The creation myth, which exists in some form in most cultures, metaphorically conveys an underlying theme of living in a heaven or hell. Each of us, and all of us together, create our own reality. The contemporary writer and philosopher Gary Zukav interprets the Garden of Eden story as symbolizing that we each have the male-female principle—Adam and Eve—and the Tree—our personal energy system and cord of knowledge—inside of us. With those we can choose "to respond to life's difficulties with compassion and love instead of fear and doubt."[6]

Depending on how we use our divinely given power, we will either "create Paradise or be Cast Out."[7] As we enter the Consciousness Age, we can cease to create with neglect. Instead we can use reverence to stand united and transform our kindergarten of learning and playing into a heaven-on-Earth, which we call Lokelani.

Lokelani, noun

Heaven-on-Earth. From Hawaiian, meaning "heavenly rose." A state of mind of living to play and enjoy life to the utmost right here and now, while learning and growing.

Lokelani above all is an internal state of mind and feeling that we can each experience anywhere on the planet, at any time. By being fully present in the moment, we can play and enjoy life to the fullest right here and now, while learning and growing. It may take some time and painful lessons to reach that point. Like a rose, we, too, only grow to maturity and blossom beautifully after working our way up a stem with many thorns.

JKLM

Creating Lokelani can only occur if we all use our free will to look deep inside ourselves, and recognize that all of us really want the same thing. We first and foremost need our survival needs satisfied: food, shelter, clothing, warmth, safety, and some minimal level of material comfort and prosperity. After that we all want to climb up the rest of well-known psychologist's Abraham Maslow's pyramid of *self-actualization* (see Figure 8-1). As we do, we reach higher and higher levels of consciousness and create greater meaning in our lives.

Figure 8-1
Maslow's Pyramid

5. Self-actualization

4. Self-Esteem and social status

3. Love and belongingness

2. Safety and physical well-being

1. Physiological survival

According to Maslow's pyramid, each of us has a hierarchy of needs. At the bottom, level one, are basic physiological needs such as food, water, and oxygen for day-to-day survival. After we have satisfied these, at the second level we seek safety, shelter, clothing and other long-term survival needs. Once we have met those, at level three we look for love, belongingness, and procreation. At level four we look for self-esteem and social status. Finally, at the apex, level five, comes the need for "self-actualization." Maslow defines this as "the actualization of potential, capacities, and talents, as fulfillment of mission, as a fuller knowledge of and acceptance of the person's own intrinsic nature, as an unceasing trend toward unity, integration or synergy. . . ."[8] Self-actualization is becoming the true spiritual self, and heading towards enlightenment.

Our lower needs—levels one and two—originate from our old brain—reptilian and mammalian—which assesses situations and persons and decides if they provide a potential: 1) nurture; 2) be nurtured by; 3) have sex with; 4) run away from; 5) submit to; or 6) attack.[9] Our higher needs—levels three and four—originate from our newer brain areas—the cortex—and serve to raise our consciousness, to rid us of emotional baggage, and to help us accurately perceive situations. When we have satisfied the old and new brains' survival concerns, we can then attend to a higher need—level five—self-actualization, where we can experience the most satisfying pleasures, those of the soul and spirit.

Overcoming the fears of the brain thus frees us to transcend the individual survival-oriented mind-set, climb the pyramid, live a right life, and discover greater freedom to create the life experiences of JKLM (see Table 9-2). Many religions consider that your reward will come after death. Yet, by following the 2nd Ten Commandments, you and all those you come in contact with are likely to lead more fulfilled lives here and now by exercising the freedom to create experiences of Joy, Knowledge, Lev (unconditional love), and Mission.

One can experience Joy through a state of mind of being "HIGH": Happy, Inwardly peaceful, Growing, and Healthy. Only by being HIGH on life can you satisfy yourself and also be of use to others. You've got to be HIGH to be free.

Table 9-2
JKLM Defined

Basic Life Experience	Definition
Joy	State of mind of being "HIGH": Happy, Inwardly peaceful, Growing, and Healthy.
Knowledge	Discovering truth about ourselves and the rest of the universe.
Lev (UNCONDITIONAL LOVE)	The unconditional emotional acceptance of all humankind, ourselves included, as part of the same whole.
MISSION	What each of us is here to do for the world in our lifetime. We learn while we teach.

Thus free, one can go on to pursue Knowledge, the discovery of truth about oneself and the rest of the universe. As we have discussed, the perennial wisdom claims that greater knowledge keeps pointing us to the oneness of all of creation. In Global Spirituality, the concept of Gev allows us to realize this fundamental connection of all mind and matter.

The spiritual tradition, philosophers, and psychologists have all spoken of UNCONDITIONAL LOVE as the glue that binds us all together as one. Again, a new word can help us grok this wisdom of the ages, and clear up the confusion caused by the word "love" and its many forms: *Lev. Lev* in Hebrew means "heart."

True knowledge gets grokked from remembering to opt for Lev over fear. Lev is the unconditional emotional acceptance of all humankind, ourselves included, as part of the same whole. Fear always results from various manifestations of ikorgance, which engender doubt and consequent pain and slavery. Choosing a combination of Lev and Knowledge instead develops wisdom. *Knowledge without Lev can be evil, while Lev without Knowledge creates stagnation. Grokking necessitates having the courage to combine Knowledge and Lev.*

> ### *Lev,* verb and noun
>
> UNCONDITIONAL LOVE. The unconditional emotional accep-
> tance of all humankind, ourselves included, as part of the
> same whole. The Greeks called this *agape.* Appropriately
> based on the Hebrew word for heart, *lev,* it is a feeling of
> acceptance, caring, compassion, and warmth toward all
> our fellow human beings. It is the most pure form of love.

Using greater amounts of wisdom in conjunction with our free will gives us the opportunity to consciously work on our Mission, the special contribution that each of us can offer the world in our lifetime. In the process of doing this we learn who we want to become while we exercise and teach who we already are. We contribute to the miraculous course of all of evolution, while at the same time furthering our own. We have the potential to bring purposefulness, meaning, and fulfillment to our lives, and eventually, to achieve self-actualization.

Our Mission directly challenges our stubbornness and temptation to decay, and instead offers us an opportunity to evolve. As the fourth cornerstone of Global Spirituality expresses, we have free will that allows us to choose how to follow evolutionary laws of nature and thereby succeed and graduate from the school of life. We can each achieve greater oneness with the rest of the universe by choosing how rapidly or slowly to grow, the order in which we learn our lessons, the situations, etc. Conversely, we can choose, for awhile, to decay and become less a part of the whole.

Happily, though, you cannot help but evolve, eventually. It's only a matter of time and how many trials, tribulations, and pains you choose to have along the way. The choice of how to grow rests with each one of us. We decide how rapidly we wish to succeed and when to graduate incrementally to higher levels of consciousness and wholeness, with their inherent rewards. The moment-by-moment vertical path leads each of us up or down, toward growth or decay. Each action and decision results in one of those two consequences.

Gev urges us all upward, as our rate of evolution depends on us to learn our lessons. Our free will means we have the choice of how and when, but not whether, to grow.

All religions of the world, when looked at deeply, have taught similar messages about the possibility of JKLM. Only the rituals and dogma they used to attempt to enlighten their followers differed.[10] In the Old Testament, God made a covenant with Moses and the people of Israel to take them to Canaan, the land of milk and honey. By highlighting the commonality and oneness among people today, we could live in harmony in a Global Promised Land, Lokelani, with an abundance of "milk and honey" for all.

IS JKLM COSMIC?

JKLM may correspond to the very essence of being human, by correlating it with the parts of our brain described in Chapter 4. Joy may relate to the oldest or most primitive part of our brain that controls body functions. Knowledge can be attained through use of the rational mind. Lev and Mission are deeply felt soul experiences of infinite creative and intuitive energy. We have spoken of this part as the higher mind, now increasingly coming into use. A wise person integrates all three of these parts, producing a harmonious, whole individual who realizes the rewards of JKLM.

Imagine that the Earth superorganism, Gaia, has these three brain parts, too: physical laws of nature, the Global Brain of humanity, and a collective consciousness (see Table 9-3). Perhaps, like us, it also has free will and desires to adhere to the JKLM Truth.

If so, we could then also correlate JKLM to the three parts of Gaia's brain and its planetary life experiences. Joy could correspond to the physical laws of nature, the harmonious expression of nature allowing all life forms to co-exist, grow, and thrive. Knowledge might correspond to the developing Global Brain and the planet's ability to manage and control its survival in a sustainable way. Lev and

Mission would correspond to the Global Soul seeking to reunify itself with the rest of the universe.

Table 9-3

Gaia's Experiences

	Human Brain	Gaia's Brain	Gaia's Experience
1. Joy	Subconscious	Physical laws of nature	Nature's harmony and growth
2. Knowledge	Rational Mind	Global Brain	Sustainable survival
3. Lev & Mission	Higher Mind	Global Soul	Oneness with the rest of the universe

Who knows, maybe the galaxy and the universe also have their own JKLM Truth.

As this cosmic picture continues to unravel in front of us, you might begin to see why we may be living in the most exciting times ever. Just as the development of our own rational brain greatly increased our individual odds of survival, the emergence of the Global Brain will fulfill that function for Gaia. We may be living in the 40-year period during which this brain turns on and awakens.

And who will participate in this massive and significant evolutionary awakening? A new type of human—Motofs—who will enjoy a newfound freedom by conquering their fears in order to help advance the planet to its destiny as the Global Brain, usher in Global Spirituality, and follow the 2nd Ten Commandments. The next chapter serves as an introduction to the detailed descriptions of these Commandments.

10

THE REWARDS OF TRUTH AND FREEDOM

And you shall know the truth, and the truth shall make you free.

—*The Bible*, John 8:32

The history of the world is none other than the progress of the consciousness of freedom.
—Georg Wihelm Friedrich Hegel, philosopher, 1800s[1]

The 2nd Ten Commandments are applicable to every action of your life. When you follow their wisdom, you will achieve increasing amounts of freedom to create experiences of JKLM, which form the basis for your success.

YOUR FEARS

To become a Motof who succeeds in this new era, you have to become aware of your patterns of thought and behavior that have resulted from individual, survival-oriented consciousness. This will most likely uncover anxiety and pain arising from your fears, denials, and doubts that you may have been unconscious of, and numb to, until now. Many self-help psychologies and therapies present ways for you to uncover and work on these issues.

Once you are more aware, the next step is to begin a transformation process to discard these fears—basically of our own death—to act in ways more appropriate for present-day situations. There will be times when old habits, based upon survival consciousness, may prevail. However, each time you make decisions using the 2nd Ten Commandments as your guide, new understandings will come to you and you will find the way. You will increasingly learn to feel and face fear, but not fall for it—not to react automatically, but rather to consciously choose a sensible action.

> *Motof Motto:*
> *Feel the fear, face the fear,*
> *but don't fall for the fear;*
> *act out of Lev.*

As you progress in your personal evolution, gradually but surely, the anxiety and pain you discover will decrease. You will grow stronger and more capable of living and being successful in the new age of consciousness and connectivity. And since you will be adjusting your being to align itself more with reality as it is now, and thus living more in truth, you will find yourself progressively freer to truly enjoy life.

According to Dr. Virginia Satir,[2] a renowned family therapist of the latter part of the twentieth century, our *freedom* comes in five basic human rights:

1. The freedom to *see and hear* what is here and now, rather than what was, will be or should be, and to be able to share it.

2. The freedom to *think* what one thinks, rather than what one should think, and to be able to share it.

3. The freedom to *feel* what one feels, rather than what one should feel, and to be able to share it.

4. The freedom to *want* and to choose what one wants, rather than what one should want, and to be able to share it.

5. The freedom to *imagine one's own self-actualization*, rather than playing a rigid role or always playing it safe, and to be able to share it.

Increased self-awareness, and then greater spiritual freedom as described above, lead to more and more success. These are the rewards of living by the 2nd Ten Commandments.

PRELUDE TO THE COMMANDMENTS

The Commandments hold together as a whole. Many of them bear on each other, so don't think of them only separately. For example, you may feel UNCONDITIONAL LOVE (Commandment No. 17), choose to act on it using what your INNER VOICE and REPAIR (No. 15 and No. 20) tell you to do, do it in FLOW (No. 11), and so on.

As previously stated in Chapter 3, the Commandments build on each other in a logical sequence. As a reminder, to move from the dependent to the independent level, an individual will have achieved a certain degree of mastery of Commandments No. 11 through No. 16. This includes finding a quality of experience that delivers happiness (11), a way of being that moves toward self-actualization (12),

135

and a healthy way of acting toward oneself (13 through 16). Then, to advance to the interdependent level and thus start to become a Motof, an individual must also have mastered Commandments No. 15 through No. 20. This includes serving others while growing individually (15, 16) and relating to others in a way that demonstrates global consciousness and responsibility (17 through 20).

As you read through each Commandment, think about how these natural laws might apply not only to individuals, but also to social groups, companies, institutions, governments, and society as a whole. How could any and all freely choose to follow them and succeed, thereby aligning themselves more harmoniously with global evolution?

PART II

THE COMMANDMENTS

Maximize your
time spent in
FLOW
and happiness

11

COMMANDMENT NO. 11: FLOW

A man's [person's] maturity consists in having found again the seriousness one had as a child, at play.

— Friedrich Nietzsche, philosopher, 1800s[1]

A cup half-empty cannot spill: a cup half-full overflows with happiness.

— Anonymous

F LOW means letting go. You allow yourself to be completely engaged in the moment.

Attitude, or state of mind, can determine one's whole outlook on life. People all over the world, from many different cultures report enjoying life the most in FLOW.[2] In this optimal psychological mode of experience, time seems to simultaneously move slowly and rapidly. You're challenged and yet completely absorbed by what you're doing. You feel strong, alert, in effortless control, unselfconscious, emotionally calm, and at the peak of your abilities.

To most people, a sport or hobby comes to mind as a familiar example of FLOW. Also, observe children's behavior. Children rarely remain stuck in any emotional state. They cry one minute, then laugh the next. They immerse themselves completely in whatever they're doing. In Zen, the concept of *satori* approaches such a state of mind: the "mind is free of thought, pure awareness; the body is active, sensitive, relaxed; and the emotions are open and free."[3]

> **"If you're not happy with what you have now,**
> **how could you be happy with more?"**
> **—Grandma**

How wonderful it is that with the right attitude we can experience FLOW in *all* of our activities. Look around you. Some people do it, usually those who "have their act together," the "winners in life." Mihaly Csikszentmihalyi, Professor and former Chairman of the Department of Psychology at the University of Chicago, spent over two decades studying the states of FLOW and "optimal experience" all over the world. He determined that "the control of consciousness determines the quality of life."[4]

With practice, we can experience FLOW anytime by being in the moment and setting challenging goals for ourselves. Challenging goals should include tasks that are neither too difficult nor too simple. Thus, learning, instead of being frustrating or threatening, becomes part of an enjoyable process. Life turns into fun as even work becomes play! Why would you want to experience it any other way? For whom, for what, and why are you doing it?

Life also presents many tough times, and we often suffer through many of the trials and tribulations that challenge us on our journey. Some things we only seem to "get" the hard way. Knowing that, we can try to maximize the times we spend in FLOW. It takes discipline and perseverance to overcome obstacles and setbacks and regain control of our life experiences. This makes discipline and perseverance the most important traits we need to hone not only to succeed in life, but to enjoy it as well. Develop and use them to increase the amount of time in your life that you FLOW, no matter what the outward circumstances may be.

> *Discipline and perseverance are the most important traits for not only succeeding in life but enjoying it as well.*

Obviously, we cannot choose to participate only in those activities that seem to lend themselves most easily to FLOW, like lying on a beach or playing a favorite sport. Pure pleasure activities do not necessarily conform to FLOW, since they don't always challenge us. Use FLOW to spend your time working in the area of your MISSION, growing and building, and also to enhance leisure activities.

Exhilaration of the spirit only exists in the present moment. Successful people not only FLOW within an activity, but also FLOW from one to the next. They still analyze the past and plan for the future, to exercise control of their lives and activities. They do not always just "go with the flow," an aimless way of passing time that lacks meaning and initiative and eventually results in boredom. Yet they allow themselves to experience the things that they choose to do with built-in flexibility and an awareness of the great and sometimes unpredictable forces of the universe.

FLOWING with the constant flux and change of the cosmos becomes easier when we use BALANCE and SURRENDER-COURAGE to determine the degree of control to exert—when to *make* things happen, and when to just *let* them happen. However, this does not mean feeling helpless. It just means accepting "what is" when you have to, and seizing the moment when the opportunity for growth and progress presents itself.

Remember, you only have one life to live, and you determine what attitude and resulting quality of experience you bring to the game. Trust the process of life. Young children enjoy the security of depending on their parents to nurture them with basic survival needs. This frees them to play and laugh.

In our day and age, we trust that we have learned to harness the planet sufficiently to meet our survival needs. This allows us to engage in furthering our knowledge while enjoying FLOW, the most pleasurable state of experience.

In the Consciousness Age you no longer have to suffer, so FLOW and take ownership of constant happiness as your birthright!

Seek
WHOLENESS
through ongoing
awareness and
lifelong
education

12

COMMANDMENT NO. 12: WHOLENESS

The body is a community, made up of its innumerable cells or inhabitants.
—Thomas A. Edison, 1880, inventor of the light bulb[1]

Not only is there but one way of doing things rightly, but there is only one way of seeing them, and that is, seeing the whole of them.
—John Ruskin, *The Two Paths* (1859)[2]

Seeking WHOLENESS means becoming successful by knowing more about yourself and the world, so that you can participate more effectively in everything around you. You can achieve this by exercising your free choice to integrate your body, mind, and spirit in a way that enhances your life and all of life.

L'CHAIM—TO LIFE

The universe values life and all living things above all else. Respect for life is Buddhism's first commandment. Other religions, such as Judaism, also espouse life as the primary underlying directive—hence the familiar salutation "L'Chaim," meaning "To Life." We all have a choice whether to add or to detract from the WHOLE. The more you get to know the inner world of you, the more you become ready to join in the process of life and contribute to the outer world of all.

As you augment life, you participate to a greater extent in Gev and project or reflect back WHOLENESS to all. You also experience the joyousness of feeling at one with all things—at-one-ment. Anything that harms life—your own included—violates WHOLENESS, and prevents feeling the deepest and most satisfying emotions. Harmony with creation has its inherent reward—your well-being.

To find that harmony, we must first become free of our barriers and resistance to living life at its fullest, barriers that keep us chained in the slavery of ikorgance. The power and COURAGE to create can then surge from within us, and add our contribution to life. "L'Chaim!"

WHOLENESS through self-awareness and education helps to free us. This freedom allows us to be and act in accordance with the other Commandments.

Breaking out to greater freedom enables us then to discover, accept, and choose a healthier life based on maximizing our potential and moving toward self-actualization. Conversely, we can also opt not to learn our lessons, and then continue to experience pain and disease—literally, "dis-ease," a lack of comfort—caught in the shackles of our old, often subconscious, emotional and reasoning patterns. This damages both our existence and our essence, and fails to contribute to the WHOLE.

Seeking WHOLENESS is a lifelong process. We get closer to it as we increasingly grok our own interdependence and our interconnectedness to the rest of the universe. As the world becomes increasingly interconnected, your opportunities to obtain knowledge and to understand how we all are interrelated will grow as well. Figure 12-1, the "WHOLENESS Circle," demonstrates our levels of interconnectedness.

Figure 12-1
"Wholeness Circle"

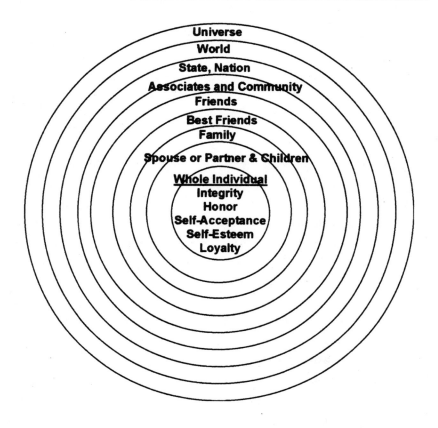

The WHOLENESS Circle shows that each individual's center has a self, or essence, that wishes to manifest its own SELF-ACCEPTANCE, integrity, honor (including honesty), self-esteem and consequently, self-actualization. In our innermost self we are aware that we co-exist with, and desire to express loyalty and reverence to, our surrounding levels of life to which we connect. That completes our sense of WHOLENESS and unity with the rest of creation. This allegiance, which creates trust, radiates Lev outwards toward (first and foremost) our spouse or partner and children, then extended family, best friends, other friends, associates and community, the state and/or nation, the world, and the universe, in this order. An equilibrium, with appropriate levels of connection to all of these outer circles, exemplifies a human being getting closer to WHOLENESS.

Wholeness helps us to develop deep levels of commitment, and to enjoy the richness of life to its fullest.

THE QUEST FOR PERFECTION

Sometime during or right after conception, but before birth, we all emanated from a spiritual place of perfection. In the womb we were totally cared for and, hopefully, received all that we needed to thrive and develop. Our quest for perfection stems from wanting to pursue our natural self-preservation instincts, and from our drive to advance our soul's evolution to higher levels of consciousness.

However, immediately after conception, the environment begins impacting and imprinting us, and thus influencing our path to perfection. This begins while we are still within our mother's womb, where noises, chemicals, and other environmental factors affect both the mother and the developing fetus. Furthermore, our genes, a result of cumulative species learning (*morphogenetics*) and early sensory inputs, inscribe us with information needed to learn the lessons we most need to evolve further. As we grow up, we also develop core beliefs, formed by our perception of what it takes to survive the game of life. All of these modify our views of how to fulfill our quest for perfection.

As a consequence of these influencing factors, each of us develops our own unique personality, which includes: predisposition; range of emotional responses; how tall we grow; the color of our eyes and skin; ability patterns; and more. Important persons such as parents and teachers, and significant events, shape many of our early ways of being, including how we relate to ourselves and others; our development of confidence and the joy of learning and doing well; how fearful we are of new experiences; and the ability to value our own perceptions and understandings.

In the process of the formation of our personality, fears also form a *shadow* side that takes us further away from WHOLENESS. Everything we learned was useful for that time in the past to help us survive. Yet much of it remains emblazoned within our mind, emotions, and body throughout our life. This learning, resulting from our animal-like, subconscious fear of death, may lead to false discernment and inappropriate actions in some situations in the present. These misperceptions create our shadow, conceived by Freud and named by Jung as "that part of the personality which has been repressed for the sake of the ego's (survival)."[3] This dark side, or "all those unpleasant qualities we like to hide, together with the insufficiently developed functions and the content of the personal unconscious,"[4] cause us to feel, and act, separate from others. It guarantees that we will violate our fellow human beings and our own WHOLENESS.

On a psychological level, the pursuit of material comfort, of drug-induced highs, of the illusion of power over others, are but some of the many futile ways our shadow undertakes to fulfill our quest to return to perfection.

But there's a light side to the shadow also: it does provide us with the opportunity to work toward even more WHOLENESS than we began with. Rather than just act as slaves to our robot-like emotional patterns, we can choose to seek, for the rest of our lives, to return to that initial stage of perfection. This is a yearning to reunite with Gev. Some Eastern religions speak of reaching enlightenment and experiencing reality as it is, undistorted, and of feeling again at one with all of creation. In the Judeo-Christian tradition, people might speak of returning to the biblical Garden of Eden.

Because we are human, and thus mortal, we all must persist in our search for the way to return to that place of total Joy, Knowledge, Lev, and Mission, as part of Oneness, by transforming the negative parts of our dualistic nature back into the Light of creation—into WHOLENESS. Jung aptly summarized the value of the shadow, or the thing a person has no wish to be, by stating that "one does not become enlightened by imagining figures of light, but by making the darkness conscious."5

RETURNING TO THE "GARDEN OF EDEN"

We can only hope to achieve ever-greater degrees of freedom and perfection by working toward more wholeness, and we do this first through heightening our awareness. Buddha proclaimed that awareness is the single most important key to becoming enlightened. Awareness can lead to some of our most beautiful and joyful experiences, and can also lead us to deep pain. Personal painful realizations, or the empathetic pain we experience as we learn about the suffering of others, represent messages from our body and mind to force us to learn and integrate new ways to think, be, and behave, so that we can awaken to a less distorted view of reality. This takes us closer to WHOLENESS.

If you think education is expensive, try ignorance!

Some people deprive themselves of the blessings of WHOLENESS by opting to remain unaware. By keeping your head in the sand, you can maintain the fiction of not knowing and not experiencing the suffering that goes on in yourself and all over our planet. Lack of awareness and knowledge insulates you from pain—temporarily. Yet, it eventually catches up with you. Meanwhile, it prevents you from becoming more **whole** and complete, because you can never realize your inherent kinship to all of life. Thus you deny yourself the deeper satisfaction that cannot be found in any other way.

On the other hand, people with increased awareness, and thus more WHOLENESS, feel better and healthier, mentally and physically. They experience greater inner peace. They stay centered and calm, so that they can act appropriately in every situation. They are always prepared to learn new lessons, always open to breaking new ground in situations not yet encountered or grokked.

Seeking WHOLENESS involves seeing everything as an exhilarating, educational experience that further advances our spirit. Some people, like those who strive to push the boundaries of their psychological and/or spiritual experiences, perhaps through near-death or shamanic rites of passage, can get unexpectedly large jolts of WHOLENESS. The rest of us have to acquire and assemble knowledge as an evolving soul, through staying as open-minded as possible while trying, through constant awareness, to educate ourselves a little bit at a time. This is a lifelong process.

In a world changing so rapidly that it produces daily or hourly future shock, our opportunity for spiritual advancement grows in proportion to the rate of change and our ability to adapt to the many new situations presented to us. For example, consider how much more we need to learn in a lifetime, when we now change careers multiple times; and partners; and the locations we call home. In the Consciousness Age, we each succeed through continuously learning how to improve our lives and grow more WHOLE in a Global Brain, and thereby accelerate our return to our own "Garden of Eden."

ATTUNING TO AND INTEGRATING THE HUMAN TRINITY AND DUALITY

Awareness attunes us to the trinity of our human makeup:

1. Our Inner Child: emotions, physical body, and the subconscious mind.

2. Our Inner Parent: the rational, conscious mind.

3. Our INNER VOICE: the higher self, or supraconscious, higher mind.

Their competing demands require us to negotiate SYNERGISTIC *win-win* agreements among all three parts. Self-actualized people, according to Maslow, "listen to their own voices; they take responsibility; they are honest; and they work hard. They find out who they are and what they are, not only in terms of their MISSION in life, but also in terms of the way their feet hurt when they wear such and such a pair of shoes and whether they do or do not like eggplant or stay up all night if they drink too much beer."[6] They pay attention to all levels of their needs, of their life, and of the world around them.

Through disciplined practice and instruction, we can grow to know the needs of each of the parts of our human trinity, and eventually to align all of them with the higher self. Fortunately, we all have built-in indicators—our health and emotions—for this process of spiritual advancement. Nature uses our sense of discomfort to urge us toward WHOLENESS. People who learn to listen to their feelings and intuition can immediately heed these messages before physical pain or distress ensues. This puts them on the only worthwhile path to pursue, the one that leads toward greater comfort and enlightenment. As we let the INNER VOICE guide our integrated inner trinity, we become more and more WHOLE.

Finally, since the days of Adam and Eve, humanity has existed in duality: male and female. To return to Gev's grace, each must realize the Eve in Adam and the Adam in Eve, to form a more WHOLE, perfect human. Remember that a human being, whether man or woman, consists of some combination of what the Chinese call Yin and Yang energies. In the future, people will exhibit a more harmonious BALANCE of these two sets of characteristics. Like everything in evolution, feminine and masculine serve a purpose, until they will perhaps someday evanesce when sufficient WHOLENESS has been achieved.

It's always better to know and increasingly to gain in consciousness, as we try to experience greater WHOLENESS, and someday, holiness.

Develop greater
SELF-ACCEPTANCE
by loving yourself
unconditionally

13

COMMANDMENT NO. 13: SELF-ACCEPTANCE

You have no idea what a poor opinion I have of myself —and how little I deserve it.

—W.S. Gilbert (1836-1911)[1]

Self-love is the instrument of our preservation; it resembles the provision for the perpetuity of mankind; it is necessary, it is dear to us, it gives us pleasure.

—Voltaire, "Self-Love," *Philosophical Dictionary* (1874)[2]

SELF-ACCEPTANCE means to feel good about yourself just the way you are right now—by loving yourself unconditionally. You're not perfect yet, and you won't be for a very long time. But you're perfect for right now.

We develop the ability to feel self-Lev by applying open-mindedness, emotional acceptance, forgiveness, and compassion to ourselves. We must understand and allow for our imperfections. We would not be human without them. In fact, the 2nd Ten Commandments differ from the original Commandments because they assume we can learn from our mistakes without societal punishment for them. They encourage you to recognize your mistakes, rectify them where possible, learn from them, and do better and better each time new situations present themselves. Rather than invoking fear, they beckon you to act out of Lev. They ask that you (really) do the best you can, as the responsible, conscious person you are at this moment in time, at this moment in your personal development.

This attitude of self-reflection represents evolution toward a higher order of mind and consciousness, as it places the burden of responsibility on you, instead of allowing you to depend on society's moral injunctions. The more that you allow yourself to love yourself unconditionally now, the more you are likely to choose right actions and consequently develop even greater SELF-ACCEPTANCE. Whether you are following the 2nd Ten Commandments, and to what degree, will be judged primarily by you, your success, and Gev.

PRESENT AND PAST PERFECTION

SELF-ACCEPTANCE consists of coming to terms with both your present self and all of your past.

First recognize that you have a unique spirit that has its own set of traits or attributes. Even if you did 100 years of personal-growth work, and peeled away layer upon layer of your outer self, you would still end up with an immutable inner core—your unique essence, *not* your personality—that will always distinguish you. These traits are neither good nor bad, but they can be used to act for better or worse. Accept and thank Gev for your special gifts.

> **Cultivate an attitude of gratitude.**

Second, embrace the perfection of what has developed as your outer layer, since the time of conception, your personality. Do this by seeing how everything in your past—your parents, your birthplace, your childhood, and the rest of your adult experiences to date—has allowed and helped you to evolve the furthest that you could. Cultivate an attitude of gratitude.

Can you not only accept, but even be thankful, to the point of saying that you would not have changed a thing in your life to get to where you are now? Take charge, as both producer and actor, of the script of the drama of your life, and recognize and thank all of the teachers who play a part in it—as trying as they may seem to make your life at times. And most of all, view your life with thankfulness to the universe for providing the abundance it affords: have SELF-ACCEPTANCE for who you are right now! Thank you, Gev.

IF I AM ONLY FOR MYSELF, WHAT AM I?

Just think, there has never been anybody, ever, that is just the way you are right now. And yet your individual journey through life takes place in an atmosphere of togetherness. You contribute to the diversity of this wonderful planet. And at this exact moment in time you can't do a thing about how you are. You can, however, choose how to be and act, and how to work on changing who you are, in the next instant in time. Hillel, the Jewish sage who lived contemporaneously with Jesus Christ, emphasized the importance of self-sufficiency while participating responsibly in your community when he said:

"If I am not for myself, who is for me?

And if I am only for myself, what am I?

And if not now, when?"[3]

So remember that to participate in the greater whole effectively, don't try to change who you are. Rather, allow your core, who you *really* are, to come out and express itself fully. Be your essence.

If not truly having SELF-ACCEPTANCE causes you to withdraw or over-express yourself, and not to bring out the best in you, who loses out? It's easy to say, "Only me," or "You really don't want to know how *I* feel." However, being as uniquely important as anyone else on the planet, you affect all. You bathe yourself and others with the glow of your heartfelt emotional self. The expression of your feelings, thoughts, and actions ripple through all your contacts like the waves in a pond from a dropped stone, the touch of wind on a leaf, and the splash of a dolphin swimming with joy. When you withhold the expression of the best in you, not only do you reduce the opportunities for others to experience you, but you also fundamentally deny experiencing your SELF-ACCEPTANCE.

Acknowledge that you value yourself, just for being, and perceive yourself as no better or worse than anyone else on the planet. One cannot have more self-worth than another, since we all have the same amount. This is true despite a hierarchy in nature, in which we participate, of each of us having evolved to different levels of advancement toward WHOLENESS. But do not allow our outer differences to cloud what can never be altered by fact or action—the even-souledness of all human spiritual beings.

Despite the basic truth of the parity of all souls, some people suffer from an inflated, egotistical sense of self-worth which amounts to arrogance—where humility would serve better. Others fall victim to their own misperceptions, and feel a lack of self-worth. All of us would do well to accept emotionally that as of here and now, everything about ourselves is as right as it can be at this instant in time.

As we have increasing SELF-ACCEPTANCE and advance individually we become more responsible, and compassionately help others to follow in our footsteps. Humans may have evolved further than other species, but we all have a long way to go to achieve WHOLENESS.

Recognize your uniqueness, embrace it, and be gentle with yourself. Develop greater SELF-ACCEPTANCE—you deserve it.

Live with
BALANCE,
priorities, and
moderation in all
things.

14

COMMANDMENT NO. 14: BALANCE

Nothing is unthinkable, nothing impossible to the balanced person, provided it arises out of the needs of life and is dedicated to life's further developments.

—Lewis Mumford, "The Way and the Life,"
The Conduct of Life (1951)[1]

How sour sweet music is
When time is broke and no proportion kept!
So is it in the music of men's lives.
—William Shakespeare, *Richard II*, 5.5.42 (1595-96)[2]

BALANCE means keeping all of your activities in perspective to everything in your life, at any given time and over your lifetime. This short journey called life lasts on average 30,000 days: 6,500 reaching adulthood; 11,000 working; and 12,500 other adult days. We consume about a third of all these days sleeping! So we should choose very carefully what to do with our time. It's each person's most valuable resource, and it's ticking away.

PRIORITIZING FOR MAXIMUM EFFECTIVENESS

Look at all the various roles you play, and the associated responsibilities you fulfill in your career, friendships, significant-other partnerships, social causes, etc., including your continuing self-development (mental, physical, and spiritual) and pleasure time. For each of these, consider what results you wish to attain in return for the precious time that you expend on them.

Set short-, medium-, and long-term goals for all these roles. Short-term might mean daily or weekly; medium-term, monthly; and long-term, yearly, 5-year, or even lifetime.

Within each category or role, continuously *prioritize* your goals and spend your time accordingly, to assure that you meet your most important ones. Stephen R. Covey, in *The 7 Habits of Highly Effective People*, calls this "Habit 3: Put First Things First."[3] He quotes the nineteenth-century German philosopher-poet, Johann Wolfgang von Goethe, who said that "Things which matter most must never be at the mercy of things which matter least."[4] So by "organizing and executing around priorities,"[5] you gain the relief that you don't have to get everything done all the time. You manage yourself to accomplish the tasks that are most in line with your goals and will bring the most happiness and meaning to your life.

The recent spiraling acceleration of technology, discussed earlier, increases the significance of prioritizing your time, as we evolve toward an interdependent world. As a nerve cell of the Global Brain, which is attempting to form and maintain itself, the connections you make, with whom, and how you interconnect, impacts the whole network.

You can expect the constant bombardment from the mass media and communications technology to escalate. Answering machine, voice mail, and electronic bulletin board messages, increasing numbers of phone calls, piles of computer-generated junk mail, advertising, and many other forms of information, will transmit an ongoing and growing barrage of input. It is up to you to evaluate the onslaught of information and decide whether to allot to it your time, money, or energy.

Many of these means of interconnecting people result from technology only put into common use a little over a decade ago. While we welcome this interlinking as being required for the formation of the Global Brain, we must beware of its hypnotic effect. Our only hope for remaining sane, and yet effectively participating in the best solution for the network, lies in prioritizing how we handle these stimuli. So only change your priorities in response to new information if you perceive it to be SYNERGISTIC with your goals. This in turn will mean you've made the optimal choice for the global system as a whole.

We constantly have to make choices that take both our own good and that of the system into account through moderation. Aristotle, the Greek philosopher who lived 2,300 years ago, in his ethics of the *golden mean*, prescribed living with *moderation in all things*. He declared that humans are by nature political animals who, by instinct, want to live in a state of union for the promotion of the good life.[6] Each individual "must preserve a balance between excessive indulgence on the one hand and ascetic denial on the other."[7] This assures that we adequately control our bodies and emotions, enjoy good health, and succeed in alignment with the whole.

PROPER PROPORTION IS THE KEY TO HEALTH

In every moment we face the polarities we observe in nature: day and night; light and dark; life and death; nothing and infinite; good and evil; the spirit of global evolution, and those forces which threaten to prevent us from connecting the health of our social institutions with the well being of the planet (Gev and "anti-Gev"). Each and all of these, in proper proportions, allow us to generate meaningful experiences in life. It seems that too much or too little of anything (whether we perceive it as positive or negative does not matter), relative of course to the matter at hand, harms us. Our health and happiness require that we judiciously determine the right measure for ourselves in each given situation. We serve our own highest good by containing ourselves within proper limits. We harm ourselves—and often others at the same time—by breaking this rule and going beyond those limits.

Discover these limits ongoingly and consciously, and adjust accordingly to maximize your success and health. Make life an exciting educational experience where you continuously learn how to fine tune your judgment of proportion. If you lack awareness, you will learn the hard way. Eventually, imbibing alcohol intemperately, working incessantly, working without meaning, eating to excess, having too much or too little sex, fun, and other physical pleasures, or a myriad of other imbalances, will force you to modify your ways due to increased stress, deteriorating health and, eventually, despair.

BALANCE, like FLOW, requires balancing a certain amount of SURRENDER to Gev with a *proactive* exercise of control and power through our free will and COURAGE. To be proactive means "to have the initiative and responsibility to make things happen" based on our values.[8] This contrasts with just *reacting* to our environment based on our feelings. And yet, we must also recognize that certain things remain beyond our control, including, for example, our essence. Like a consummate gymnast on a BALANCE beam, we must walk a fine line to stay on a destined course, dictated by our INNER VOICE.

We must combine faith in Gev and ourselves with the will and self-confidence that assures us that we can do it!

PSYCHOSPIRITUAL PERSONALITY TYPING (PSPT): A MEANS TO BALANCE OUR "GIFTS" AND "SINS"

Believing in ourselves includes honestly understanding our individual pluses and minuses and acting with them in an appropriate BALANCE. Philosophers and psychologists have long attempted to categorize people into personality types, to map human nature and to guide us in assessing ourselves, especially our strengths and weaknesses.

Ancient mystical teachings about personality types attempted to help us to evaluate our individual "gifts" and "sins." They described basic personality types, with a continuum of subtypes, to encompass the spectrum of humanity, using what we call *Psychospiritual Personality Typing*, or *PSPT*. Kept secret globally for thousands of years, many of these ancient methods have now emerged to assist us with self-evaluation. Significant among these traditions in Western culture are: the *Enneagram* (Mesopotamian),[9] the "Seven Deadly Sins" (early Christianity),[10] and the ten "Sefirot" or "Faces of God" of the Kabbalah (medieval Jewish mysticism).[11] As one might expect, all of these observations about the fundamental nature of humans seem to relate rather well to each other, and to modern-day psychology. They contain an abundance of truth and wisdom.

Recent analyses by psychological experts of the wisdom contained in these ancient teachings have also revealed strong parallels to twentieth-century personality theories such as those of Sigmund Freud, Carl Jung, and Karen Horney.[12] They have correlated with personality evaluation tests, such as *Myers-Briggs* and the *Riso-Hudson Enneagram Type Indicator (RHETI)*.[13]

These kinds of tools, regardless of their imperfections, can help us to gain a better understanding of ourselves and of each other, and to attain BALANCE. As the Global Brain evolves, it is necessary for us to have a minimum global standard of how to discuss and understand personality issues that will always exist in our inner psychological states and in our interactions with others. It is time for as many of us as possible to use these tools and to "know thyself," including our strengths and limitations, so that we have better insight into how we can all live and work together.

Ultimate transformation toward greater WHOLENESS depends on finding the most appropriate BALANCE of the notable characteristics for our type as revealed to us by the PSPT that we choose to use. As most of us know intuitively, each person has strengths and weaknesses, or "gifts" and "sins." While we are all composites of many different personality traits, usually one trait, or at most a few traits, seem to predominate and become obvious in our psychological makeup. By paying close attention to BALANCING our most predominate personality traits we become stronger in many ways.

For example, a PSPT frequently referred to as a "Leader" (in the tradition of the Enneagram), must seek to BALANCE their power, strength, and self-confidence with a compassion for vulnerability and weakness, including their own, thereby overcoming their temptation for lust and abuse of power. When they have a high degree of BALANCE, people of this type can be transformed into magnanimous, historically great leaders such as Martin Luther King, Franklin D. Roosevelt, and Mikhail Gorbachev.[14] If left to stray to their extremes, and by failing to act in moderation, some leaders can and do become ruthless, tyrannical dictators, and cause great harm to others, and eventually to themselves.

Use your understanding of your PSPT, and the spirit of BALANCE, to determine to what degree to moderate your behaviors, as you follow all of the 2nd Ten Commandments.

Act true to your
INNER VOICE
and fulfill your
MISSION

15

COMMANDMENT NO. 15: INNER VOICE-MISSION

Your vision will become clear only when you can look into your own heart. Who looks outside, dreams; who looks inside, awakes.

—Carl Jung, psychologist, early 1900s[1]

What I mean by a religious person is one who conceives himself or herself to be the instrument of some purpose in the universe which is a high purpose, and is the motive power of evolution, that is of a continual ascent in organization and power of life, and extension of life.

—George Bernard Shaw (1856-1950)[2]

NNER VOICE-MISSION means awakening your higher mind within and aligning yourself and acting in accordance with the greater intelligence that connects all of us together, Gev.

USING YOUR HIGHER MIND

As the Consciousness Age dawns upon humanity, greater numbers of people are becoming aware that within each of us flares a spark of divinity. This soul or spirit, essence, higher mind, or speck of the life force, fuels our existence. As our core, it is also a part of the Higher Power—Gev—and the source of all inspiration and creation. The gateway we use to contact and align ourselves with this greater intelligence within us is called our INNER VOICE.

Although most of us hear a cacophony of many voices and messages, through disciplined evolution of our spirit and personal-growth work, we can learn to distinguish the voice that knows best. The INNER VOICE represents a deeper and truer knowing. It always knows what's right for each of us. Adhering to it automatically honors not only what's best for ourselves, but for others, too. It represents what you *know you know,* deep down inside.

Acting in accordance with your INNER VOICE's directions may bring up difficult emotions such as guilt, anger, sadness, and fear. These emotions may lead you to want to fool yourself and to choose an easier path. However, you can't fool your true self, at least not for very long. Sooner or later, with new insights or, more often, due to increasing discomfort and pain, you recognize the benefits of your INNER VOICE's message and heed it. Each time you realize the gains reaped from acting rightly the time before, it becomes increasingly easier to follow your INNER VOICE the next time. Eventually, with sufficient experience, you always feel wonderful immediately when you do act true to it. The ultimate goal of every person's spiritual path is to constantly do what their true self or INNER VOICE really urges them to do, and to feel good about it.

For the last six thousand years, the religions of the world have attempted to link each of us with what we are calling the INNER

VOICE and Gev, and to realize their benefits. Aldous Huxley, who studied the wisdom common to all the world's religious teachings, summarized in *The Perennial Philosophy* that truth can be found only through the exploration of, and identification with, the deep Self.[3] Ghandi, the liberator of colonial India, said: "Truth resides in every human heart, and one has to search for it there and to be guided by truth as one sees it."[4] Enlightened religious teachers and some non-religious leaders in history not only knew this, but let most of their actions be guided by this truth.

Despite the wisdom common to all of these religions, why haven't more of us come to rely on our INNER VOICE? Because we continue to act based either on our animal-like emotions or on the rational mind that has developed over the past several millennia, rather than employing the higher mind.

Science tells us that we employ less than ten percent of our brain's faculties. Evidence would indicate that much of humanity's future will rely on even further progress in the utilization of the brain, rather than the body. Over the past tens of thousands of years, the size and weight of our brain, relative to our bodies, have continued to grow. The ratio now stands at more than double that of other comparable mammals, who have remained stagnant in that respect.

What will enable us to learn how to use our higher mind more frequently? Completely new ways of thinking. This kind of transition also occurred about 10,000 years ago, when we began to use logic. Until then our hunter/gatherer ancestors scavenged like animals in their quest for food. They survived from one meal to the next. Imagine the "revolutionaries" who suggested to their fellow tribespeople that they cease their roaming and settle down into agrarian societies. Surely many of the hunter/gatherers thought they were crazy. But over the course of the next several thousand years, the gears of the rational mind increasingly began to turn, and more and more "followers" turned into farmers. As they planned and planted, they reaped what they had sown. (This may also have served as the first metaphorical introduction to human consciousness of the law of Karma.) The harvest rewarded them with sustenance that lasted for months or years. Even smart animals that stockpile food have not as yet demonstrated the capacity for this kind of proactive survival adaptation. Logical processing then began to spiral further, as inventions like the wheel rolled humanity forward on an ever-accelerating course.

As we advance to the next level, how do we begin to tune in to, and really listen to, the INNER VOICE? By harnessing both centuries-old techniques and new methods made possible by technological advances. Often we act true to our INNER VOICE, but haphazardly. We sometimes say we followed our "gut feeling" or intuition, and it seemed to pay off.

Learning to use our INNER VOICE more methodically involves practicing techniques such as: meditation, yoga, Feldenkrais, scientific prayer, dream interpretation, self-hypnosis, computerized biofeedback, brain-stimulating medical machines and drugs of the future,[5] virtual reality, and other technologies that mimic reality on multiple levels. All of these train us to more quickly induce a state of mind in which we can clearly hear our INNER VOICE. They also help us overcome our fears and doubts, and reduce our need to use toxic substances such as alcohol and some drugs, that chemically disconnect us from the neurons needed to tap into our higher mind.

INTEGRITY, HONESTY AND LOYALTY PROMOTE SELF-ESTEEM AND TRUST

By heeding the INNER VOICE, we maintain the highest level of *integrity*, the value we place on ourselves. This follows naturally, because it represents the true, unique aspect of the self. Expressing the realizations you have from attending to your INNER VOICE feels right and good because all parts of you—physical, emotional, and rational—can align with a greater purpose.

Some refer to sticking to one's higher integrity as submitting to and following the path of the heart. Whenever we do, life works. At times this requires humility and to SURRENDER our ego's wishes to circumstances outside ourselves, which transcend us. Our rational and subconscious minds may resist aligning with our INNER VOICE, but in the long run we will feel unrest until we fix our ways and tune in.

Listening to your heart and soul also urges you always to tell your truth. This *honesty* includes full disclosure. Both truth-telling and relevant disclosures must occur in a timely manner. Ken Keyes, Jr., founder of the "Science of Happiness," and the author of *Handbook to Higher Consciousness*, says that "the love that total honesty can create is worth whatever pain may be triggered when your honesty evokes the other person's embarrassment, fear, jealousy, resentment, or anger—or your own."[6] Unveiling the truth always inspires new creation, and can break old patterns.

The INNER VOICE also reminds you to remain *loyal* to others by keeping your word and commitments both to yourself and to them. In some instances, you may need to renegotiate your commitments. At those times you can still maintain your loyalty as long as you arrive at a mutually satisfactory resolution by using SYNERGY.

As the world gets tied together into the Global Brain, the importance of doing what you say you will do increases. Betrayal causes systemic dis-ease that ripples around the globe. What already occurs at the human-body-system level now begins to manifest in Gaia. For example, imagine that the stomach communicates to our brain that it is hungry, and that it agrees to digest food if it receives it. After getting food it decides that it doesn't feel like processing it just now. This causes what we commonly refer to as an "upset stomach." The system-level organism—the person—experiences it as a discomfort that disrupts productive activity as a whole. Such disharmonies also happen worldwide to Gaia, such as when a company supplying goods fails to meet its promised delivery times.

When we claim integrity, honesty, and loyalty as a result of even imperfectly following our INNER VOICE, we feel good about ourselves and thus experience *self-esteem* and joy. Every cell in our body experiences harmony with a powerful energy force, and senses an unparalleled vitality. But when we doubt or disobey the INNER VOICE, our ability to listen to it diminishes, as does our self-esteem. We first and foremost hurt ourselves, and then others.

Our self-esteem is further enhanced by using our individual, unique talents with an attitude of service and MISSION. Combining our best efforts at the tasks we choose to undertake, with a sense of purpose, results in accomplishments and rewards—internal and external.

Our integrity, honesty, loyalty, and self-esteem also promote other people's *trust* in us, which is ultimately the key factor in any successful relationship—with ourselves, with others, and with Gaia.

SERVICE AND THE FEATURES OF A PERSONAL MISSION

As a part of the Global Brain or nervous system, each person has a role or MISSION to fulfill for the benefit of the integrated whole.

Each of us must discover this MISSION through a process of listening to our INNER VOICE, and choose to what degree to carry it out. In the past, our society often assigned our role and subsequent MISSION, based on birth, parents, social status, religion, and other factors beyond our control. If your mother was a homemaker, or your father was a fisherman, you probably would follow in their path, based on your gender.

In the Consciousness Age, however, as we more often claim our free will, we *find* our MISSION instead of being given it. While the MISSION comes from Gev, it does not come with exact instructions, a blueprint, or an imperative to execute it. That would require us to abdicate a part of our free will, and would lessen the inherent richness of living out the essential mystery of life.

Once on the track of unearthing our MISSION, we continuously fine-tune our understanding of it. Knowing it somehow makes sense out of most of the things we've learned, experienced, and done in our lives until now, and prepares us for the tasks yet ahead. While we can't explain everything, we do in fact seem to participate in part of an ingenious and incomprehensible master plan. We're never quite sure where our higher self will lead us next, and we can't wait to find out.

After we have sufficiently discovered our personal MISSION, the following features about it become clear to us:

1. MISSION gives meaning to our lives.

   Some even claim that the search for meaning is our very purpose for wanting to live.[7]

2. We can perform our MISSION in FLOW and happiness.

   It takes advantage of our most actualized self, challenges us, and often exacts from us every last bit of our globally unique skills, knowledge, character, and personality traits. The process becomes like playing a game we know how to play extremely well but still continue to improve at. Like champions in any arena, doing what we do best allows us to make maximum impact with minimum effort, and eventually to earn other people's appreciation. Each of us enjoys and loves most of the "work" required to be done. Confucius, China's most famous teacher, said around 550 B.C.: "Choose a job you love, and you will never have to work a day in your life."[8]

3. Our MISSION teaches us the exact lessons we most need to learn to evolve spiritually.

   Amazingly, these acts of self-expression also teach us experientially the exact lessons that our soul must learn to succeed in its continuing evolution. We teach who we are and thereby learn what we wish to become. In some ways the MISSION actually feels like an integral part of our very life and breath.

When we consider that we are a nerve cell in a global nervous system, this makes perfect biological sense.

4. Our MISSION rewards us with sufficient money to survive and thrive.

Do what you love; money and all else will follow!

Once we fall in line with serving Gev by fulfilling our MIS-SION, a life filled with Joy, Knowledge, and Lev comes to us. Genesis records that God breathed life into us humans, having already created all the matter and energy in the universe. As we inhale each breath of air, in every moment of our lives we breathe out our expression of yet another rearrangement of the original creation. This regenerates the process of life—change and evolution—in every instant. Taking our place in history, even in small, seemingly insignificant ways, by fulfilling our MISSION, creates a happiness that no amount of money can buy—or ever does!

If you think you're too small to be effective, then you've never been in bed with a mosquito.

5. Carrying out our MISSION excites us with the exercising of authentic power as a co-creator with Gev.

Assuming authentic power means acting unselfishly in ways that may have a lasting positive impact on creation as a whole. This is the only form of real power. It simultaneously gives us a burden of responsibility and an unparalleled privilege. It can seem like both a curse and a blessing. It requires SURRENDER-COURAGE to achieve maximal results.

FOLLOW YOUR BLISS, FOLLOW YOUR SONG

Joseph Campbell, the twentieth-century Jungian psychologist/mythologist, said:

> And so I think the best thing I can say is follow your bliss. If your bliss is just your fun and your excitement, you're on the wrong track. . . . Know where your bliss is. And that involves coming down to a deep place in yourself.[9]

To figure out how to follow our bliss, we find ourselves at every twinkle in time trying to decide which path to take in our lives. Robert Frost, the twentieth-century poet, wrote about this ongoing choice: "Two roads diverged in a yellow wood,. . . . I took the one less traveled, And that has made all the difference." To choose the right road at every moment, look to prayer. Praying does not mean crying out, "Lord, Lord," but rather doing the divine will.[10]

Yogi Bhajan, the contemporary religious leader of the Sikhs of the western world, when presented with this Commandment, spoke movingly and paraphrased it astutely:

> I am your consciousness [God or Gev]. I am your existence. I am in every cell of you. Hear me oh human, hear me. Behold, I set you on a journey with destiny. You must walk distance, with my light within you.[11]

Follow your INNER VOICE-MISSION, intuition, or spirit guide to claim your bliss.

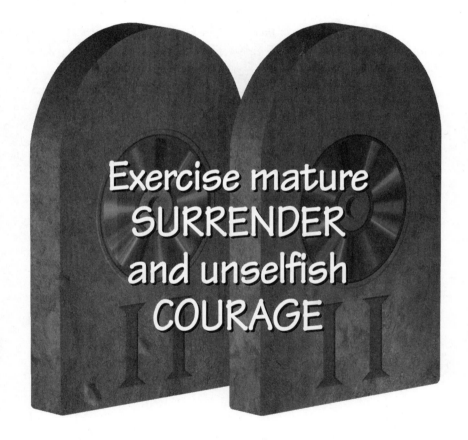

Exercise mature
SURRENDER
and unselfish
COURAGE

16

COMMANDMENT NO. 16: SURRENDER-COURAGE

There's a divinity that shapes our ends,
Rough-hew them how we will.

—Shakespeare, *Hamlet* (1600)[1]

Courage is not freedom from fear; it is being
afraid and going on. Once you have looked fear in
the face and have overcome it, you can do it again
and again and again.

—Unknown

SURRENDER-COURAGE means to grok when to have the peace of mind to accept the things you cannot change, and when to have the fearlessness to act boldly and impact the things that you can change. This is a paraphrasing of the "Serenity Prayer": "God grant me the serenity to accept the things I cannot change; the courage to change the things I can; and the wisdom to know the difference."[2] Developed by organizations concerned with helping people to recover from substance and other kinds of abuse, it asks that we each make a responsible choice in every situation we face.

ACCEPT, OR CONTRIBUTE AND GROW

Conscientious people, aware of their role in creation, bear tremendous responsibility in all situations. Upon reaching higher levels of growth on their journey to becoming their higher selves, they come to terms with when, if, and how to act responsibly in each moment and in every circumstance. They know that every action they take influences everyone else and global evolution, and that they must therefore take all consequences of their actions into consideration.

With each free action that stems from Lev, not fear, we make a contribution to the world, grok new truths, and grow ourselves. The actions we take from Lev further the process of evolution, and allow us to understand more of the universe and Gev. As we achieve more WHOLENESS, our own growth comes not so much from fighting past our baggage and fears, but from facing the unknown and conquering our fear of it. We step forward with our heart and soul onto new ground, thereby letting go of our hold on the familiar and the traditional, to discover new truths appropriate for current situations.

Thus every action requires a careful BALANCE of SURRENDER to the circumstances presented to us by the universe, with the COURAGE and proactiveness of exercising control and power through our free will. Before acting we must contemplate, and discern where our effort will run head on into a brick wall, and where it will bear fruit.

This ultimately gives us the freedom to create productively and efficiently, without unnecessarily wasting energy.

The universe seems to favor those who know when to go forth boldly, leaping into action as co-creators and molding the future in both small and large ways. They better their own lives and those of the rest of the world. Winston Churchill, the heroic British Prime Minister, claimed: "COURAGE is the first of human qualities because it is the quality which guarantees all others."[3] Similarly, a recurring theme in ancient Greek mythology asserts that "the gods help those who help themselves." We achieve what was previously believed to be impossible, and metaphorically slay dragons along the way.

Sometimes we must recognize when to hold back and wait for a more opportune time, and when to SURRENDER altogether and pursue other goals. Sometimes elements beyond our dominion and control affect our lives. Why should we exhaust ourselves wrestling with them?

> *"Do birds fight the seasons?*
> *Do flowers fight rain?"*
> —"I Can Surrender," Living Love Songs[4]

Once we acquiesce to what we don't have power to change, there's no limit to how far we can grow, or to how great a list of accomplishments we can amass. Like birds, we're free to build nests, and like flowers, to bud petals. *Like ocean waves, humans can flow forward with steps of COURAGE, and ebb back with SURRENDER to the tides of time.* Some of us choose to break early, and need another chance to rebuild and try again. But each of us has the opportunity to reach the shore of our destiny.

MATURE INACTION AND UNSELFISH ACTION

Mature SURRENDER occurs when evolved individuals, who can clearly perceive reality, recognize and choose to accept their power-

181

lessness to change a situation. Unclouded vision under these circumstances may dictate exercising patience until a time when action will lead to positive results. An idea ahead of its time may or may not fit in with evolution. But when the time is right, the pursuit of thought-to-be-impossible dreams can change the course of events, and of your life.

Beware of immature SURRENDER. That means taking the easy way out due to laziness or cowardice, not believing that you have enough strength, Lev, knowledge, or resources to act successfully. This stems from fear and inaccurate perceptions, not mature inaction, and leads to paralysis of thought and action.

The Gods help those who help themselves.

Unselfish COURAGE means acting and exerting power and influence for the sake of others and Gev, rather than only for yourself. This can include extending yourself in situations where you try to help others grow, and thereby helping yourself, too. Again, this means that you accept the burden of making a decision that until now only the Creator and relatively few individuals in history dared to make: influencing events and people in a constructive manner.

The Information Age gave all of us access to data, and allows each of us to act Gev-like in the Consciousness Age. Listen to your INNER VOICE to decide when to observe passively, and when to take a proactive leap of faith, using SURRENDER-COURAGE to make miracles happen.

Feel UNCONDITIONAL LOVE and recognize the oneness of humanity

17

COMMANDMENT NO. 17: UNCONDITIONAL LOVE

It is only with the heart that one can see rightly;
what is essential is invisible to the eye.
                    —Saint-Exupéry, *The Little Prince* (1943)[1]

One cannot be strong without love. For love is not
an irrelevant emotion; it is the blood of life, the
power of reunion of the separated.
                    —Paul Tillich, *The Eternal Now* (1963)[2]

UNCONDITIONAL LOVE means treating every human being as though they were members of the same tribe, whom you care about as deeply as you should care about your own spirit or soul. You see beyond their immediate behavior to the positive, beneficial intention behind it.

WE ARE ALL ONE PEOPLE

UNCONDITIONAL LOVE, or Lev, can be experienced as the most pure love. According to Ken Keyes, Jr., it is "a heart feeling of acceptance, caring, and warmth. [It] is not action—although it can lead us to helpful actions. It is a heart bridge from separateness to oneness. And from this love feeling, our most beautiful and noble moments unfold."3

Most of the great philosophers and religious leaders throughout history, and leading modern psychologists, such as Carl Rogers, have in one way or another attempted to explain how to live by this seemingly simple, yet difficult to achieve, concept. The difficulty arises because people only understand love in their immediate relationships, such as toward partners, family, and close friends. They have a hard time seeing how these feelings of love would apply in relationships with acquaintances, strangers, people they've never met, people they will never meet, and certainly "enemies," or people they dislike. They don't grok that love manifests itself in many different forms, only one of which, Lev, we can feel for all people, and which substantially enriches our own lives when we do.

With few exceptions, languages of the world further complicate and limit our ability to comprehend UNCONDITIONAL LOVE by having only one all-encompassing word for all the different types of love. The ancient Greeks recognized this problem, and invented the word *agape* to describe what we have called Lev, a type of love that they specifically distinguished from *eros*, sexual love, and *philia*, the friendship or fraternal kind of love. Other peoples have also seen the importance of describing vital elements of their lives with many words, thereby affording subtle but relevant differentiation. For example, the Eskimos of the Arctic circle invented 42 different words for snow. The natives of the Hawaiian Islands have dozens of words for ocean waves. Portuguese is one of the very few modern languages that explicitly names the multiple genres of love, with 14 words that delineate the various types.

Think of the relationship between two neurons in the Global Brain. You don't necessarily have to like the other person or cell, you may or may not like what they do or say, but you *can* view them as necessary elements just playing their role and trying to evolve. Like them, you are playing your role and trying to make your life "work" the best you can. Such *openness* to all others, coupled with Jesus' attitude of "Love thy neighbor as thyself," gives you an *acceptance* of the other person's problems and programming. And by even "loving thy enemy as you love thyself," another of Jesus' fundamental teachings, you might see something in them that you dislike in yourself, and learn and grow from it. Besides, in a Global Brain, their problems are yours, too; until they solve theirs, your total well-being can never be completely assured.

EMOTIONAL ACCEPTANCE AND OPENNESS

True acceptance of all people as your sisters and brothers most importantly includes your *emotional acceptance* of them: a liberation from your addictive emotional needs, rooted in your childhood programming, which enables you to act wisely and appropriately toward your fellow human beings.

Emotional acceptance subsequently buys you internal peace, since you no longer feel like you *have to* control anybody else. As long as someone is not infringing upon you, be and let be. This freedom stops us from constantly judging others.

Fear-driven judgment, not hate, is the opposite of Lev. Hate stems from your passing judgment on somebody else for something they do or say that you find totally unacceptable in yourself, and which causes a subconscious, fearful reaction. Their action engenders rage in you, whereas at the level of your higher self you desire to adhere to spiritual law, which requires that no matter what, you still feel Lev toward all. As the Native Americans recommend: Do not judge your fellow humans until you have walked a mile in their moccasins (in the snow)!

While we feel UNCONDITIONAL LOVE, we give our involvement and time spent in any sort of interaction with another person conditionally. Lev does not demand any particular action or interaction with others. We may still choose never to associate with certain people. When we do share experiences with others, we use SYNERGY to voluntarily give of our time in a way that delivers mutual benefit and enjoyment. Learn to separate the person from the problem: Work lucidly with the problem, Lev the person!

This kind of *openness* and UNCONDITIONAL LOVE does not create martyrs of us all, as some people claim, since we still reserve our right to preserve our own well-being. The critics, perhaps unwittingly, defend and promote separation amongst people. Do not mistake a state of mind for action, by linking the two.

Lev does not imply allowing ourselves to be rolled over by the irresponsible and immoral acts of transgressors of societal or natural laws, just because we're supposed to keep loving them, an inaccurate interpretation of Jesus' "turn the other cheek." Remember that UNCONDITIONAL LOVE does not preclude us from having a sense of right and wrong about other people's actions, simply not judging them as good or bad. Jesus did not imply that we should allow physical or emotional harm to ourselves, but rather that we should not judge another person's worth based on their behavior, and should recognize the evenness of all souls.

Everyone is trying to do the best they can. Nonetheless, as individuals and as a society, we still have the free will to have two important responses to other peoples' actions: first, not to allow anyone to push us around, so that we may freely choose our own actions if they don't infringe on anybody else; and second, to determine and enforce consequences to other people's actions, such as serving justice to people who break society's laws.[4]

FORGIVENESS AND COMPASSION LEAD TO LEV

As we bring greater quantities of UNCONDITIONAL LOVE into our hearts, we develop increasing amounts of *compassion* for our fellow humans. This means really feeling what it might be like to be in their shoes. We may remember times when we actually were in situations similar to theirs. Or we may realize that if they only knew a little more, they would not find themselves in this unhappy circumstance. We must even view what we consider evil behavior as nothing more than a result of ignorance by people who don't yet see it that way. Franklin D. Roosevelt proclaimed, "There's nothing to fear but fear itself."[5]

> *Namasté (Hindu for peace):*
> *The most pure part of me that loves the most pure*
> *part of you, and in that relationship, we are One.*

Sometimes situations that most stretch our ability to forgive open our hearts the most. *Forgiveness* means releasing our critical judgment, putting behind us injurious behaviors that we didn't like, and returning to loving ourselves and others in the same way that we did before an incident happened. By forgiving painful occurrences, we internalize at a deeper level our understanding of the human predicament, and can feel Lev more intensely.

Perceiving and acting based on compassion and forgiveness open our own gateway to moving into the planes of higher consciousness. Until this time, shamans and mystics have been some of the dedicated few who have taken the time to develop and unfold the experiencing of this at-one-ment, and have reached ecstatic states. We can all feel these states as we recognize the oneness of humanity, hone our abilities to feel Lev, and get closer to seeing reality as it truly is.

Grokking Gev's glue—Lev—allows us better to comprehend the second cornerstone of Global Spirituality: that we are all connected as one people, one tribe, to one planet. We, too, can each then feel more daily, natural, ecstasy.

Of all the Commandments, this one most defies a written and intellectual explanation: ultimately, UNCONDITIONAL LOVE or Lev must be felt and experienced through the heart.

Base your level of
relationship
commitments on
BOTTOM LINES
—what you can't
live with and
can't live without

18

COMMANDMENT NO. 18: BOTTOM LINES

If you drink too much one more time. . . .
I really will leave this time. And I'm never
coming back!
> —Many fed up people, throughout history

Almost all of our relationships begin and most of
them continue as forms of mutual exploitation, a
mental or physical barter, to be terminated when
one or both parties run out of goods.
> —W.H. Auden, "Hic et Ille," *The Dyer's Hand* (1962)[1]

BOTTOM LINES means grokking for each of your relationships, and for how much you put into and expect to get out of them, what you can't live with and what you can't live without.

In today's world we meet and connect with many people, and have ever-greater opportunities to form relationships with others who are interesting, attractive, healthy, and, like us, want to enjoy life to its fullest. In the circle of WHOLENESS (see Figure 12-1), each person commits to, and thereby creates, different levels of significance of relationships within each of their concentric circles of eight rings (listed in decreasing order of priority): spouse or partner and children; other family; best friends; friends; associates and community; state/nation; world; and universe.

Depending on the level of relationship we wish to form, and on what we hope to receive in return, we decide what degree of our energy, emotions, and effort, and how much of our time and money we will invest. This does not conflict in any way with UNCONDITIONAL LOVE, which we feel for everyone, in every situation, regardless of how much or how little we choose to invest in our relationship with them.

We don't have much choice with our relationships with the seventh and eighth rings of the circle of WHOLENESS, our world and our universe: we SURRENDER to the BOTTOM LINES preset for us with both our planet Earth—basically "Love it or leave it. . ."—and with the cosmos—stuck here, as far as we know. . . . But we wield the sword of responsibility in deciding what forms our relationships will take, and the levels to which we want them to develop, in the innermost six rings of the circle of WHOLENESS.

WHAT'S REALLY IMPORTANT

Adhering to our BOTTOM LINES guarantees that we invest in all of our relationships only in a manner that assures our own joy and well-being and which will further our growth and success at a satisfactory pace, and with a tolerable level of pain. Every one of us has at least one essential BOTTOM LINE in any of our relationships: our own physical safety. The rest of our BOTTOM LINES allow us to develop criteria regarding how to commit to relationships that will teach us new lessons, rather than to slavishly go through the motions over and over again, as we fail to grok current lessons. When we don't stick to our BOTTOM LINES in our relationships, we end up wondering, "Why does this keep happening to me?" and experience increasing—and eventually intolerable—levels of pain.

> **We have the right to choose BOTTOM LINES without feeling guilty.**

Consciously or not, we each have two types of BOTTOM LINES: the maximum negative acceptable to us, and the minimum positive we need to have. Some people already have an understanding of this commandment without realizing it, for example, when they say that a commitment to a certain relationship "doesn't feel right." When they probe further, they eventually discover a violation of one or more of their BOTTOM LINES.

Your assessment doesn't judge the other person in any way. It only asserts what's important for you to receive for your investment in a given level of relationship. Either the other person acts in one or more ways that to you are negative or unacceptable—*what you can't live with*—and/or they don't provide one or more essential positives—*what you can't live without.*

A BOTTOM LINE sets each person's minimum requirements for committing to a particular group or person. For example, most people tend to stay away from cannibals altogether. Some of us will only live in a country that has no military draft, or won't perform work for defense-related companies. Others will only commit to a monogamous sexual relationship, and will terminate it if this BOTTOM LINE is violated—but may alter the commitment level to friendship only. As crazy as it may seem, some people will only become intimately and sexually involved with someone who loves to go skiing.

195

The better we know ourselves, the more aware we become that we have BOTTOM LINES, of what they are, and that *ultimately* they must be satisfied for us to commit wholeheartedly. Whereas we may initially get involved with others based on only some of our BOTTOM LINES being met—such as attraction, opportunity, or convenience—for the relationship to be maximally satisfying and enduring *all* of our BOTTOM LINES must be met.

Once we've committed to a certain level of relationship using BOTTOM LINES, we set *boundaries* and use SYNERGY to determine the amount and quality of time to spend with others. *Boundaries* are psychological semipermeable membranes, limits that you set and use to define and communicate the terms under which you will or will not participate with others.

For example, our best friend may set a *boundary* that they don't wish to share a particular activity with us, such as going scuba diving. In this instance, both people understand that this would not alter either our friend's or our own level of commitment to the relationship based on the BOTTOM LINES we satisfy for each other, none of which includes having to go scuba diving together. (*Boundaries* will be discussed more fully in the next Chapter on SYNERGY.) Learn to distinguish your *boundaries* from your BOTTOM LINES.

FEATURES OF BOTTOM LINES

1. Relationships work far better when both parties communicate their BOTTOM LINES to each other.

2. BOTTOM LINES may or may not be absolutes; at times we change them.

> *Be careful what you ask for—*
> *Gev might help you get it.*

3. Depending on the levels of relationship that you are trying to create, having too few BOTTOM LINES will waste your time playing games that you should have evolved beyond, while having too many will lead to a monastic and solitary existence.

4. Depending upon other people's actions—meeting or violating our BOTTOM LINES—we might upgrade or downgrade the level of our relationship commitment to them.

5. The BOTTOM LINES you are aware of, combined with your preferences—items we would like to have but don't insist on—serve as your criteria for entering a certain level of relationship.

   When competing opportunities satisfy all of our BOTTOM LINES, we can choose among several options (jobs, partners, etc.). This is wonderful! In that case, we can satisfy more of our preferences and choose the best overall combination.

6. You frequently discover new BOTTOM LINES while in relationships.

7. When violated, BOTTOM LINES require attention and action, since violation often evokes strong emotional responses and can flare up into a relationship crisis.

   As a guideline, consider allowing only one or two violations before altering the level of your commitment, unless an event threatens your physical safety, in which case you may well decide only to tolerate one violation.

8. The BOTTOM LINES that truly serve each one of us best also serve the world best, as they help the Global Brain evolve more positively and rapidly.

By insisting on and adhering to your BOTTOM LINES, you encourage others to discover *their* BOTTOM LINES, modify their behavior, and grow that much more quickly themselves.

KNOW THYSELF AND THY BOTTOM LINES

Your can also think of BOTTOM LINES as the biochemical laws of cellular interaction in the Global Brain. Adherence to Commandments No. 11 to No. 17 creates an evolving individual striving for WHOLENESS, enjoying increasingly more FLOW, SELF-ACCEPTANCE, BALANCE, integrity, honesty, loyalty, self-esteem, and trust, while attending to their INNER VOICE in the quest to fulfill their MISSION, exercising SURRENDER-COURAGE, and giving and receiving UNCONDITIONAL LOVE. This ever-changing neuron/person participates in networks with many others—individuals, groups or clusters, and social systems. By nature, these attachments and relationships are temporary, based on circumstances and the needs and level of growth of each cell and group.

For two cells or people to healthily interact and attach to each other requires that they mutually satisfy each others' BOTTOM LINES and *boundaries*—a kind of "chemical" compatibility—for the duration of the relationship. For the superorganism to thrive, the semi-permeable membranes must link and exchange matter and energy agreeably. As in cellular biology, certain cells are toxic and may actually feed on and/or destroy their neighbors; others use SYNERGY to enhance each other and create higher levels of complexity and efficiency.

Learning to live successfully by using BOTTOM LINES demands some SURRENDER to who we are, and the psychological and natural laws of intra- and inter-human chemistry. Chemistry recognizes each of us as a unique composition of genes, personality, and spirit, different from everyone else on the planet. Thus our reactions to specific stimuli, at specific times, will depend on an interaction with another organic (living) or inorganic (inanimate) object. As in all of nature, to varying degrees and specific to the individual, some situations cause us discomfort and harm our well-being, while others enhance our sense of comfort and happiness. By figuring out and living according to our limitations, we maximize our vitality and longevity.

As we evolve further and further, we learn to avoid many situations altogether, namely those which represent lessons already learned. The more we know ourselves, grow, and grok each successive lesson, the more we learn to put our being into more and more meaningful and desirable situations.

ROMANTIC LOVE

People learn their most challenging lessons, which also reveal many of their BOTTOM LINES, in *romantic* love relationships, to which everything stated in this Commandment applies. *Romantic* love functions as nature's stickiest glue for learning, for evolving, and for regenerating the species. It gives you the opportunity to confront many issues in yourself. The chemical feelings that falling in love sets off, and the bells and alarms that start ringing throughout our bodies, urge us into these relationships that help us succeed—if we consciously use them for growth.

Ever since the Garden of Eden, nature has intended for many Adams and Eves to return to paradise hand in hand. This means that special persons exist who complement you so fully that when you relate together a greater WHOLENESS emerges. The combination of male and female energies merges in the dance of Yin and Yang to come closer to Gev. Modern family psychologist Harville Hendrix has put forth the concept of "Imago Match,"[2] to help describe this phenomenon.

The "Imago" is a set of traits that our subconscious mind scans for as it perceives people with whom we come in contact. (Hendrix posits that the Imago consists of our parents' positive and negative traits, but especially the negative ones). When we lock in on a person who resembles the image we search for, we have an "Imago Match," and we trigger that body chemistry and feeling within us that only a romantic attraction can kindle. Our Imago Matches have the potential to provide us with the lessons that will complete each of us in a manner that can hardly be accomplished in any other way, and which lead us to Lokelani.

However, not everyone we feel romantic love for, and who tests positive as an Imago Match for us, merits creating a partner, significant-other, or special relationship. In the Global Brain, numerous opportunities present themselves, based on a high degree of intermingling. In order for the relationships that we ultimately choose to last, and for mutual growth to continue, we can't allow ourselves to "marry" every person we fall in love with.

To reap the maximum benefits that nature intended for romantic love relationships, make sure that your candidate satisfies the following five criteria:

1. First and foremost, they satisfy your BOTTOM LINES.

2. They express total commitment to spiritual evolution as the top priority and purpose of their life.

3. They can communicate using effective, skilled, higher levels of interpersonal communication. Global Brain cells can't interact without this, particularly in a situation that calls for frequent and intense conflict resolution.

4. They want to play the same "games"[3] in the "great adventure of life": compatible missions, views on raising or not raising children, preferences of geographical living area, hobbies, and any others that are important to you.

5. They use this same process to evaluate *you* as a candidate for *them*. Unrequited love doesn't fulfill nature's expectations.

Remember, though, that each evolving cell's journey in this life begins and ends alone. As you advance and perhaps live into your 100s, you will continually change all of your temporary relationships as your BOTTOM LINES change. This doesn't preclude a life partner, lifetime job, and so on, but it doesn't require it, either.

So *first* discover and set your BOTTOM LINES for traveling as far as you can to grok the lessons you need. Then live what you've learned, and have fun, by giving yourself the chance to relate to others in the most enduring and complete way possible.

Create SYNERGY by using win-win and setting boundaries

19

COMMANDMENT NO. 19: SYNERGY

One man may hit the mark, another blunder; but heed not these distinctions. Only from the alliance of the one, working with and through the other, are great things born.

—Saint-Exupéry, *The Wisdom of the Sands* (1948)[1]

For where two or three [or more] are gathered together in my name, there am I in the midst of them.

—Jesus Christ, *The Bible*, Matthew 18:20

S YNERGY means synchronizing energy and effort expended so that in all of your interactions the outcome produced by the participants in concert exceeds that which would be produced by the sum of the participants by themselves.

Using *win-win* strategies for thinking and doing means that you figure out how to interact with others in a way that is mutually satisfactory—no one loses and everyone gains.

Boundaries are psychological semipermeable membranes, limits that you set and use to define and communicate the terms under which you will or will not participate with others. Your *boundaries* must not violate your own BOTTOM LINES or societal laws. You can only create a positive interaction with others when your *boundaries* do not violate their BOTTOM LINES or *boundaries.*

THE PASSAGE FROM A POWER-BASED TO A HIGH-SYNERGY SOCIETY

1 + 1 = 3 or more

Every interaction, any time spent involved with others, should take into account both the implicit and explicit good of the individuals, and the greater good of the whole. Biologists have found that SYNERGY occurs naturally among groups of living organisms and leads to higher levels of complexity. Simply stated, we can think of this process in nature as one plus one equals three or more.

Most of nature automatically follows this law to evolve further. Within humans, the organs in the body work together as a whole, to comprise a well-functioning organism. At the inter-human level, we have the free will to choose how to interact with each other, and whether or not to create SYNERGY, and thus collectively to evolve to the next level of complexity—the Global Brain superorganism.

When as individuals we set our *boundaries* and opt for *win-win* strategies, we manifest a marvelous characteristic of our higher mind, as we consciously create SYNERGY, cooperate in the acceleration of evolution, and produce the miracle of a higher form of life—a more intelligent Gaia.

> **Old way:**
> **"It's either my way or the highway"**
> **New way:**
> **"It's my way and your way combined—the biway"**

At the societal level, the formation of the Global Brain translates to a shift away from individual or group power-based, survival interaction, to global use of high-SYNERGY, to ensure cooperative community and planetary survival. Technology provides the links that give us the opportunity to create this collaborative rather than competitive global society, by virtually putting us all together into one room with each other. Our use of the higher mind, or INNER VOICE, instead of the lower, individual-survival-oriented mind, can guide us to maximize the benefits of these links.

These links to each other bring us some of our greatest joys and opportunities for learning in life, by allowing us to spend time and connect with others in a myriad of ways. This includes using the multitude of new technological communication media developed in the twentieth century. Phones, faxes, videophones, and computer networks help us to stay in touch, even at a distance. The boom in transportation and mobility has contributed to the exponential increase in the number of people we can contact and the interactions we can have with them. We also have much more free time available for socializing and playing, due to conquering the survival challenge—at least in the first world—and soon in the rest of the world, too (see Chapter 5).

Most leisure activities we engage in today, such as "flying to the Caribbean," competing at Monopoly, riding roller coasters, "veging" in front of the television, going to the cinema, playing videogames, bargain hunting at shopping malls, and many others, didn't even exist a century ago. We will doubtlessly innovate a plethora of new ones in the coming centuries of the Consciousness Age.

UNDERSTANDING AND SETTING *BOUNDARIES*

To understand these interactions better, we must first learn to differentiate types of relationships from how we spend time within a relationship. BOTTOM LINES define what type of relationship we choose to have with another person or group, if any, and our level of commitment to it. Within this framework we set *boundaries* to identify how we wish to participate in any given situation. We exercise our free will to choose what we want to do, how we want to do it, and with whom. *Boundaries* assure our physical and emotional security and, if we reciprocate by honoring others' *boundaries*, theirs, too.

Boundaries assure *win-win* and allow SYNERGY by preventing situations in which one individual or group "loses"—i.e., their self-interest is not satisfied—in an interaction with another individual or group. A win-lose or lose-win actually detracts from the whole system and fails to produce SYNERGY. This leaves one or both of the involved parties dissatisfied. To avoid such cases, communicated *boundaries* establish our level of essential preferences, and of reasonable intolerance to situations we don't want to repeat, since we may have already learned those lessons.

Violated *boundaries*, especially if they are frequent or recurring, may lead to new BOTTOM LINES and subsequent alterations in the level of commitment to a relationship; as when you decide to break up with a boyfriend when he repeatedly dishonors your agreement to stick to your *boundary* and not "surf the remote control" during an argument. You would continue to Lev him and perhaps even suggest that you "just be friends," thereby altering your level of commitment to him. In your quest for your next boyfriend, you'll set a new BOTTOM LINE that he must actively and willingly work through an argument with you.

CLEAR INTENTION LEADS TO COMMON VISION AND SYNERGY

In the South Pacific, scientists have observed flocks of 50,000 birds turning in the same direction in 1/70th of a second.[2] Even more astounding is the apparent absence of any leader to signal their course alteration. They all seem to be tuned in to each other, perhaps at some frequency we have not yet detected. Most of us have experienced situations with other people where this seems to occur, too. We all flock in the same direction with a common vision, while we FLOW in the most enjoyable manner and have the feeling of something magical or even miraculous transpiring. This is SYNERGY which, as a principle, allows us to construct our nests together most creatively, whether at home, work, or play.

Clear intention with stated *boundaries*, communicated effectively, with *win-win* agreements, lead to common vision, which when executed leads to responsible creation with SYNERGY, and spiritual ascension and success for the parties involved.

Our desire to allow SYNERGY to occur, with these inherently large payoffs, prompts us to develop good habits of healthy give-and-take negotiating for *win-wins*. We don't compromise our underlying needs, just our ideas of how we can have those needs met, and to allow another party to have theirs met. Practicing effective habits can increase the chance of a very favorable outcome in our lives and in the lives of others with whom we relate. At some point they happen almost without a second thought. Then they become the way we naturally think and act, rewarding us with joy.

Following the combination of *win-win* and SYNERGY as habits, superbly described by Stephen Covey as habits number four and six of his *7 Habits of Highly Effective People*, will help us adhere to the spiritual law described in this Commandment as SYNERGY.[3] The concept of *win-win* has enjoyed increasing popularity since it was pioneered by the Harvard Negotiation Project in the 1970s, and published in the national bestseller *Getting to Yes: Negotiating Agreement Without Giving In.*[4]

To effect a *win-win*, each person or group must enter the situation with clear intention regarding what they wish to create. The more we live by Commandments No. 11 to No. 16, and thus know who we are and what we want, the better focused our intention will be. Otherwise, we engage with divided consciousness, with different parts of us trying to forge different realities. As co-creators with Gev, each of us wields tremendous power with our thoughts and actions. We must bring our whole being into alignment to know our intention precisely, and to establish a personal and group vision of what we wish to create.

Only with clear intention can we create responsibly and ascend the ladder to greater overall success (see Figure 19-1). We first state our intention, along with our *boundaries*, and communicate with others about theirs. *Win-win* negotiating may then require mutually discovering creative new alternatives which include some of the original positions of the parties involved, but may also include new positions that satisfy all of them. This leads to a common vision or set of goals. On the other hand, if no clear agreement can be reached, we should always opt for the "no-deal" option rather than win-lose or lose-win, or certainly lose-lose. "No deal" means the parties respectfully bow out of jointly engaging in the particular situation, because no jointly-acceptable terms were found. If a *win-win* did prevail, then of course the parties involved have accepted the responsibility for carrying through as agreed, to preserve their integrity (based on INNER VOICE), or to request a renegotiation, again based on *win-win*. The goal always remains to create SYNERGY. This method will promote a more rapid and responsible evolution toward a cooperative, global environment, and allows each of us to ascend spiritually as we grow, succeed, and feel good about what we've created.

Figure 19-1
Ladder of Spiritual Success

Spiritual Ascent and Success

Responsible, SYNERGISTIC Creation

Common Vision and Execution

Clear intention with *boundaries*

→ Effective communication

→ Unambiguous *win-win* agreements with yourself and others

Free will to choose to obey the 2nd Ten Commandments

The woman whose boyfriend resorted to channel-surfing during arguments would hopefully go on to create a mutually supportive partnership, where both she and her new partner would learn from each argument in which they fully engage. Perhaps they would not only resolve their immediate conflict, but also sprout an idea for starting a new business together. This is an example of SYNERGY. One can only hope that as a result of her sticking to her BOTTOM LINE with her ex-boyfriend, he will now also have the opportunity to create a more SYNERGISTIC relationship, in which he feels free to enjoy watching television, but not during an argument.

A SYNERGISTIC world order benefits everyone, since it fosters harmony between the goals of individuals and those of the system as a whole.

REPAIR the world
by treating
others reverently
and fairly
and doing
good deeds.

20

COMMANDMENT NO. 20: REPAIR

Each little thing that we do passes into the great machine of life which may grind our virtues to powder and make them worthless, or transform our sins into elements of a new civilization, more marvelous and more splendid than any that has gone before.

　　—Oscar Wilde, "The Critic as Artist," *Intentions* (1891)[1]

Life is really simple. What we give out, we get back.

　　　　　　　　　　　—Louise Hay, modern-day healer

REPAIR means that you act consciously to effect an ever-renewing Lokelani by believing that everything you do either hurts or helps you and everybody else, too.

Jesus Christ, a paragon of the enlightened "universal human,"[2] reduced all of his teachings to two basic spiritual laws:

1. Obey and love God with all your heart—follow your INNER VOICE.

2. Love your neighbors as yourself—feel UNCONDITIONAL LOVE for them.

As a result of these two maxims, he promulgated his "Golden Rule": "Therefore all things whatsoever ye would that men should do to you, do ye even so to them. . . ." (Matthew 7:12) Most people have heard this commonly paraphrased as: Do unto others as you would have others do unto you. Millions of people, over many centuries, have progressed from barbaric ways toward higher consciousness as a result of following Jesus' two basic laws and the Golden Rule.

DO UNTO OTHERS AS YOUR *INNER VOICE* WOULD HAVE DONE UNTO YOU

Due to gross and repeated misunderstandings and misinterpretations over the last 2,000 years, many have criticized and refused to follow Jesus' Golden Rule. His words urge you to choose to behave toward your fellow human beings exactly as you would like them to act toward you. But this assumes that you already consider them and yourself as human beings who live by a similar set of ethical and spiritual rules.

For example, Attila the Hun would not hesitate to pick a fight with you, since he wouldn't mind it at all if you provoked him. Thus, he would apparently be following the Golden Rule, but not if you had a different set of morals. Your morals might set a higher standard, but you would still suffer at his brutal hands. Christians who have "turned the other cheek," attempting to live according to a higher standard, have frequently turned into martyrs.

On the other hand, some Christians have interpreted the Golden Rule as allowing them to force their ways onto other, unreceptive cultures and individuals, with the argument that, "if I were a heathen, I would like to be shown the one true way to God, too." Misguided applications of the Golden Rule have thus resulted in centuries of inquisitions and crusades, and produced many martyrs.

REPAIR brings out Jesus' original meaning behind the Golden Rule in a way that we can all grok. In a Global Brain the truth of his guideline becomes more readily apparent as we realize the interdependence of all humanity. And remember, REPAIR applies only in conjunction with the rest of the 2nd Ten Commandments, which solves the problem of taking into account a common set of morals.

> **"We are not human beings having a spiritual experience, but spiritual beings having a human experience."**

If you insert the term INNER VOICE into the paraphrase of the Golden Rule, it becomes: Do unto others as your INNER VOICE would have done unto you. This stretches the Golden Rule to include spirituality. It asks that, for the Consciousness Age, you proactively search for opportunities to be of service to others. It states that at a minimum, use *reverence* to avoid bringing harm to others, even more than that to let *fairness* guide your actions, and at a maximum, to voluntarily do *good deeds* for other people. This makes perfect sense in a society with high SYNERGY.

REAL REVERENCE, FAIR COMPETITION AND KARMIC COMFORT

At the time of Jesus, the Jewish sage Hillel stated that at the very least, "*Don't* do unto others what is hated unto you." He thereby correctly solved the practical issue of how to maintain a delicate BAL-ANCE between self-sufficiency—which may require competing with others—and having reverence for all of your fellow human beings, in a way that lays the groundwork for a society with high SYNERGY. His maxim reminds us that if you can't do something positive for someone else, then at least don't do something harmful. And since "Don't do unto others" establishes a reasonable philosophical basis for a moral code, adherence to it also keeps you in conformance with most of society's written laws. This includes abiding by the Ten Commandments, which guarantees protection for individuals from one another. For example, since you would not want to be killed, stolen from, or lied to, don't do these things to anyone else.

But to truly honor reverence necessitates also listening to your INNER VOICE, so that the self-imposed "Don't do unto others" system of justice *also* precludes acting toward others in ways that you *should not* act toward yourself. For example, sado-masochism violates WHOLENESS and thus harms life; if you want to violate your INNER VOICE and do this to yourself, then at least stop short of doing it to anyone else. If you had a gun in your hand, would you shoot to kill a person holding your infant and about to slit its throat? Only your INNER VOICE can answer that question for you, in that moment.

Thus, to treat others with reverence, we have to assume that a universal sense of good and evil exists, that a set of spiritual laws governs everyone, that when we truly listen to our INNER VOICEs, at some level, they all tell us the same truths, because we are all kindred spirits. So before you do or say something to somebody else, pause and attune empathically: How would my WHOLE self feel if that was said or done to me? How would I feel if I were in their place?

Once we have reverence, we move on to the next level of REPAIR by treating others with fairness. This means not only *not* doing bad things to them, but going out of your way to do things that they will perceive as being good and equitable to them—things that if you were in their shoes, you, too, would appreciate as being fair. You will therefore sometimes need to act in ways that you may not like, but that you know will assure a just and optimal outcome for all concerned. You may, for example, tell a prospective buyer of your used car that you had had an accident, knowing full well that this disclosure may result in a lower—but more equitable—sale price.

> **Karma: You can fool some of the people some of the time, many people a lot of the time, but not Gev, eventually. Your biological counters keep score, and make sure that you get what you deserve, sooner or later.**
> **—Those who have been around**

"Karma," one of the spiritual laws that has guided humanity for centuries, particularly in the East, presents people with a straightforward and clear motivation to act with reverence and fairness. Karma promises that what we call "good" that you do to others will come back to you (in this lifetime or the next) as something positive to your well-being. The same holds true for evil: something that we call "bad" that you do to others will come back to you as something harmful to your being. Karma gives you the opportunity to learn lessons of importance toward your spiritual evolution.

Karma would indicate, then, that giving and receiving are the same. Intuitively, most people believe that "What goes around comes around"—sooner or later.

If we wish, we can choose to take a scientific approach to confirm our intuition, by viewing everything in a nonjudgmental way, without believing either in a punishing, morality-based God or in a spiritual principle that enforces karma. As biological organisms, we can adopt a chemical and psychological comfort model, where we don't label "good" and "bad" as such, but rather as physically "pleasant" or "unpleasant." Then, if giving and receiving are the same, wouldn't our reasoning tell us to make ourselves as comfortable as possible, by choosing to act in ways that have the most "pleasant" consequences, both to ourselves and to the Global Brain super-organism?

Remember, you reap what you sow!

GOOD DEEDS OR MALIGNANT BEHAVIOR

Once we treat others with reverence and fairness, we can advance still further up to the next level of responsibility and consciousness, and to the highest level of REPAIR, by proactively choosing to do good deeds and make the world a better place for everybody. These actions we take, using SURRENDER-COURAGE, assist others to grow and the planet to progress. Since giving and receiving are the same, as we help others we help ourselves.

An evolved person first meets their own needs. They never make a "sacrifice" at their own expense.[3] They BALANCE satisfying their personal short-term needs, with taking whatever actions—even risks—will contribute to the betterment of the interdependent world in the long term. If you look far enough into the future, in most circumstances what's best for you is best for all, too. Knowing this, and wholeheartedly feeling Lev, generous actions and gifts—unconditional giving—entail no loss to yourself, when given in amounts appropriate to your level of relationship.

Jewish mysticism refers to *Tikkun,*[4] which means REPAIR or correction in Hebrew, as the vehicle for raising the soul to its highest peak, by doing good deeds that each eliminate yet another small slice of the evil pie in the world, both in ourselves and in others. It teaches that each of us has our own dark side, and that collectively we manufacture all of the evil that exists in the world. Good deeds ultimately serve and elevate us as the doer as much as, if not more than, the recipients. These gifts we give help us heal and, through this process, REPAIR the world.

Ironically, every *bad* deed not only disrupts the Global Brain and threatens the health of Gaia with a rapidly spreading malignancy, but also eliminates sustenance from the offending neuron or person. Consider how in the human body, a "highly successful" cancer which takes over and destroys the whole organism also writes its own death sentence—it has nothing left to feed on. Naturally then, the healthy cells, whether in our bodies or neurons in a Global Brain, will always feel the urge to act responsibly. They will attempt to prevent malignant and short-term selfish behavior, and REPAIR and restore both the harm done *and* the dysfunctional cell, for the well-being of the superorganism.

By continuously REPAIRING the Global Brain, the nervous control system, we ensure the proper caretaking of the planet, its environment, its people, its other living beings, and its longevity. Some American Indian chiefs in the past had to have "a skin seven times thick" in the face of criticism, to control their own negative thoughts and feelings in order to calculate the effects of their policies "down to the seventh generation."[5] Imagine thinking that way!

> **In all our deliberations we must take into account the well-being of the seventh generation to follow ours.**
> **—The Great Law of the Haudenosaunee, Iroquois Six Nations**[6]

As we evolve, we realize the ramifications of each of our actions for the interconnected whole over the course of time. We gradually develop a greater sense of responsibility, the consequence of everyone's personal development and success, as we shall see in the next Part.

A letter written by a survivor of the holocaust, the genocide of the 1940s, states, "All that is necessary for the triumph of evil is for enough good men to do nothing."[7] Universal adherence to the REPAIR principle has the potential to root out all evil and create and sustain Lokelani.

PART III

GETTING ON
THE PATH TO
THE GLOBAL
PROMISED
LAND

21

ACCEPTING THE RESPONSIBILITY OF BEING A MOTOF

Nothing is as profound as an individual acting out of his/her own conscience, thereby awakening the collective conscience.

—Norman Cousins[1]

Our loyalties must transcend our race, our tribe, our class, and our nation; and this means we must develop a world perspective.

—Martin Luther King, Jr.[2]

Motofs have monumental evolutionary tasks: to raise humanity's consciousness to a higher level, to form a Global Brain, and to elevate Gaia to the next order of complexity, within about 40 years. Organizations and individuals are arising whose purpose is to respond to this overwhelming challenge.

> *"The price of greatness is responsibility."3*
> *—Winston Churchill*

For instance, the "Foundation for Global Community," a non-profit, educational movement formerly called "Beyond War," whose mission is to "discover, live, and communicate what is needed to build a world that functions for the benefit of all life," understands the overwhelming nature of such a challenge. They have seen the difficulties firsthand, as they facilitated both the original discussions leading to the end of the Cold War between the United States and the Soviet Union and the peace-process dialogue that brought Israel and the Palestinian Liberation Organization (PLO) together.4

At the same time, they acknowledge how simple it would be if everyone would just cooperate at the individual level. In their charter, they explain that:

> . . . change of this magnitude, involving whole societies and cultural systems, paradoxically depends on change at the level of the individual person. Each of us holds part of the consciousness of the whole planet within our soul, and each of us is thus responsible for making the shifts in our thinking, in our actions—in our very being—that will secure the future. It is these profound changes that will affirm our wholeness as individuals and our oneness with the Earth.5

This oneness and wholeness with the Earth, a result of taking individual responsibility, will ultimately bless Motofs with previously unprecedented levels of health and happiness. This is their reward for agreeing to accept and shoulder their destiny. In the past, only a select few members of society enjoyed the material and physical comforts that Motofs will soon take for granted. As technology unleashes more of its potential to better the human condition, Motofs will cease to worry about individual survival, and will be free to find joy and well-being in all their endeavors. So becoming a Motof is as much an honor as it is a commitment.

As we strive to be worthy of this honor and enlist in the mission, each of us attempts to gain a deeper meaning of responsibility. In Dan Millman's *Way of the Peaceful Warrior: A Book that Changes Lives,* the wise old teacher Socrates gives the 1960s hero a comprehensive lecture on responsibility that we, too, can learn from:

> It is better for you to take responsibility for your life as it is, instead of blaming others, or circumstances, for your predicament. As your eyes open, you'll see that your state of health, happiness, and every circumstance of your life has been, in large part, arranged by you—consciously or unconsciously. Habit itself—any unconscious, compulsive ritual—is negative. . . . Activities . . . are bad and good; every action has its price, and its pleasures. Recognizing both sides, you become realistic and responsible for your actions. And only then can you make the warrior's free choice—to do or not to do. . . . Responsibility means recognizing both pleasure and price, making a choice based on that recognition, and then living with that choice without concern.[6]

AN HEROIC RIGHT OF PASSAGE

Finding guidance in the twentieth century (and beyond) on how to make these choices has become both formidable and trying, as many of the traditions handed down to us by our ancestors have broken down. This shouldn't surprise us, given the changes that have occurred in the world, and the unrelenting pace of continuous change.

The pressure caused by these changes has thrown most people off balance and increasingly led them to question the sense of meaning in their lives. It has reduced their sense of stability and security, which was based on old paradigms, whether in occupation, marriage, geographical location, or friends. This pressure is responsible for the fear-based frustration that results from rigidly holding on to the old ways.

By early in the twenty-first century, most of humankind will be feeling a bit, and in many cases a lot, like Tevya, the main character in the musical *Fiddler on the Roof.* Like him, our lives will seem as precarious as that of a fiddler trying to stand on a slanted rooftop.

Tevya lived in the early 1900s in a tiny, poor, Jewish, Eastern European village called the *shtetl.* The villagers were holding on to the past for dear life and they were about to get overrun by the first waves of the Russian Communist movement. Tevya and his little tribe had found what in their minds was a historically proven solution to cope with the situation. In the musical, he tells us in the opening song: "We keep our balance by TRADITION! And where did we get these traditions? I'll tell you [pause]. I don't know. But it's a tradition. And because of our traditions every one of us knows who he is, and what God expects him to do."

But what do we do today, devoid of traditions and rituals to rely upon for guidance as we approach the next millennium? Who can we turn to? Do we, like Tevya and his faithful and ever-hopeful kinsmen, forever try to hold on to the past and refuse to recognize the new world? Do we, too, need to get hit by a nuclear, chemical, or biological war, the *third* World War, the modern-day equivalent to a *pogrom*, or massacre, to wake us up enough to adapt to the present?

No. Not if we attend inside to become conscious beings and learn to find our balance and meaning, keep everything in the proper perspective, and live by the 2nd Ten Commandments. We take the best wisdom from past traditions, which no longer help us today, and let those traditions go. We can then create new traditions.

In fact, we're all very much like that Fiddler on the Roof, who while tottering in a very precarious situation, had the ability to awaken and see the bigger picture from above. In the cosmic scheme of things, we can each choose to use our free will to weave our web and to find our course, through inner and outer work, to respond to the new realities.

Don Riso, a modern-day psychologist and author, reminds us that, "We are all prisoners in an unguarded jail cell."[7] Only we hold the key to the lock that lets us break free. It is up to each of us to choose whether to adapt to the new world and become a Motof, or to stagnate and perish from stress. Socrates, Millman's teacher, speaks universally when he reminds us: "You are too willing to change anything except yourself, but change you will. Either . . . open your eyes or time will, but time is not always gentle. Take your choice. But first realize that you're in prison—then we can plot your escape."[8]

The key to the first step in our escape is to venture on an heroic journey, face the dangers and perils of the unknown, and bear the responsibility for the decisions we make along the way. This spiritual path, recommended by this book as the "yellow brick road" to true success in life, is almost always the hardest one to take in the short term. However, it always brings the most rewards in the long term. As this becomes the "road more traveled," more of us will find it almost impossible to turn back. Only by wasting away into oblivion could we opt to abandon this adventurous and challenging trail.

An old Chinese curse says: "May you live in interesting times."[9]

We do. So did Adam and Eve. When they left the Garden of Eden, Eve may have exclaimed, "Adam, I think we are living in a time of transition and change. Perhaps we should take an apple for the road." Humanity has been traveling on that trek for a long, long, time ever since.

Sheer determination, humanity's eternal hope for success since the Garden, must somehow keep us going. As Gary Zukav reminds us, "Responsible choice is the conscious road to authentic empowerment."[10]

And once we are on the path, where can we start looking for empowerment? Joseph Campbell comments:

> With the secularization of our social life . . . no one is telling us you've got to believe this, you've got to believe that. We're left each to find his own beliefs. Nobody can give you a mythology. You don't have one. You are in the process of making it, and your life will be your mythology.[11]

Images that mean something to you will come from your dreams, creative work, and every new moment. You're on your own heroic journey. The initiation or heroic right of passage for an adapting Motof must commence first and foremost by believing in a *world dream*. This is not only an interesting time, but also the *most exciting of times*.

TRADING IN THE AMERICAN DREAM FOR A WORLD DREAM

In 1991, an article in *The Wall Street Journal* reported that "the death of the American Dream is greatly exaggerated." The "Conference Board Consumer Research Center Survey" reported that, "among husbands and wives between the ages of 25 and 35, the average income is about 40 percent higher, adjusted for inflation, than that of their parents when they were the same age." Furthermore, over 70 percent believe that they have greater opportunities than their parents did. To give just one example of why people of this generation have more disposable income, we can look at how much less they spend on food today, adjusted for inflation.

"Americans spent 11.4% of their incomes on food in 1992, down from 17.5% in 1960, thanks to improvements in food production and increasing personal incomes."[12] *Financially speaking then, the average person in the first world lives better today than ever before in history*—the American Dream is alive and well.

Then why do we perceive the American Dream to be a myth? Why do we hear as many complaints about it as about the weather on an average day on Main Street, U.S.A.? Because the American Dream, as people have understood it for the last two centuries, has always given them a purpose and meaning in their lives that now, for the first time, it no longer does.

What is the American Dream, really? Since the "discovery" of the New World, people have sought to land on its shores in search of freedom and opportunity. Since the founding of the United States of America, they have flooded its gates in the hope of making a better life for themselves, and so that their children, and their children's children, will each successively build on the previous generation's accomplishments and achieve an ever-improving standard of living. And this has actually happened, for the most part. Generation after generation, aided by the Industrial, and then the Information, Revolution, Americans have raised their standard of living and constructed one of the most prosperous and powerful countries on earth. These goals, in and of themselves, gave the products of these generations meaning in their lives. They found "life, liberty, and the pursuit of happiness," as stated in the Declaration of Independence, to also include prosperity and growing material comfort.

Today we experience a crisis in meaning. The quest that sent Europeans in the sixteenth and seventeenth centuries to seek life, liberty, and the pursuit of happiness in the New World, and then sent subsequent generations to chase after prosperity and the American Dream, no longer motivates or gives purpose to young people. In the first world, and increasingly in the rest of the world, we take political liberty as a given. Likewise, the majority of the population in the first world has a sufficient quality of life to address survival concerns reasonably well. Countries in the non-first world are very rapidly achieving this, too. The game has now changed to rising expectations for material comfort and leisure, based on procuring the latest and greatest technical innovations. But since survival really isn't that difficult anymore, this new game ultimately fails to provide meaningful purpose to people's lives. At some point, people discover that the "s/he who dies with the most toys wins" approach doesn't lead to more happiness or fulfillment, unlike in the past when material gains improved basic comforts.

A study in the 1990s across all of the economic strata of the United States, from poor to rich, found that at every level, people reported that what they thought would make them happier would be ten percent more income. Clearly, money and material wealth do not satisfy any of us sufficiently in the long run, nor provide us with meaning in, and passion for, life.

What will provide meaning? Future generations still need a guiding vision, albeit a new one, with which to mold their personal and societal lives. We will want to have the same sense of adventure, zest, and exploration of a frontier, that fulfilled our forefathers' and their children's and children's children's dreams, as they explored the New World and transformed it into a prosperous land for all.

Today, perhaps people all over the planet can find an analogous mission in the quest to form the Global Brain, combined with the aspiration for a Lokelani to come into being in the best possible way. With this guiding vision we can begin to weave a world dream that seems real enough for us to live for.

Buying into this world dream, and accepting the responsibility for helping to create it, is the first step in becoming a Motof. The next chapter will look at some ideas on how to take further steps.

22

NINE GREAT IDEAS FOR BECOMING A MOTOF

If you always do what you always did, you'll always get what you always got.
　　　　—Anthony Robbins, *Awakening the Giant Within*[1]

The difference between a successful person and others is not a lack of strength, not a lack of knowledge, but rather in a lack of will.
　　　　　　　　　　—Vincent J. Lombardi[2]

1. Strive to consciously apply the 2nd Ten Commandments in your daily living.

2. Practice a daily mind/body discipline.

3. Keep yourself physically fit.

4. Explore aspects of your personality type using the *Enneagram*.

5. Develop *better bad habits* to substitute for ones which have outlived their usefulness, and to help you act principle-centered.

6. Plan what you would *do* if you won the lottery.

7. Write a personal constitution and mission statement.

8. Set prioritized goals by roles, but be process-oriented.

9. Engage in personal-growth education to grok deeper.

1. Strive to consciously apply the 2nd Ten Commandments in your daily living.

Humans are creatures of habit. Habits help us cope with the constant changes and unpredictability of our lives. We begin to form them at birth, and continue to accumulate them throughout our lives. Habits are patterns of behavior that we have learned through our particular life experiences, that lead us to approach or avoid situations and consequently effect outcomes in ways that we prefer.

While useful, habits can keep us from acting freely, based on a conscious choice, and prevent us from making the best possible decision in a given situation. By acting habitually, we may subconsciously act without deciding, and perhaps in a different way than how we would consciously choose to act if we were completely free to choose.

The goal for Motofs is to act consciously and responsibly in every situation, and to follow the 2nd Ten Commandments. Through awareness of your behavior and thoughts, you can leave behind old habits which limit your ability to develop further. While we perceive many situations as being similar to those we've previously encountered, in reality each situation presents us with a unique set of circumstances—particularly in a fast-changing world. Therefore, each situation may deserve a different response on our part, in order to maximize our success.

Try in each moment to adhere to the principles of the 2nd Ten Commandments. Just by invoking the name of each commandment, and remembering its meaning, you might choose a different, more creative, and more effective response in any given situation.

While this seems like a reasonable starting point, it may take many years and a lot of repetition to accomplish. The subconscious and rational minds safeguard many of the patterns that keep us chained to our current modes of behavior. While this may make change harder, it assures that once we've grokked a lesson thoroughly, we're less likely to go back to our old ways. If change came easily, it might be "easy come, easy go." To accelerate our change process, we need ideas that will enhance our ability to permanently integrate desirable new ways, and allow us to adapt more quickly to life as a Motof.

2. Practice a daily mind/body discipline.

How, then, do we become more conscious and aware? By altering and transforming the subconscious and rational minds, and strengthening the connection to the higher mind. This leads to more rapid personal development. The subconscious mind is like a filter we look through, a clutter of excess thought, imagery, and impressions of the past and of future possibilities, that limits our functioning in the present. If we can get a snapshot of what's behind the filter, progress comes much quicker.

Modern psychology and spirituality have given us many tools that can help us with this task. Undoubtedly the future will deliver many more, particularly as technology begins to assist us in developing a growing field of *psychotechnology*, or tools that develop the mind and thereby put us in touch with our INNER VOICE. Some examples of techniques currently available include: meditation, hypnosis, computerized and other forms of biofeedback, various types of yoga, Feldenkrais, Hakomi therapy, Inner Child work, breathwork, psychoanalysis, the Course in Miracles,[3] and other daily spiritual practices.

The goal of meditation, or any of these techniques, is to quiet the lower minds' activity, to allow experiencing a state of higher mind, and to listen to the INNER VOICE. By silencing the lower minds it becomes easier to attend to and be directed by the higher mind. After sufficient practice, one can begin to come in contact with the INNER VOICE with open eyes, during regular activities.

Music, art, poetry, and nature provide other great vehicles to enter higher states of consciousness. Traditionally referred to as the languages of the soul, these seem to have the power to alter our state of mind almost instantly. A great calming may occur after the activity. It is then that you may find yourself most open to the deeper messages from your innermost self. Our goal is to re-create this peaceful existence and to live constantly in this state of mind of Gev-consciousness.

3. Keep yourself physically fit.

What replaces the manual labor of working in the fields and factories in the survival-oriented times of the Agricultural and Industrial Ages? Exercise. The Information Age and our technology threaten to turn many of us into "vegetables" as we live more sedentary work- and life-styles. In the past, you probably would have walked to a store (marketplace, etc.) to obtain anything you needed.

As of the twentieth century, we drive cars instead. In the Consciousness Age, we are likely to sit at home, order everything we need on a computer, and wait for it to arrive at our door—as others of us deliver it, not as messengers on foot, but as drivers of commercial vehicles.

To circumvent the decay of our physical selves, engage in routine physical exercise. Find ways to exercise that you enjoy and that will keep you fit. Bear in mind the importance of some amount of daily activity and at least four times a week of moderately strenuous aerobic exercise—with a properly elevated heart rate—lasting 20 minutes or more.

Explore resting or sleeping for shorter periods of time several times a day, rather than for one long sleeping period—a leftover from the dawn-to-dusk, survival-oriented days when electricity didn't exist. Many people find that two 20-minute, meditative "power naps" during the day keep them sharper all day long, and reduce their night sleep time by more than 40 minutes.

Eat healthily. Experiment with eating smaller quantities, more frequently, rather than "three large meals a day," another habit left over from survival-oriented days. Explore eating foods that are in keeping with the latest nutritional recommendations. Reduce or stop altogether your use of cigarettes and your consumption of alcohol, caffeine, sugar, fat, and other substances that you know, but have not grokked, don't keep you fit.

Remember that your mental fitness requires that your mind and soul have a physically fit and tuned-up vehicle, your body, for your travels.

4. Explore aspects of your personality type using the *Enneagram.*

To begin deep-rooted, fundamental transformation, the *Enneagram* PSPT provides an easy-to-use map for getting to know yourself, and a shortcut to fast personal growth. A spiritual wisdom handed down orally for over 4,500 years, and recorded only recently, its truth stares you straight in the face—if you have the courage to really look in the mirror. If you do, it will clue you in to the areas in which you need to do the most work for your personality type and level of advancement. It can give you a wonderful opportunity for transcendence of the limiting framework within which you may have operated, unaware, for your whole life.

By identifying which of the nine major personality types fits you best, and at which of approximately nine levels of health you operate,[4] you can begin to free yourself of rigid patterns of behavior. The personality types in the Enneagram have had sufficient practical application and research to show that they can be of use to persons as a starting point to greater self-understanding. No type is better or worse than any other type. Each type comes with a set of strengths and weaknesses.

Use the Enneagram to perform an honest self-appraisal of your "gifts" and "sins." This may at first deal a blow to your self-image, as it paints an ugly picture of your dark side or less desirable traits, no matter which type you are. You must own this side, too, in order to integrate it and strengthen yourself even further. Thus, the Enneagram provides the opportunity for quick personal evolution, if you choose to use it.

Our inner spirit calls on each of us to transform our dark side into more greatness. If we remain unconscious of our "sins" or weaknesses, they will eat us alive. In every moment that we act out of fear or darkness our being decays. Instead, choosing awareness allows us to confront our fears and work on evolving. By truly acting freely, we can enhance our "gifts" or strengths, and use them to co-create the world's future, as a Motof. As you use spiritual growth to ascend through the nine levels of health within your type, you will experience greater success and happiness, and contribute more to the world. At the highest level, any of the nine types expresses the Gev consciousness in a way that makes you a paragon of humanity, and maximally adds your uniqueness to the whole.

The Enneagram's depth and combination of simplicity and complexity makes it the best PSPT to date, and an invaluable starting point for your journey. As more of us use the Enneagram, we will further evolve its potential as a model to serve this purpose. Use the Enneagram's power to understand yourself, and to accept others as they are, not to manipulate them. Learn more about the model and your type and subtypes, and amaze yourself by how these seemingly general descriptions can help you to see yourself much more clearly. Previously, it may have taken people great expenditures of time, resources, and energy to come to many of the realizations about themselves that the Enneagram affords almost immediately.

Perhaps the Enneagram's time-saving ability explains its popularity and rapid spread. You will find many best-selling books on the subject. In 1994, two of the nation's highest-rated academic departments, Stanford University's School of Psychiatry and Graduate School of Business, sponsored the first annual international conference on the Enneagram, with four times as many attendees as expected. You, too, should look into it.

5. Develop *better bad habits* to substitute for ones which have outlived their usefulness, and to help you act principle-centered.

Some habits keep us focused better than others toward pursuing the right direction in our lives. Right direction, as we have already discussed, requires acting according to a set of principles, such as the 2nd Ten Commandments, that take us to higher levels of personal success. We already know that habits are "bad," as they can chain us to ways of acting, even if our ways of behaving do not accomplish what we really want. They can prevent us from acting in a given situation according to principles in which we believe. It is essential to recognize that even if we can't make all the changes we would like to at this very moment, it may be possible to shift a habit slightly, or to develop a new activity into a habit that can substitute for what we are currently doing. This process enables us to move in the direction that we want to go, even if we have been stuck for a long, long time.

"Better bad habits"[5] conveys the concept of finding better and better habits that are more likely to align us to universal principles. Stephen Covey, in *The 7 Habits of Highly Effective People*, has found seven such significantly *better bad habits*, of which we can all make use.

Covey summarized two thousand years' worth of literature on how to be a successful person in the form of seven habits. You can use these over and over again to become a highly effective person and to help you follow the 2nd Ten Commandments. One caveat, however: remember that when faced with a choice between acting based on habit or principle, always claim your freedom. Exercise your free will choosing to abide by universal law instead of following your more comfortable, customary way.

6. Plan what you would do if you won the lottery.

Most people find themselves too preoccupied with their daily lives to let themselves dare to think as if they were financially independent. However, as our technology allows our standard of living to increase, many people will have more time and money, and more choice about how to spend it, than ever before. Once survival needs have been met, and minimum levels of comfort satisfied, shouldn't you step back and think about why you would want to win the lottery?

Think about it. If you won the lottery, say $10 million, what would you do? Within a couple of months you would probably quit your job. Then you might buy a yacht, the car of your dreams, and a multitude of other possessions, including caring gifts for your loved ones to make their lives a little more comfortable, too. Then you might travel for awhile. You would cruise, fly, wine and dine yourself, lie on beaches unaware of the passing of time (or when you have to be at your next meeting), play golf all day long without worrying about how long 18 holes actually take, and enjoy the nectars of life, until you had had enough of that. But then what?

Anecdotally speaking, the initial period of unabashed freedom to indulge lasts for about a year after people become totally free of financial concerns. Then what?

Then you'd be more or less right back to where you are now, trying to figure out what *really* makes you happy in life; what kind of work or life-passion, friendships, relationships with loved ones, hobbies, and so on. Amazingly, you'd probably find that pursuing the things that really make you happy doesn't take $10 million, after all. And that your MISSION or work that brings you fulfillment can mostly likely be accomplished in a way that pays more than enough money to keep you comfortable.

Make a list of what you would do if you did win the lottery, and try to figure out how you could implement most of it now. With a few alternative scenarios, and creative thinking, you will probably find that you don't really need the $10 million to be happier and more fulfilled. Granted, you might have to make some compromises along the way, that having more money would have made easier.

But you might surprise yourself by discovering how fantastic you can make your life right now by just starting to imagine what it would be like to be totally free, and living life in a way that you really enjoy the most. This can also be a little scary—removing the money excuse leaves you naked to the possibility of real freedom, and of a departure from just fitting a mold. But the rewards are commensurate; remember, happiness is your birthright as a member of the generation of the Consciousness Age—if you claim it.

7. Write a personal constitution and mission statement.

Once you've imagined your total freedom and happiness, and have a stronger sense of who you are and what you want out of life, you're ready to write your personal constitution. Just as a country has a document that defines its belief system and values, you, too, could have a guiding vision that keeps your life sailing in the direction that's best for you. You can amend this document yearly, and perhaps monthly at first. But a powerful vision can last and endure— the United States Constitution has been amended on average only once a decade in the 200 years since 1789.

Since spirituality attempts to continually discern the temporary from the lasting, sticking to your personal constitution will lead you toward fulfilling your dreams in the most meaningful and successful way. It can prevent you from staying stuck in the aimless temptation of daily distractions, and keep your life progressing on a course you wish it to follow.

The personal mission statement, contained within your constitution, declares the purpose of your life, in terms of both finding your meaning and making your unique contribution to the world. It simply states what listening to your INNER VOICE has revealed to you as your MISSION, as discussed previously in Commandment No. 15. You may continually refine your understanding of it, a process analogous to a sailboat that repeatedly adjusts its course based on weather, wind, its physical condition, and sometimes commands from headquarters (inspiration from Gev). But putting your MISSION down in a sentence or two will help you to reach your destination.

Here's a checklist for writing your personal constitution:

a. Look in Stephen Covey's book, *The 7 Habits of Highly Effective People*, under the chapter on "Habit 2: Keeping the End in Mind." In other words, look at your life as if you had already lived all of it, and think about how you would like to have passed your time here. He also gives further information on creating a personal constitution.

b. Identify all the roles in your life, such as career, partner, parent, friend, community member, etc. Then write down your goals in each of these roles for the next year, five years, ten years, or even your lifetime.

240

c. Look at the example provided in Appendix A (which includes the author's personal constitution).

d. Ask other people—friends, family, colleagues—how they see you, and what they would like from their interactions with you in the long term.

e. Remember to see this as an evolving document. Just get something down on paper, and let it change frequently for awhile. Don't let intimidation deter you from starting. Initially everyone has a hard time with this assignment. But then again, it'll be more than worth it once you've done it.

8. Set prioritized goals by roles, but be process-oriented.

To keep yourself on track once you've established a personal constitution and mission, set prioritized goals by roles for each week, quarter (3 months), year, and five-year period. These will help you to translate your lifetime aspirations into manageable increments of accomplishments. This idea will help you tremendously toward achieving BALANCE in your life. By paying attention to all your different roles, and prioritizing the goals within each role, you attend to the most important items in the wide spectrum of your existence.

Like your constitution and mission, you will want to assess your progress toward goals, and continually reset them. In this world of incredible change and mobility, it seems impossible to set goals for more than five years. Nonetheless, five years gives you a reasonable window to plan your lofty achievements. Then reducing those to goals for the year makes them a little more definitive. The quarterly goals, called *objectives*, describe a set of expected outcomes, and provide the easiest increment in which to make concrete commitments to yourself and others, while leading you toward the accomplishment of your longer-term goals.

One way to determine your effectiveness is to grade your goals and how well you accomplished them on a scale of 0 to 100 percent, with 80 percent as the desired minimum, 100 percent being nearly impossible to hit. It takes a lot of practice to realistically set meaningful objectives, and then to learn to consistently achieve 80 to 100 percent.

Finally, you can break down your quarterly objectives into a short-term action plan, namely weekly goals or objectives, also prioritized by roles.[6] Here it is especially important to plan your time in such a way that you don't waste too much of it, or over-commit by scheduling too many tasks. Remember to also schedule growth and pleasure activities as a routine part of your diet, too.

While getting organized in your time management, remember to keep your focus on the process through which you accomplish your goals. A Motof's success depends on maintaining a continual spiritual ascension through personal evolution. Setting prioritized goals can help you to stay on track, but above all, you want to pay attention to the process of your experiences, rather than to focus primarily on the results. The only result that really counts in the long run is your continued growth, and the REPAIR and new creation you bring to the world. These are inseparably linked together, and matter most.

9. Engage in personal-growth education to grok deeper.

Further your understanding of *The* 2nd *Ten Commandments* by engaging in educational activities aimed at personal-growth and improvement, such as: reading books and magazines; attending seminars and workshops; and doing related therapies. As you begin to accept educational activities as a lifelong endeavor, rather than just a childhood experience, this idea will seem obvious to you.

Of course you have to invest your time carefully in the areas that will benefit you the most. In addition to the books suggested to you on the list in Appendix C, go to the bookstore and see what draws you most; sample activities listed in your local community events calendar; see what the local video store or library has to offer;

access Internet; or do whatever else appeals to you most, and appears to have the potential to further you the fastest.

If you repeatedly hear about a book or workshop from several sources in a short period of time, consider that the universe may be "leading the horse to water." It's up to you to drink or not. Unlike the Israelites in Moses' day, it is *each of our* decisions that will determine whether we reach the "Promised Land" or not, as we shall see in the next chapter.

23

MOTOFS: THE ADAPTERS SURVIVE AND SUCCEED

To survive, to avert what we have termed future shock, the individual must become infinitely more adaptable and capable than ever before. He must search out totally new ways to anchor himself, for all the old roots—religion, nation, community, family, or profession—are now shaking under the hurricane impact of the accelerative thrust.

—Alvin Tofler, *Future Shock* (1970)[1]

We didn't inherit the Earth from our parents. We're borrowing it from our children.

—Chief Seattle

Fewer than 50,000 years ago, *Homo sapiens sapiens*, our current species, replaced those Homo sapiens who did not adapt to their harsh environment, by developing language and tools. This newer breed could make better use of the power of groups to cope with their environment. Throughout prehistory, Cro-Magnon man and many other humanoid types had come and gone. No matter how much control we think we have over our environment, evolution will still favor those of us who can cope with and thrive on what is available at the time.

NATURE (EVENTUALLY) SELECTS NOVELTY OVER HABIT

In the impending Consciousness Age, increasing numbers of people will awaken to their role within a *planetary* clan. These humans, many of whom are alive today, are learning to live within and to thrive on the emerging intercommunicative society, the Global Brain. We call them Motofs, but in reality these are, and will be, those of us who understand what is happening on our planet and what needs to be done to preserve our chance to have a future home worth living in. We have already presented the case throughout this book for why these people will opt to use the principles of the 2nd Ten Commandments to guide their actions. Those who do will become Motofs.

As more Motofs learn to function as Gaia's nervous system—the Global Brain—they will act as global scouts helping to transmit the information that leads all of humanity into the new Promised Land. This will create and maintain a sustainable living system for all. *As you shall see, even by a conservative analysis, by the middle or at the latest by the end of the twenty-first century, only Motof humans will live on planet Earth.*

This may seem implausible to many. But change is running rampant on the planet now, causing tidal-wave-proportion redesigning of society and its people. How many people 40 years ago would have believed that the Berlin wall would come down, the Cold War between the United States and the Soviet Union would lose its chill, or that Israel and its Arab neighbors, including the PLO, would sit at one table and discuss terms for a peaceful co-existence in the Middle East?

Changes in our attitudes and interests are also occurring at astounding rates. Figure 23-1 shows an estimated growth curve for people who are likely to become Motofs from 1980 to the middle of the twenty-first century. We estimate that in 1980 about 1,000,000 people had the values, interests and knowledge to want to participate as members of a world-consciousness movement. These relative few began the fast rate of increase now occurring, in which we can start to see the impact of the greater and greater numbers of Motofs developing across the globe.

We predict the rate of growth to increase the number of Motofs by a factor of ten in each of the next four decades. This is shown in Figure 23-1 by using a linear graph, with a logarithmic scale on the vertical axis (multiples of 10 instead of 1). This means 10 million Motofs in the year 1990, 100 million in 2000, 1 billion in 2010; somewhere between 2020 and 2030, there would be 10 billion Motofs, about the expected population of the entire Earth at that time.

The "Motof Movement" is well underway, albeit by many different names. Look around. Notice how you are communicating with more people at a faster pace. This is happening right now.

The shift of the population to a global consciousness was discussed in Chapter 7 (see Figure 7-1) and was shown to follow the characteristics of an S-curve. These are the Motofs. Figure 23-2 now fits their S-curve growth to a 40-year period, the 1980s to the 2020s.

In the S-curve of Motof growth, the number of Motofs had stayed constant at a very small number for many years before 1980, probably much less than a million. Moses, for example, may have been one of the first Motofs, and Jesus and other great teachers were far ahead of their times, too. Then, as is characteristic of S-curves, suddenly, in a relatively short period of time, the rate of growth

Figure 23-1
Global Brain Participation (Motofs)

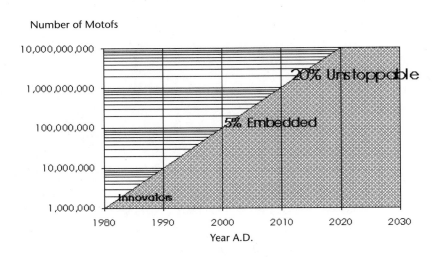

Year A.D.

Figure 23-2
S-Curve Growth of Motofs

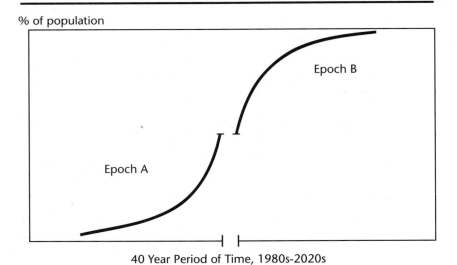

40 Year Period of Time, 1980s-2020s

explodes exponentially. This part of the S-curve was shown in the earlier graph, Figure 23-1, on a linear scale.

While hard to identify definitively, we estimate that *in 1995 about 50 million* people had enough of the traits described in the next section to be considered Motofs, putting us right on schedule. Within decades, the growth tapers off toward a maximum value, the population of the planet. After the twenty-first century, the number of Motofs will remain constant at this peak value of 10 to 12 billion. Thus, in "Epoch A" in figure 23-2 the Motofs are in the minority, and in "Epoch B" they constitute the majority and, eventually, the whole.

Sociologist Everett Rogers[2] found that new ideas or innovations tend to get adopted according to S-curves, such as Figure 23-2. Figure 23-3 shows how this creates a bell-curve distribution of adopters.

Figure 23-3
Adoption of Innovations/Ideas

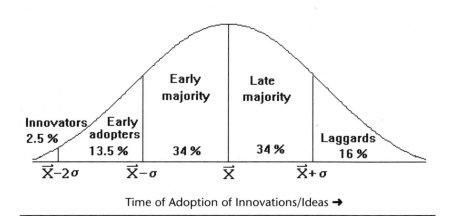

Time of Adoption of Innovations/Ideas ➜

First, 2.5 percent of the population, called *innovators*, venture forth and try an idea. Then 13.5 percent, the *early adopters* or *pacesetters*, carry it to the majority by serving as respected and successful role models. Next, the *early majority*, 34 percent, and the *late major-*

ity, also 34 percent, go along, the former by choice and the latter by economic necessity and network pressure. And finally, the traditional *late adopters* or *laggards* give up their strongholds, having at times even slowed the innovation-decision process to a crawl, and give in to the new idea.

In the first world, Motofs have reached the early majority phase on the S-curve (50 million out of a little over one billion is slightly over 2.5%). Rogers further found that once 5 percent of the population has embraced an idea it becomes permanently embedded, and when 20 percent of the population adopts the innovation, it is virtually *unstoppable*. If Figure 23-1 correctly predicts the rise of the Motofs, the trend would become unstoppable, coincidentally or not, around the year 2012!

The concept of adapting populations is not new. Charles Darwin wrote in the late 1800s about the principle of natural selection:

> In any population of self-reproducing organisms, there'll be variations in the genetic material and upbringing that different individuals have. These differences will mean that some individuals are better able than others to draw the right conclusions about the world around them and to act accordingly. These individuals will be more likely to survive and reproduce, and so their pattern of behavior and thought will come to dominate. It has certainly been true in the past that what we call intelligence and scientific discovery has conveyed a survival advantage.[3]

Every person alive today can choose to become a cell in this new order of complexity in nature. But of course all change encounters massive resistance. Even awareness of the need to change doesn't always sufficiently prompt many people to abandon habitual, comfortable behavior patterns.

TRADING IN HABIT FOR SALVATION

Let's look at the bad habits of drinking and smoking, as examples of how difficult people find it to kick habits. In the United States alone in 1992, 60 percent of all premature deaths occurred as a combined result of alcohol consumption (100,000 deaths) and tobacco smoking (450,000 deaths).[4] Many parts of the world would report even worse statistics. Excessive alcohol consumption is to blame for two-thirds of the homicides in the United States, and one-third of the failed marriages. Mothers get M.A.D.D. (Mothers Against Drunk Driving organization) and campaign against drinking and driving, advertisers advise designating a sober driver, and yet *half* of the over 42,000 automobile accident fatalities in 1993 and in every other year are drunk-driver-related. By comparison, only 40,000 Americans were killed over the decade of the Vietnam War. And despite over 30 years of warnings about lung and other cancers, and admonitions to quit, a full 27 percent of the population still smokes (although 30 percent of the population has kicked the habit over the last 20 years). Overall, substance-related problems currently cost the United States over $238 billion per year[5]—almost the amount of the defense budget.

This tragedy exemplifies how slowly we give up old habits, even after knowing what harm they cause us. While lack of awareness and education can excuse some of these self-destructive behaviors, sheer stubbornness and fear of change, or fear of the new, account for the rest.

Consider as another example the advent of novel technological conveniences that increase productivity. A study in the early 1990s found that "55% of Americans are either resistant to or actually phobic about such modern-day electronic devices as personal computers, cellular telephones and even digital alarm clocks."[6] Interestingly, and not surprisingly, teenagers are far less technophobic, and have a much easier time operating these gadgets (especially compact disc players).

So imagine how hard people will have to struggle for the next 40 years to overcome their own backward, survival-oriented thinking and stubbornness. Those who don't change may become an extinct group. Those who face and overcome their fears will become the Motofs.

For a whole society to accept a major new paradigm usually involves waiting for the next generation, as did the Israelites in the days of Moses. Remember that of all the slaves who fled Egypt, only three brave men completed the 40-year journey. Moses, who lived to be 120 years old, got to see, but not enter, the Promised Land. (He was denied admission as his punishment for having doubted God early in the mission.) The other two, Joshua and Caleb, were two of the 12 scouts sent ahead by Moses many years earlier, and were the only ones who believed in the feasibility of conquering Canaan. As their reward, they led the new, open-minded generation in blowing down the walls of Jericho, winning many more battles, and triumphantly claiming sovereignty over the land of Israel. But before that, in a time when the average life-span was about 30 years, clearly one whole generation of slave-mentality people had to die in the desert during the 40 years en route.

We face a similar situation today.

However, life-spans today extend to 80 years or more. In the twenty-first century it is quite possible that millions of centenarians (100 years of age or older) will populate the world. Given the accelerating pace of evolution we discussed, a great impetus will drive individuals to personal-growth and change. The rest will die in many ways, often prematurely, due to "stress" and other so-called natural causes. Many will want to return to the "comforts of Egypt"—after all, the slave-driving pharaohs did provide sufficient food and other basic needs, whereas in the harsh desert many starved for lack of food and water. In the current times this metaphor translates into not wanting to participate as a Motof in the Global Brain—refusing to use computers or the Internet, for example. The old, known ways always seem preferable to many.

As a result, Motofs will continually have to face many people who insist on hanging on to the old, more familiar, ways. They can find comfort in remembering that the resistance and hostility that surface from these seeming forces of darkness are nothing more than the actions of people in fear, who operate out of ikorgance. Motofs must not fear, but rather respect, those who feel threatened by the new and who are prisoners of their own lack of understanding.

With the disappearance of nationalistic or racial enemies resulting from political changes in the modern era—such as the end of the Cold War—people need a new sense of purpose, a cause to peacefully pursue. Viewed in this light, the resisters, both passive and active, present Motofs with an opportunity to strengthen themselves and further develop the traits that will allow them ultimately to survive the evolutionary process. By spreading a higher consciousness and bringing more knowledge to light, Motofs can offer salvation— health, happiness, longer life-span, etc.—to all.

MOTOF TRAITS

What traits and attributes will characterize Motofs? Here is a partial list:

1. *Most importantly, Motofs will display an openness towards new knowledge, the world, and its people.* Motofs expect constant change, and do not rule out anything as impossible. Humanity put a person on the moon in a decade, and can now grow babies in test tubes. The Berlin Wall came down with almost no advance notice. Anything can and will happen, and fast.

   Therefore, Motofs greet new gadgets, concepts, and activities with interest and enthusiasm ("Cool, I might try it, too,"), rather than with judgmental, immediate criticism. They

253

accept all others, no matter how strange or different, as a contributing, necessary part of the whole.

2. *Motofs will agree with Global Spirituality and the Global Brain paradigm.* This requires gleaning the best of past religions, and integrating their traditions into a new mind-set.

3. *Motofs will live to a high degree by the 2nd Ten Commandments.* Unlike the first Ten Commandments, the 2nd Ten Commandments can never be fully achieved. They are goals to strive for.

   By the way, according to one source,[7] 64 percent of the people in the United States believe they follow all of the first Ten Commandments. Individual Commandments, like the fifth—respecting one's parents—achieve a 95 percent adherence rate. Reassuringly, 91 percent say they wouldn't murder anyone, thereby sticking to Moses' sixth Commandment, and 86 percent wouldn't violate Commandment number seven by committing adultery.

4. *As a result of traits one and two, Motofs will act appropriately towards their fellow Motofs, engendering great mutual trust.* Robert Heinlein, in his science fiction classic *Stranger in a Strange Land,* talks about "grokking a wrongness"[8] causing the offended Martians such self-harm that they choose to "discorporate"—die and start over in a new body. Even King Solomon and Confucius strained to discern proper versus improper behavior. But as Motofs, we realize how dramatically we affect each other in a global community; that we all operate under the same natural laws; and that how we behave in a physical form can conform to higher levels of spirituality. Motofs act from the standpoint that everyone is in it together.

5. *Motofs will recognize the benefits of technology in combination with consciousness.* By itself, technology is neutral. Used with-

out Lev and caring for what happens to others as a result of its development, it can be corrupt, if not outright evil.[9] Used properly, it can free us from our survival concerns and help to link the inhabitants of the planet through the use of the tools of the Information Age (see Figure 23-4). Motofs realize that, if properly synergized with right values, technology helps further the creation of a Global Brain and Lokelani.

6. *Motofs will believe in an emerging set of interdependent values that have been latent until now.* For Motofs, collaboration will dominate over competition, and the whole over the parts. The individual *and* the group will triumph over just the individual. Consensus will win over old-fashioned power; it will be interdependence, not just independence. Balance will rule over extremes, and an attitude of "both/and" will replace "either/or."[10]

7. *Motofs will believe in their immortality and agelessness, with physical death becoming a more conscious choice in the future.* Either we perceive that we are fundamentally connected to all of the planet or we don't. If so, then our eternal spirit survives in ways that we have only begun to comprehend. Subsequently, Motofs will discover new ways to think about their physical bodies and life expectancies. We can also expect great advances in controlling the aging process of our bodies, whether with our minds, technology, or a combination of the two. We are at a junction in history where humans have learned how to physically survive, and the rules of the game may very well change now.

8. *Motofs will speak English, the Global Brain's official language, reasonably well.* This will allow Motofs, anywhere on Earth, to communicate with and understand each other.

9. *Motofs will partake in a "supra-culture," new customs and mannerisms that appear globally, cutting across lines of race, religion,*

Figure 23-4
Motofs Getting Plugged Into
the Information Age to Interlink

and nation. An example of this might include the use of global products; like Coke and Pepsi. Motofs may end up not wearing ties or high-heeled shoes regularly—it's time for humanity to "loosen up," to get down to earth and be comfortable, and for it to be perfectly acceptable for everyone to be themselves and be happy.

10. *Motofs will exert personal influence, to varying degrees, by acting as leaders who affect outcomes in specific domains.*[11] We define *leadership* as: interpersonal influence, exercised in situations and directed through the communication process, toward the attainment of a specified goal or goals. Motofs,

aware of their roles as co-creators, will invoke Lev, guidance, and discipline to try to reshape the world in their image.

In summary, Motofs will act from Lev, face their fears responsibly, be open, gladly seek new adventures, be joyous, and above all, radiate the smile that emanates from the faith that life is good, and can only get better. Isn't it about time that we humans, after thousands of years of hardship, finally evolve enough to deserve this?

In 1270 B.C., the Pharaoh's horse-drawn chariots chased the fleeing Israelites across the Red Sea, which parted for the Israelites but closed upon the drowning Egyptians. Three thousand years later, modern-day Israel was founded in 1948, after a military defeat of modern-day Egypt. One generation later, in 1973, Egypt successfully crossed the Red Sea and avenged a three-millennia-old score by attacking Israel, this time with tanks. The Yom Kippur War, combined with the initiative of President Sadat of Egypt and Prime Minister Begin of Israel, who aspired to give hope to future generations, eventually led to the 1978 peace treaty between the two countries. As former masters and slaves, they now attempt to live side by side as equals.

Perhaps Motofs can accomplish this, today, globally. Patricia Watson calls them all in her song:[12]

> Come to the year 2000,
> Come join the human race,
> Come where the modern lovers
> Fill the air with sweet grace.

Ken Carey invites them to participate in the *Third Millennium*:[13]

> You are the template, the prototype of a new and universal species, part solar, part material, both temporal and eternal, the species that will span the gulf between the visible and the invisible, bringing new worlds into form. Through you a new and unprecedented cycle of creation will occur.

So bring your global passport, sign a "Declaration for Universal Alliance through sharing our highest common ideals,"[14] and get on the path of no return to believe, think, and act as a Motof. You are a citizen of the world. You know that as a Motof, "Gev and we are one," since "we are all one people, a part of Gaia."

This is the spirit of the *Gevolution*: the process now occurring which will effect the transition from the current, survival-oriented world, to the new Consciousness Age. It promises a peaceful, non-violent form of revolution.

Gevolution, noun

The process now occurring which will effect a transition from the current, survival-oriented world to the new Consciousness Age. A peaceful, nonviolent form of revolution, that will result in Motofs creating Lokelani and functioning as the Global Brain.

MAKE A LEAP OF FAITH, TRUST, SMILE, AND LAUGH

The gates to Lokelani and Motofland beckon and call to you: one turn of the doorknob and anyone on Earth can jet into Heaven-on-Earth. Realize that with a single leap you could live your life in Lokelani all the time, if you just allowed for that possibility and then worked towards it. By valuing every moment of your life here and now, you will live life to the fullest, make the most of every day, and stretch yourself to the peak of your capabilities.

Once in the flow of this higher stream of consciousness, life becomes much lighter and more humorous. Each and every activity has its lessons for you, and everything really does work out in the long run. Things that happened to you that you thought were bad, turn out to be great opportunities, and vice versa. As long as you keep a good attitude, one of success through just growing and learning from every experience, you take life and yourself less seriously. You begin to see the unfolding cosmic drama, and your small but significant part in it—you are nobody and everybody, simultaneously. And as you start enjoying life, giving the utmost of importance to every moment, you can't help but smile and laugh at the marvel of all of creation.

Have *spiritual faith,* and trust that the universe will provide you with a wonderful playground to partake in. *Spiritual faith* means having an unprovable belief in the "perfection" of all things—that everything happens for a reason, often unknown to us, and is exactly as it's supposed to be.

Faith implies three things: first, it implies grokking that everything in the past and present was and is "perfect": you needed it to get to where you are now and wouldn't trade it for anything. If you don't see it this way, your thinking needs to change as you adapt to reality. Healthy, older people often say that if they had their life to live over again, they wouldn't change a thing. So why not take that attitude now?

Second, faith implies realizing that if you follow the laws of the universe, both physical and spiritual, you have complete choice from this moment on to participate in creating a spectacular future for yourself and others. And third, faith implies accepting whatever outcome results. If you know who you are, what you want, and do your best, you trust that Gev will take care of the rest. You've made it this far, haven't you? The future looms even brighter, as you see the perfection and marvel at the oneness of all creation and the universe. This will be the subject of the next chapter.

Spiritual Faith, noun

An unprovable belief in the "perfection" of all things— that everything happens for a reason, often unknown to us, and is exactly as it's supposed to be.

Once we acquire a frame of mind filled with faith, we should expect that ". . . [Gev] will disturb us when we're comfortable, and comfort us when we're disturbed."[15] Our spirit alternately shakes our foundations to help us grow, and rewards us with the nectars of Lokelani. Life is change and evolution. In reality, we, symbolized by Adam and Eve, never actually left Paradise. We just forgot that we're already in it.

24

ONE IS ALL, AND ALL ARE ONE[1]

I pledge allegiance to the Earth,
and all the life which it supports.
ONE PLANET, in our care, irreplaceable,
with sustenance and respect for all.

—Janina Lamb, 1992[2]

Let me not forget myself is nothing,
but my Self is all.

—Foundation for Inner Peace,
A Course in Miracles, 1975[3]

261

What might the Global Promised Land be like? It will be a place where all of us have our survival needs met, where we can each pursue JKLM, (Joy, Knowledge, Lev, and Mission), where we can all co-exist in peace and harmony, and where we can all help each other to grow and succeed.

SCOUTING OUT THE GLOBAL PROMISED LAND

Recently, 25,000 participants at a World Game Workshop composed a vision for the year 2009 of "What the World Wants."[4] They concurred that 100% of humanity would have to have the following items on a sustainable or ongoing basis:

Abundant supplies of nutritious and culturally appropriate food,

Abundant supplies of clean water,

Adequate housing,

Local comprehensive health service,

Healthful sanitation facilities,

Abundant, clean, safe and affordable supplies of energy,

Employment opportunities, and fulfilling work,

Vocational alternatives, and on-the-job training,

Literacy, and access to advanced educational opportunities,

Access to communication facilities so that anyone can communicate with anyone else on Earth who wants to be communicated with,

Access to transportation facilities, enabling anyone to go anywhere,

Access to decision-making processes that affect their lives,

A peaceful, secure, nuclear/chemical/biological weapon-free world,

A crime- and drug-free world,

A clean, self-regenerating environment, free of toxic wastes, pollution of all kinds, soil erosion, and damaging practices that don't sustain the biosphere,

Easy and equitable access to the materials and information needed to produce the above,

Freedom of speech, press, and religion,

Absence of all forms of prejudice—race, religion, gender, age, sexual preference,

Respect and celebration of the diversity of all cultures and nations,

Strong social supports for individuals, families, and communities,

Strong social incentives that foster initiative, trust, cooperation, respect, and love,

Absence of all forms of torture, or degrading treatment or punishment,

Access to full equality before an independent and impartial tribunal,

Access to the right to nationality,

Access to the right to perform public service in one's own country,

Access to rest and leisure,

Access by mothers and children to special care and assistance,

Access by children to special protection,

Access to spiritual growth and fulfillment.

Sounds utopian? Not if we all head there together.

SPIRITUALITY SEEKS ONENESS

In a Global Promised Land we would realize that the following seeming opposites are actually one and the same:

Our mental and physical health are one.

Giving and receiving are one.

Learning and teaching are one.

Doing and being done unto are one.

Working and playing are one.

Individual and global community happiness are one.

One and all are one.

Adopting the 2nd Ten Commandments and Global Spirituality provides a paradigm shift to viewing things this way.

SCIENCE, TOO, SEARCHES FOR ONENESS

Every day scientists get closer to discovering the oneness of creation. Physicists have reduced all known forms of energy to two primary forces. They continue to search feverishly for a unifying theory to combine those two into just one.

Out on the edge of the frontier, some mathematicians and physicists have found that all matter seems to contain the same "stuff." At the University of California at Berkeley, George Smoots' discovery of "wrinkles in time" (in outer space) has generally been seen as a validation of the big bang theory.[5] This theory suggests that all matter arose from a single point ten to twenty billion years ago, and has expanded ever since then to form the entire universe. In his book, *Wrinkles in Time*, Smoots claims that his find indicates that there's a clear order to the evolution of the universe. And furthermore, that it's moving from simplicity and symmetry to greater complexity and structure.

One evolutionary, creative force, that we have called Gev, pushes it all forward in a purposeful way—although we do not fully know in which way. We humans are the "I" and "eye" of the universe—intelligent beings, perhaps like others elsewhere, that question and attempt to understand creation.

If everything is made of the same "stuff," in a sense the "microcosm" and the "macrocosm" are one and the same. One astronomer says: "Quantum theory physics and chaos theory are letting us look with new eyes at the idea that the universe is mirrored in each of us."[6] Harriet Witt-Miller, in an award-winning science paper, explains how "fractals" help us to bridge the gap between the seeming paradoxes of chaos and complexity in nature, resulting in the uncovering of a unity in the cosmos. Fractals, or patterns mathematically described by a new form of geometry, were pioneered by Benoit

Mandelbrot in 1975, and map the shape of nature's processes. They have two outstanding characteristics: they are independent of scale, and self-similar. Add to this the *non-locality* principle of quantum physics, and that all subatomic particles in the universe emanated from the big bang, and Witt-Miller drives home two conclusions: "a) No object is located just where its physical form appears; and b) all objects, including our own bodies, are in instantaneous contact with the entire universe."[7]

Some current biological theories also seem to indicate this kind of oneness, such as reported by Joseph Chilton Pearce in the *Magical Child*:

> Brain researchers are now beginning to consider the brain as a form of hologram. A hologram is a kind of photography that contains the entire photograph within any part or piece of the whole. (You must see this to believe it.) There are many uncanny properties of holography, but this phenomenon of the whole within the part is the property that seems similar to the brain. For example, take a hologram plate of a vase of flowers, and break it in half. You do not have a picture of two halves of a vase; each half is still the complete picture. Break the plate into quarters, and you will have four complete pictures, and so on, down to small fragments. The problem is that the picture gets fuzzier at each reduction. A tiny piece still contains the whole picture, but the clarity is gone.
>
> When we speak of the brain as a hologram, we mean that any part of the brain, even a single thinking cell, reflects or encompasses the workings of the total brain. An even more intriguing implication is that the brain may be a hologram of the entire planet earth. That is, just as you can divide a holographic plate and find the whole picture in any piece, so the brain can be considered just such a piece of the earth, reflecting within it the picture or workings of the whole life system. The human brain may be a kind of micro-miniature replica of

the living planet itself, just rather fuzzy at the edges, needing clarification.[8]

On a grander, and even more curious, cosmic scale, considering what we have discussed in Chapter 6 regarding ten billion brain cells in the human brain, and ten billion people as the maximum number for our planet, it is interesting to know that scientists believe that there are about ten billion planets such as ours in our Milky Way Galaxy.[9] And furthermore, about ten billion galaxies in the universe. And who knows, perhaps ten billion universes? Perhaps some time in the future we will discover that we are all just part of one "humongous" super-super-organism? One "You-niverse?"[10]

One can only speculate on whether the spiritual laws presented here as the 2nd Ten Commandments also apply to higher-order superorganisms such as the planet Earth, the solar system, the Milky Way Galaxy, and even the universe(s). Regardless, they definitely present a golden pathway for humans to continue their search for truth and freedom, and to tap into a great source of energy and inspiration that authentically rejuvenates and empowers. They help get individuals, and all of us collectively as a planetary society, on the path to success in a Global Promised Land. They lead us all together toward . . . greater oneness!

Our hearts are one,
We are one with our planet,
We are one.

DO YOU WANT TO SAVE CHANGES? [YES, NO, CANCEL, HELP]

You can no longer save your family, tribe, or
nation. You can only save the whole world.

—Margaret Mead

No one is safe until everybody is safe.
No one is free until everybody is free.

—Orion Kopelman

YOUR CHOICE

We are human, thus we have choices. As you are coming to the end of this book, you can choose one of the following responses to retain the changes that have happened to you: Y̲es, N̲o, C̲ancel, H̲elp. Each implies your having related to the material in different ways. "Yes" means you valued what you learned or concluded and wish to complete your use of the book at this time. You can always come back to it another day, just as you can with any computer file. Should you choose "N̲o," i.e., to exit without saving, it seems regrettable. We feel certain that this work will prove highly useful to people wishing to succeed and thrive in the twenty-first century, and that this will become increasingly apparent in the years to come. So we implore you to reconsider carefully.

If you choose "C̲ancel," please enjoy whatever parts you have chosen to go back and re-read. It means that you recognize a continuing need to engage with the materials of *The 2nd Ten Commandments*. As authors of these materials, we still find that we select this option most often and will continue to do so. We hope that you will, too, and that your re-reading will catalyze both external and internal dialoguing about it for days, weeks, and years to come.

Finally, "H̲elp" signifies that you're unsure of how to proceed. As the impact of *The 2nd Ten Commandments* takes you out of your habitual ways into new territory, you may need assistance. Discuss the book's influence on you with trusted others. Seek other educational opportunities. Explore. You may need some time to digest the material and its impact on you. Take this time and then ask again, "What is my next step with the 2nd Ten Commandments?"

Regardless of which option you choose, we hope that you will seriously consider trying the ideas presented in Chapter 22 on how to become a Motof. By no means do these contain the last word on the subject. We all need more help in figuring out how to accelerate our paths toward freeing ourselves and adapting to the new era dawning upon humanity, the Consciousness Age.

To assist with this, our society needs a new brand of primary care physician—a *growthologist*—someone who helps us grow simultaneously in all ways: physical, emotional, mental, and spiritual. These "doctors" will refer some of us to a new kind of therapist, a spiritual psychologist. Spiritual psychologists will support our search to see how our innermost selves create our realities, and show us how to do this in a healthier, more functional way, one coherent with living in our upcoming global society. Both kinds of healers already exist in sparse, but increasing, numbers. We urge you to seek them out, and/or to become one yourself.

Time will not stand still, as evolution screams at us to adapt. The time is now. Heed the call and become the kind of person—of whatever race, sex, color, nation, or religion you may happen to be— who chooses to serve as an example to others in this most worthy task of all, the redemption of our species and our planet.

Choose to venture out on the journey, and find your success. *The 2nd Ten Commandments* can serve as a great road map for your trip. It will shed light on your path to a maximally satisfying and balanced life in all domains; health and happiness, career, relationships, family, finances, and community. But exactly how to implement and live by what you have read will greatly depend on you as an individual. As long as you keep moving forward and don't look back, you will find greater fulfillment than you ever believed possible, despite what appears to be a more tumultuous world than ever before. This is what we are all learning together.

OUR CHOICE

An old Chinese proverb warns: "Unless we change the direction we are headed, we might end up where we are going." Collectively, we are at a crossing point: one where we have to choose a different direction if we are to save the planet and the species; one that resembles the Israelites' moment of choice 3,000 years ago, when they stood at the edge of the Red Sea, caught between Pharaoh's chariots closing in from behind, and an apparently uncrossable barrier in front of them.

As in any crisis, various factions formed, each with their own response:[1] "There's no hope, we give up—let's jump into the sea or surrender." "The past was better—let's return to Egypt." "Let's be practical—we'll wage war upon the Egyptians." "It's beyond our control—let's pray to God." Moses, their leader, rejected all four of these factions and commanded, "Go forward," as he parted the Red Sea.

We, too, must choose "not to escape reality, not to submit to it, not to wage war on it, not to deal with it only on a spiritual level,"[2] but to look for creative solutions and move forward. We, too, may have seemingly insurmountable barriers in front of us that will yield, and face ominous threats that will fade away, when we believe that together we have the power to wave our wands and create a different future. Our planet and humanity are in a "condition red" alarm zone, and we can't count on a miracle to save us. Rather, it is up to each and every one of us, and all of us together, to find the courage to move forward, to seek and find the Global Promised Land. This is what we mean by Gevolution.

To figure out how best to move forward together, we solicit your comments in the most genuine and open-minded manner. Please, send your input to the address provided below—or call, fax, or send electronic mail. Please encourage others to read the book and do the same. Please tell us and everyone you know what you have discovered. We intend to continue publishing new understandings, as we integrate and synthesize what we learn. This way we can keep updating this guide, and help ourselves and others by providing more accurate trail markers to the fastest path to Motofhood. As a result, we expect that collectively we can create rapid planetary development, and produce a Global-Brain-kind of world that's not only worth living in, but also worth bringing new souls into.

Best wishes in your hard work on commencing or continuing your most Rapid Personal Development, and see you in Lokelani, as we mutually join and live in tomorrow's global world, today.

Orion Moshe Kopelman
Marc Lehrer
Feb. 14, 1996

GLOBAL BRAIN™, INC.
555 Bryant St., #369
Palo Alto, CA 94301-1704
USA

Orders: 1-800-U-GO-GLOBAL
(1-800-846-4562)
(within the United States)
Tel. 415/327-2012
FAX 415/327-2028
E-mail: GloblBrain@aol.com
http://www.globalbrain.com/global/2ndten

APPENDIX A

ORION'S JOURNEY OF DISCOVERY

Where there's a will there's a way.
—Theodore Herzl,
founder of the Zionist movement of the late 1800s

A man must rise above the Earth to the top of the atmosphere and beyond, for only thus will he fully understand the world in which he lives.
—Socrates (circa 399 B.C.),
on a plaque at Mission Control Center, Houston, Texas

I n 1988, at the age of 26, I had met many of my life goals, and had seemingly achieved "success" in the form of the "American Dream." It turned out to be a mythical and only partially fulfilling success. In this section I will recount the events of the next seven years of my life, events which led to the discovery and writing of *The 2nd Ten Commandments*. I will describe the journey that led me to trade-in the fleeting and unrewarding success of my original dream for a new, far more fulfilling "World Dream," in the hope that it may also help you find a path to your own *lasting* success.

THE WOUNDED HEALER

Since my teenage years, I had only thought about life as a game in which one tried to figure out how to most swiftly climb the ladder to the American Dream-kind of success. Ironically, just as I reached "the top," and was finally supposed to be able to start enjoying life, I developed an increasingly nagging, and then almost constant, irritation and pain in my neck that caused me to have daily, severe headaches.

I used to curse the fragility of my neck. Nothing seemed to provide relief. Today, I thank the universe for this pain which I couldn't get rid of with medications, or with the variety of other standard treatments I tried, because it led me directly to learning how to achieve a much healthier, more meaningful, balanced, and happier life for myself. Healing my emotional pain, manifested physically and lodged in my neck, I discovered the principles of the 2nd Ten Commandments, and freed myself from my bondage to pain.

Many spiritual traditions contain stories about shamans and other teachers who first struggled with and conquered their own monumental suffering and pain, and then became known as *wounded healers* who could help others. When I began my efforts to heal myself, I did not know of these traditions, nor did I attempt to seek this type of solution. My suffering did not allow me to rest. I had to keep trying different paths until I found methods that made a difference for me. It was only during the latter parts of this process that I discovered that what had helped me to heal might also help others. *I pray that I can steer many of you in a right direction, before you, too, have to suffer as I did. Although suffering may be highly useful in motivating you to significantly change your life, why suffer more than you have to?*

FOUR CORNERSTONES OF ACHIEVING THE AMERICAN DREAM

By 1988 I felt that I had climbed to the top of Mount Everest. Only later did I find out that I had really only discovered peaks, and that perhaps the process of life matters more than where you end up. Nonetheless, while traveling what I believed to be the path to my eventual "success," I chalked up in the victory column the following four significant accomplishments, which are typically associated with the cornerstones of having achieved the American Dream:

1. Respectable career status

2. Some financial independence

3. A wealth of material possessions

4. Marriage to a "desirable" woman

1. Respectable career status

I was Vice President of Engineering of Mountain Computer, Inc. in Scotts Valley, California, and co-founder of its Media Equipment Division. From 1984 to 1990 I helped this high technology company grow from 50 to 500 people, and from $10 million per year in sales to over $100 million, with a string of consecutive profitable quarters throughout my tenure there. Among other things, this adventure earned me selection as a member of "Who's Who in America," and the honor of serving as Chairman of the International Electrical and Electronics Engineers (IEEE, a non profit, worldwide association) Engineering Management Society in California's Silicon

Valley. The engineering education I had obtained and financed myself at Stanford University clearly had born fruit.

2. Some financial independence

In 1988 we sold Mountain Computer, Inc., to Nakamichi, Inc. of Japan. The long-anticipated payoff for the stock, that many of us owned (paid over the next two years), allowed me to not have to work for quite a while, if I chose not to. I left the company in 1991, became an "investor," and had quite a bit of fun with the stock market. I discovered that the same devotion to details, while keeping an eye on the big picture, that I had successfully used when I went to the "Mountain," also let market success come to me. I couldn't lounge in retirement on the beaches and golf courses of the world forever—someday I hoped to have children and be able to afford to send them to college—but I could take it easy, while figuring out what to do with the rest of my life.

3. A wealth of material possessions

I managed to gather plenty of proudly- and self-earned material possessions and toys. This included, of course, the fulfillment of the American Dream, a beautiful wooden house in the beach resort town of Santa Cruz, California, with a spacious yard, a hot tub, and a two-car garage, with two shining foreign cars—status symbols— parked in it. I competed with other "nouveau riche" friends in the race to acquire the largest compact disc collection. While dining lavishly at expensive restaurants, I laughed regularly, albeit with a bittersweet feeling, about how as a child I used to look forward so eagerly to our monthly treat at McDonald's.

4. Marriage to a "desirable" woman

The house was not devoid of another part of the American Dream, a childhood sweetheart. Yael, an intelligent, charming, and attractive woman whom I had already courted at age 13 while going for ice cream in Israel, fell into my lap at a "chance" meeting six years later. (I now believe there are no random coincidences.) My friends, her professors, and my family all told me how lucky I was to have "such a woman," who not only cooked an excellent spaghetti bolognaise, but who had also received an A+ in her freshman logic class at the University of California, Santa Cruz, where she graduated with her bachelor's degree in 1988. We loved each other dearly.

Indeed, I had climbed to the top rung of the ladder of "success," as I understood it, only to discover that the ladder rested on the wrong wall. I was about to find out that true success comes only from spiritual growth.

SOLVING FOUR "MINOR" PROBLEMS THAT AROSE FROM THIS SUCCESS

What shattered my American Dream? What went wrong with the success picture as I've described it? Four "minor" problems arose, one in each of the areas of accomplishment:

1. My work seemed most directly to cause my daily headaches, which prevented me from doing any of the things that I really enjoyed doing in life.

2. My financial independence begged the question: What would I do with the rest of my life?

3. The wealth of material possessions wasn't making me that much happier. I had discovered the fallacy of the bumper sticker that claims: "He who dies with the most toys wins."

4. My marriage to a "desirable" woman got into trouble when I realized that she wanted to move to and live only in Israel, her homeland.

I finally discovered what most wise people already know: that the most important things in life are your youth and your health—with those you can get everything else. I had the former, but suffered greatly from debilitating headaches, and I felt very confused about how such a seemingly young and physically fit person, who had won the Michigan State Doubles Championship in tennis only eight years earlier, could have fallen this ill. I decided that I would make recovering my health the only priority in my life.

After two years—and thousands of dollars spent on treatments—I failed to get much physical relief from my headaches. Doctors officially diagnosed my problem as a "chronic cervical strain" in my neck, a leftover from an earlier tennis injury that had worsened over time. Even the Magnetic Resonance Imaging (MRI) scan had indicated only a minor amount of actual damage, which experts concurred did not merit the risk of surgery. And yet, clearly the symptoms not only persisted, but seemed disproportionate to the damage as diagnosed. I went to many medical doctors, used numerous prescribed drugs and pain-reducing injections, and was pushed and pulled by physical and mental therapists, a chiropractor, and an acupuncturist.

In October 1989, things finally took a turn for the better, thanks to Dr. Svetlana Keyser, an unusual M.D., a physiatrist—a specialist in rehabilitation medicine—and as it turns out a godsend ("Gev-send"). At her recommendation, I embarked on a mind/body therapy, similar to Yoga, called the Feldenkrais method of "Awareness through Movement and Functional Integration." I didn't know it at the time, but here my real healing began, and my first steps toward discovering the 2nd Ten Commandments. I began to realize that something about *me* would have to fundamentally change. I finally understood that doctors could only provide temporary fixes and tools. I, the patient, would have to take responsibility for healing myself.

For the next two years, I suffered and yet endured, finding the methods and approaches that worked best with my "problem." I learned through dozens of Feldenkrais sessions about how all the parts of my body interacted and influenced each other in simple actions such as sitting, as well as in complex movements. In a myriad of ways, a hundred times a day, my state of mind was causing me to tense my back, shoulder, and neck muscles, which compressed the spine and its nerves and induced my headaches. I must admit that I greatly resisted this concept for many months. Fortunately, Marcia Margolin, my teacher, exercised amazing patience and compassion with me, and worked on relaxing and reprogramming my body, rather than trying to argue with my strong-headed, stubborn rational mind.

To address the mind-body connection more directly, Dr. Keyser suggested that I try computerized biofeedback combined with hypnosis with a unique practitioner, Dr. Marc Lehrer. Looking back, not only am I infinitely grateful to Marc for leading me on my healing journey, but I still marvel at his patience in working miracles with me. Through more than 100 subsequent sessions, over a period of a year and a half, other aspects of my awareness began to awaken. I began to ask the standard mid-life-crisis-type of questions, such as: "Who am I? Where am I going? Why?" I attended numerous personal-growth workshops; developed a home self-practice set of routines that included meditation, Feldenkrais, self-hypnosis, and muscle stretching and strengthening; and took countless notes of what happened from all the experiences I had. My very way of being was shaken to the core, daily.

During this time, I was still quite limited by pain. I couldn't write or type, do athletics, or wear sunglasses or hats for even short periods of time, without paying for it with more extreme headaches, which would start either immediately or after a while, and sometimes last for days. By now I was prepared to admit that my pain, in addition to being related to some form of soft-tissue damage, was also very much psychologically based.

At this point my pain began to unveil to me many agonizing but simple facts that you might recognize as correlating to the consequences of not following the 2nd Ten Commandments.

First, I was not enjoying life, because I had *hurry sickness*—a compulsion to do and accomplish. I had become a "human doing," symbolized by lack of blood and oxygen flow and excessive tightness and immobility in my neck muscles that produced spine compression and lots of pain, of course. My life lacked FLOW. I pushed; I struggled; I never noticed the many times I could have let the momentum carry me. One day, on my way to a lunch plaza that I frequented often, I descried many beautiful bouquets, at what I surmised must have popped up as a new flower shop. I congratulated the woman behind the counter inside for their grand opening. Surprised, she let me know that they had been there for about two years. How much I had missed along the way!

Second, my tremendous focus on needing to achieve had caused me to ignore other needs in myself. My lack of WHOLENESS kept me always wanting more, without any sense of what more would really accomplish, a combination destined to fall short of providing any degree of deeper satisfaction. I came to see this symbolically as the squelching of my inner child, or the animal part within me, who was attempting to yell out of my throat. Fortunately, I heard this part of myself before we both died.

Third, although I had tons of self-esteem, my impending divorce, and the absence of someone else to love me, kept creating doubts about my SELF-ACCEPTANCE, my ability to really love and care for myself.

Fourth, since my college days I had lost the BALANCE in my life. Correspondingly, the muscles on the right side of my body were always tight, and those on the left stretched to the point of pain, causing a structural imbalance and subsequent pain in the vertebrae of my cervical spine.

Fifth, I had also lost touch with my INNER VOICE in my race to "be successful" in the world. While I had never been religious, in earlier years I had had that feeling of just intuitively knowing what was "right," and following it.

By following the principles later written down as Commandments No. 11 to No. 15, which took lots of transformation work through discipline, I started figuring out who I really was and what I wanted in my life: what kind of relationships, my MIS-SION, and my relation to the physical and spiritual worlds around me.

I found that Commandments No. 15 to No. 20 helped me to feel better and better as my health kept improving. I discovered the seemingly biological link, like nerve cells in a Global Brain, to adhering to and living and breathing these natural laws. It is a different way of *being*. Today I use my slight neck pain as feedback to monitor my adherence to these Commandments. I hardly ever get headaches, and I am unreasonably happy and healthy.

As I progressed in my understanding of how to abide by all of the 2nd Ten Commandments, and regained my health and vitality, I began to solve the other three "minor problems" that I faced. I can now easily see myself spending the rest of my life enjoying my MIS-SION, and have an idea, albeit constantly evolving, of what kind of relationships I wish to have with my fellow human beings. All of these are stated in my personal constitution below, which I have included to help others gain a sense of who they are and what they want out of life. We're all different, and that's OK. We're also allowed to change with time. I update my constitution a bit every year.

I still enjoy material possessions but am no longer addicted to them—I'm not unhappy without them. They still add to my quality of life, and I think that's OK. Many spiritual people have fallen on their heads on this one. They have "thrown out the baby with the bath water." Eliminate the compulsion and addiction, don't buy too much on credit, but by all means enjoy the abundance that centuries of human ingenuity and technology have created for all of us.

And as to my fourth problem, in June of 1991, after a two-year separation, I finally got divorced in Israel, where Yael and I had been married seven years earlier. While we settled everything amicably—no lawyers—and remain friends to this day, we realized that despite our great love, we didn't meet each other's BOTTOM LINES: she chooses to spend the rest of her life living in Israel, and I don't. As our Rabbi Rick Litvak said, "You're both wonderful people, but an elephant and a giraffe can play together but aren't meant to mate." I had just met my symbolic inner child, who I think of as a giraffe, two months earlier at a phenomenal workshop lead by Ken Keyes, Jr., in Coos Bay, Oregon. I hadn't realized how, unconsciously, I had enslaved my inner child to many traditions and ideas of the past that my parents and others had handed down to me, and which no longer served me. My survival-oriented drive for success, and the whole era of my seven-year marriage, culminated with my personal exodus from the bondage of Egypt, much like Moses' and the Israelites' 3,000 years earlier. It was arduous and trying, to say the least— although I, unlike the Israelites, never had to worry about starving, thank Gev.

GIVING IT ALL UP TO GET MUCH MORE BACK

Undoing programmed beliefs and myths that we live by and that reach back thousands of years is hard—almost undoable. I unraveled them a bit at a time. Much to my good fortune, my parents were still alive and supported me admirably and with a lot of caring through my process of undoing many of the beliefs they had taught me. In the three decades since they had brought me into this world, they, too, had found that some of their "hand-me-down" teachings had created problems in their own lives.

As my journey progressed further, I realized that I would just about have to give up everything that had been meaningful to me. By "giving up" I mean removing my psychological attachment to, and belief in, its value to me. I had to put all of my status symbols of the American Dream's fulfillment—my house, my BMW, my wife, and my job with a six-digit income—"up for sale." Some of them I physically gave up. All of them I had to mourn over. A few of them I ended up keeping. For example, to abate my neck pain, I even had to give up playing tennis for several years, but what I really had to give up was my competitive attitude to playing tennis, which stemmed from the importance to me of "winning at all costs."

I got tennis, and much more, back. Once I had shifted my attitudes and overcome my survival-oriented approach, not only could I enjoy the external objects but also have my health and an inner sense of richness and satisfaction.

Another example: Shortly after buying my BMW 535i, the culmination of a childhood dream of one day owning an expensive car like my rich Uncle Jozsi in Europe, and a symbol that "I had now made it" like he had, I noticed that I got severe headaches as a result of driving it. How aggravating and unfair! I observed that I could drive any other car without pain. I couldn't figure it out. I experimented with many different types of seating options, thinking it might be posture-related. Nothing worked, and a direct physical cause didn't seem to make sense, since I would bring on a headache, lasting for hours, within even a five-minute drive to the convenience store.

In desperation, after a year of being perplexed, I advertised the car for sale in the local newspaper. It didn't sell, as a result of a recession in California in 1990. Then, one day, a curious idea popped into my head: to try a hypnosis session in the car (not while driving—I don't recommend that). Dr. Lehrer sat in the passenger seat and hypnotized me while I sat in the driver's seat. Within an hour I learned that my subconscious mind wouldn't allow me to enjoy driving *that* car as long as it carried the myths of the rich car of my uncle, and of the car that proved to my wife what a good provider I was. Dr. Lehrer suggested what seemed to me to be a preposterous idea: to name my car and form a relationship with it, so that I might really revel in it free of my baggage. On my way home a name came to me, "Terminator," perhaps a symbol of the end of my suffering about this issue. Terminator and I have zoomed to many places and have had a blast. And neither of us has gotten a speeding ticket or a headache in the five years since.

This occurrence, and dozens of similar instances involving a willingness to surrender what used to have meaning for me, have completely re-engineered my being. You can only begin to imagine the unparalleled health and unreasonable happiness that I now experience as a result of living much more in line with Gev's laws.

REFLECTIONS ON MY PASSAGE TO THE GLOBAL PROMISED LAND

While the heroic journey I undertook stretched me to the limits of my courage, once one gets into the path of a higher river of consciousness, much assistance comes one's way. Today I try to accept everything that happens to me, knowing that I will later see its perfect usefulness.

I can't emphasize enough the late mythologist Joseph Campbell's point about looking all around you for signposts along your journey. Whenever I contemplate the dozens of books I'm always intending to read, some messenger invariably appears that makes a compelling case for me to read one of them. It ends up being exactly the one that has what I need to grow further at that moment, or to complete a portion of my work.

One kind of help came in the form of a software program that uses the principle of *synchronicity* to tell fortunes. Originally, I laughed it off, until it repeatedly gave me the same reading, out of the hundreds possible. It told me that to cruise on an airplane at 500 miles per hour at 35,000 feet, one must grab "catnaps." I started to engage in two or three 10- to 20-minute meditative sessions each day, and not only reduced my sleep by one or two hours per night, but also now feel awake and vital all day long, on most days.

I reached one milestone when I finally grokked, months later, a statement that a total stranger had made to me while we sat in a sauna, that my friends and I had laughed about to no end at the time: "Everything is Yoga, and everyone's a mystic."

Dreams serve as another great source of inspiration. I was trying to leave a relationship with a woman during a trip to Maui, and had already visualized, during meditation, the word "Courage" rolling off an ocean wave, with the "C" in the curl of the wave, and the rest of the letters strewn across the water. At the same time the word "Surrender" kept popping into my head as missing from the Commandments (at that stage of their evolution). How to combine these two words eluded me. Finally one night I woke up from a dream and spoke the words: "Exercise *mature* SURRENDER and *unselfish* COURAGE." I don't believe that in a million years of waking hours I would have chosen the adjectives "mature" and "unselfish," without which the Commandment can be grossly and dangerously misinterpreted.

In another dream, I saw an elephant passing through a large ring and turning into a giraffe. After deciphering it, I felt euphoric when I realized that I had made it through the marriage and divorce, symbolized by the ring, with Yael, the "elephant," who likes to hang out with her tribe in Israel, and had rediscovered my inner child and my own happiness, symbolized by the transformation to a "giraffe." From that point on, I have ascribed to the philosophy of following one's bliss. In other words, every person's path should result in unreasonable happiness. It's a good universe we were born into, if we can but see things clearly.

The table on the following page gives a summary of survival-oriented myths of the male-based society in which I grew up, and which I have replaced in my belief system with truths of the heart, that serve me far better.

Changing our ways of being to use more functional roadmaps of understanding our behaviors and consciousness takes a lot of hard work. Habits die slowly. Our minds feel satisfied that we have survived using the old habits, regardless of how dysfunctional they may have made our existence.

During one of my many miraculous hypnosis sessions, my INNER VOICE predicted that I would embark on seven trips of three

Male Myths	**Truths of the Heart**
Work should be hard.	Work should be challenging but fun.
What matters is to be individually successful and make money.	Value service to the world and making it a better place for everyone.
Happiness, your own and others', may or may not result.	Don't do anything that doesn't make you happy and healthy.
The goal is to win at all costs—the ends do justify the means.	Immerse yourself in a process of learning and teaching while achieving goals.
"Just the facts, please"— feelings aren't important at all.	Feelings and facts combined result in making the wisest decisions.

weeks or longer away from my home in Santa Cruz, with about two to four months between trips. On the sixth sailing, at the Turtle Bay Hilton on the main island of Hawaii, I assembled the 2nd Ten Commandments from all that I had learned up to that time. The seventh journey, of forty days in Maui, Hawaii, my current home, gave me the inspiration to develop many of the other ideas for this work, an expression of a monumental phase of my inner work.

Subsequently, I visited the pyramids in Egypt and climbed Mount Sinai, to grok the first Ten Commandments' history. I then retreated to neutral ground, and wrote other parts on another mountain, in the Swiss Alps (which many Israelis joke that Moses should have chosen, instead of the deserts of Israel, for the Jews' Promised Land). The rest of the book evolved through meticulous and painstaking work over the next three years. Marc Lehrer helped me tremendously for the last two of those years, spending innumerable hours ensuring that everything holds together as much as possible and propels the reader toward wanting to adopt these principles into his or her life.

I now realize that over the last few years I have had to suffer the consequences—pain and its enslavement—whenever I violated a Commandment, and that I have enjoyed the rewards of freedom— creativity and joy—when I have adhered to them. Each situation I've faced has taught me exactly the right lesson, at the opportune time to provide yet another sentence or paragraph in this book. Much like a Jedi warrior in the movie *Star Wars*, I felt that I would be repeatedly tested until I completely grokked a lesson that I needed.

For example, my departure from Nakamichi, Inc., and its management, who had bought Mountain Computer, Inc., the "baby" I had nurtured with all my heart for almost seven years, was not amicable. I subsequently sued them, and reached a satisfactory settlement out of court two and a half years later. What an ordeal! I didn't need the money, or do it for that reason, but I now know why I put myself through it: I learned once and for all that one has nothing to fear if you just speak the truth and seek justice. Throughout depositions, threats, and many unpleasant legal proceedings, I found that I progressively got calmer because I was simply stating the truth. For my own peace of mind, I resolved that I would just tell the truth and leave the outcome up to Gev and the legal process. I used the settlement money to start a company called "Global Brain, Inc.," which published this book.

As another example, Gloria St. John, my first fabulous content editor, kept sending my description of Commandment No. 20 back as "unfinished." A reading group at Abbott Labs, Inc., also expressed a lot of concern about it. This feedback plagued me. In retrospect, I can see that I had not sufficiently learned the gist of the Commandment to do its explanation justice. Another relationship, with additional help from yet another meditation session, taught me the difference between "Do unto others as you would have done unto you," the original version of the Commandment, and interpreting this more deeply, so as to state it in terms more relevant to the modern-day, interdependent world of the Global Brain. Thus arose the current version.

I ventured into three trying but amazingly rewarding significant-other relationships in a four-year period, which taught me what perhaps only tens of thousands of dollars and years of therapy would have done. My two years with Debi re-connected me with my feelings and emotions, showed me FLOW and WHOLENESS, and forced me to practice SELF-ACCEPTANCE and SURRENDER-COURAGE. My year with Megan, who exemplified BALANCE, helped me re-enter the world, of business especially, and reconfirmed to me the importance of listening to one's INNER VOICE. Finally, my relationship with Olivia gave me an opportunity to cement my new-found values of using BOTTOM LINES, *win-win*/SYNERGY, and REPAIR, and therein she taught me faith and freedom and to love myself—and others—enough. I'm very grateful to all three of them. Each of us benefited greatly from our times together. How could it have been any better?

I'm now in a relationship in which I can be myself, do the things I want to do, and live by the 2nd Ten Commandments. Thank you, Pattie. I "sprove" (spiritual, romantic love) you.

I rewrote this section for the last time in my condominium in Maui, called Lokelani, the week I passed into Motofhood, 33 years, 3 months, and 3 days after I left my mother's womb. Probably no coincidence.

Since all inspiration comes from a single source of higher intelligence, I thank Gev for the gift and responsibility of having these 2nd Ten Commandments "transmitted through me." Thank you for reading my story and what I have learned. I hope you will learn, as I did, to harness the power in Gev to lead more successful lives—the 2nd Ten Commandments can lead the way.

POSTSCRIPT BY MARC LEHRER, PH.D.

My contribution to this incredible project has grown from the seeding of ideas of how to create change and ways of being whole in an ever-complexifying world, to the fruit grown as *The 2nd Ten Commandments*, which is meant to provide the necessary nourishment for even more seeding to occur. Only five years ago, at our first biofeedback session, I told Orion that he was starting to discover his spirituality. A polished executive in a suit and tie, he had a blank look on his face—a what-in-the-world-does-that-mean type of look— and he later told me that he almost didn't come for any more sessions after that. A mere year later, when he was already feeling much better, he told me that he thought he could write down the ten rules for life. I responded, only half-jokingly, "Given these issues we have been talking about for a while, and the power that they have for you, why don't you go to Mount Haleakala in Maui, and come back with the 2nd Ten Commandments." He did.

It has been a privilege to have had the opportunity to watch and to participate in the amazing process that has followed. Each Commandment came into being as a birth, through dreams, visions, and struggle, until it had grown and formed sufficiently, and could finally be stated and named.

There is power here, meant to be used wisely. My life has been immensely enriched. May yours be also.

ORION MOSHE KOPELMAN'S PERSONAL CONSTITUTION
Revision 6, May 29, 1995

1. INDIVIDUAL VALUES, GROWTH AND EVOLUTION:
Follow the 2nd Ten Commandments to an exemplary degree!

2. PERSONAL MISSION:
Act as a prophetic leader and as a spokesperson for raising consciousness and accelerating synergistic technological development, as humankind evolves upward from the Information to the Consciousness Age, thus forming the Global Brain. This will make use of the following unique combination of skills:

1) *Leader: Outrageous, self-confident, obsessed, big-picture integrator, wise, resourceful, courageous,* intense, determined, analytical, having good people skills, achiever, enthusiastic, producer, organizer and builder, visionary, innovator (not inventor), hilarious.

2) Broad knowledge of both technology and consciousness psychology.

3) International bent, can interact and communicate effectively with people from every developed country.

4) Strong technological salesperson, excellent speaker and writer.

3. PARTNER
Be committed, loyal, provide for as needed, passionate, and best friend. Always look to grow, learn, and improve status quo and build higher and higher levels of trust.

4. FAMILY

Make other members proud: be there for them if needed: be their best friend.

5. FRIENDS

Be loyal and fun to be with: listen well and give good advice. Be one who can be counted on, reliable.

6. COMMUNITY AT LARGE (INCLUDES WORK-PLACE, HOME TOWN, COUNTRY, WORLD)

Be seen as a person who follows the 2nd Ten Commandments, and who is consequently happy, achieving, effective, successful, healthy, and helpful. Be one who always finds a way to get things done, never gives up, is respected, likes to build, and is followed as a leader. Help the world selflessly, but not at the expense of my own health and needs, or those of my family and friends.

7. PLEASURE AND RELAXATION

Achieve balance in life: attach equal importance to physical, mental, spiritual, and social health. Especially enjoy sports, both as a participant and as a spectator.

APPENDIX B

RELIGIONS OF THE WORLD

Principal World Religions	World Membership (millions)
1. Christianity	1,870
2. Islam	1014
3. No affiliation	913
4. Hinduism	751
5. Buddhism	334
6. Atheism	242
7. Chinese folk religion	141
8. New religions	124
9. Tribal religions	100
10. Sikhism	20
11. Judaism	18
12. Shamanism	11
13. Confucianism	6
14. Baha'i	6
15. Jainism	4
16. Shintoism	3
17. Other religions	19
Total Population	5,576

Source: 1994 *Encyclopedia Britannica Book of the Year.*

APPENDIX C

RECOMMENDED READING

Peter Russell, *The Global Brain Awakens: Our Next Evolutionary Leap*, Global Brain, Inc., 1995. Foundation for the paradigm used for many of this book's ideas. Top-notch, scientifically oriented approach to consciousness.

Ken Keyes, Jr., *Your Life Is a Gift, So Make the Most of It*, Love Line Books, 1987. A very short, cartoon book which serves as an excellent primer on personal growth. Written by the founder of the "Science of Happiness," who has over 5 million books in print internationally. Who says we have to suffer?

Stephen R. Covey, *The 7 Habits of Highly Effective People, Powerful Lessons in Personal Change,* Fireside, 1990. Great book for successfully managing one's personal life and career, while also getting along with people, and living with fairness, integrity, honesty, and human dignity.

Don Richard Riso, *Discovering Your Personality Type: The NEW Enneagram Questionnaire*, Houghton Mifflin, 1995. The best general introduction to the Enneagram, featuring the most reliable test, which will reveal to you a lot about yourself that you may be blind to.

Key Keyes, Jr., *Handbook to Higher Consciousness*, Love Line Books, 1975. Excellent tools and methods for understanding our individual evolution from cave-person days to now. Million-copy bestseller.

Harville Hendrix, Ph.D., *Getting the Love You Want: The Guide for Couples*, First Perennial Library, 1990. Great book on romantic relationships and how they are meant to help us grow and develop.

Gary Zukav, *The Seat of the Soul,* Simon and Schuster, 1990. An eloquent, at times poetic, treatise on understanding the truths of the spiritual world.

M. Scott Peck, *The Road Less Traveled: A New Psychology of Love, Traditional Values and Spiritual Growth,* Touchstone, 1978. The classic (over 5 million sold!) on how to get onto a path of no return toward self-actualization.

John K. Pollard, III, *Self-Parenting: The Complete Guide to Your Inner Conversations,* Generic Human Studies Publishing, 1987. A practical guide to integrating the different parts of your personality, specifically your "inner child."

Louise Hay, *You Can Heal Your Life,* Hay House, 1987. Find out how you can cure almost any persisting physical problem by linking it with an emotional cause!

Renee Baron and Elizabeth Wagele, *The Enneagram Made Easy: Discover the 9 Types of People,* HarperSanFrancisco, 1994. Easy, fun, and humorous—lots of cartoons—but useful. One person said about it, "I wish I would have known all that about myself ten years ago."

Robert Muller, *New Genesis: Shaping a Global Spirituality,* World Happiness and Cooperation, P.O. Box 1153, Anacortes, WA 98221, USA, 1982. Available through the United Nations bookstore, by calling 1-800-553-3210. Written by the "UN's prophet of hope" who served for 40 years at the UN and was Assistant Secretary-General.

FURTHER READING SUGGESTIONS, LISTED ALPHABETICALLY:

John Bradshaw, *Bradshaw On: The Family: A Revolutionary Way of Self-Discovery,* Health Communications, Inc., 1988. How to understand and fix the dysfunctional baggage we've got. Select this or any of Bradshaw's later books.

Mihaly Csikszentmihalyi, *Flow: The Psychology of Optimal Experience,* Harper Perennial, 1990. A whole book on Commandment No. 11. It goes hand in hand with living a balanced life, by showing what state of mind to experience time in for maximum enjoyment. Why bother living otherwise.

Richard E. Cytowic, M.D., *The Man Who Tasted Shapes: A Bizarre Medical Mystery Offers Revolutionary Insights into Emotions, Reasoning, and Consciousness*, Warner Books, 1993. The title says it all, almost. An excellent discussion of the biology of the brain and how it affects our ways of being.

John Gray, *Men are from Mars, Women are from Venus*, 1992. A bestseller on relationships.

Willis Harman, Ph.D., *Global Mind Change, The New Age Revolution in the Way We Think*, Warner Books, 1988. Solid analysis of consciousness and science merging to synergize a new science.

Robert A. Heinlein, *Stranger in a Strange Land*, Berkeley Books, 1961. Dubbed as "the most famous science fiction novel ever written," it seems amazingly close to an emerging reality.

Gerald G. Jampolsky, M.D., *Love Is Letting Go of Fear*, Bantam Books, 1981. Simple, yet true. A very short book that can transform people.

Barry Katz, *Technology and Culture: A Historical Romance*, Stanford Alumni Association, 1990. Does an excellent job of putting the experiment of civilization in longer-term perspective. Fun to read, too.

Ken Keyes, Jr., *The Power of Unconditional Love: 21 Guidelines for Beginning, Improving, and Changing Your Most Meaningful Relationships*, Love Line Books, 1985. All your important relationships can work. This shows how.

Abraham Maslow, *Toward a Psychology of Being*, D. Van Nostrand Inc., 1962. The original on self-actualization theory and satisfying physical and psychological needs at higher and higher levels.

Dan Millman, *Way of the Peaceful Warrior: A Book that Changes Lives*, H.J. Kramer, Inc., 1980. More on getting onto a different, more rewarding path.

Melvin Morse, M.D., *Closer to the Light, Learning from the Near-Death Experiences of Children*, Ballantine Books, 1990. Amazing. Provides insight into the bigger picture of life.

Helen Palmer, *The Enneagram in Love and Work: Understanding Your Intimate and Business Relationships*, HarperSanFrancisco, 1995. Fascinating discussion of the dynamics between types.

Ayn Rand, *The Virtue of Selfishness*, Signet New American Library, 1961. Often misunderstood, nonetheless one of the originals on individual wholeness, consciousness, and goals as prerequisites for synergy with societal goals.

Peter Russell, *The White Hole in Time, Our Future Evolution and the Meaning of Now*, HarperSanFrancisco, 1992. A dazzling and innovative picture of humanity, that integrates evolutionary perspective and a startling vision of what the future means to the living in today's eternal present.

Marsha Sinetar, *Do What You Love, the Money Will Follow: Discovering Your Right Livelihood*, Paulist Press, 1987. Shows how to self-actualize through a spiritual yet practical approach to following your heart and making a living.

Adin Steinsaltz, *The Thirteen Petalled Rose*, translated by Yehuda Hanegbi, Basic Books, 1980. A discourse on the essence of mystic Jewish existence and belief. A great summary of the spiritual world and humans' place in it.

Alvin Tofler, *Future Shock*, Bantam Books, 1970. A classic original on the hypnotic society and the racing pace of evolution. At the time "far out," now seems obvious. Look for other books by Tofler, perhaps the leading prophet of change alive today.

Connie Zweig and Jeremiah Abrams, *Meeting the Shadow, The Hidden Power of the Dark Side of Human Nature*, Jeremy P. Tarcher, Inc., 1991. Read and understand this about your self before taking on causes like saving the world. Save yourself first!

ACKNOWLEDGMENTS

First and foremost I'm indebted to my parents, Raoul and Chava Kopelman, who not only brought me into this world, but also gave me everything I needed to succeed on my path. My mother's incredible love, idealism, zest for fun, and spirituality were coupled with my father's wisdom and career success as a professor of physical chemistry. I had a unique crucible to grow up in, and it took lots of growth work on my part to realize how perfect for me—even with our home's imperfections—my parents really were.

I can never return enough love to the rest of my family—brother Leeron, sister Shirli, aunt Franzi Alt, and ex-wife Yael—especially for their undying support and encouragement during a difficult five-year transition period of my life. I'll never forget it, and I hope I can give enough back.

I am infinitely grateful to Dr. Marc Lehrer for leading me on my healing journey. Time and again I marvel about our miraculous biofeedback/hypnosis sessions. He also put me in touch with my spirituality and encouraged this writing. As a co-author, one could not ask for a more cooperative, wise, helpful, and knowledgeable authority on the fields of psychology and spirituality. Or for a bigger believer in this work as a mission.

My best friend of over 25 years, Mark Lorentzen, not only introduced me to personal growth, but also philosophically led me step by step through much of my thinking. I love you, Mark, and hope we'll remain best friends for life.

I'm indebted to Dr. Svetlana Keyser for almost five years of alternative treatments, and to Marcia Margolin for Feldenkrais sessions. Ken Keyes, Jr., had a tremendous influence on my philosophy of life and on my healing. So did Art and Rainya Dann, who brought lots of light into my life.

Patricia Watson and Maury Swan made the beginning of this writing project in Maui both fun and significant. Patricia has also been a great source of inspiration, UNCONDITIONAL LOVE, fun, learning, and support for my growth, as a *mission-mate* and *soul-sister*.

I'm very grateful to many friends who helped me along my journey, stuck with me through trying times, and supported this work. They include: Megan Beachler, Debi Mack, Harris Moku, Kerim Khayat, Konrad Knell, Dave Levy, and Olivia Stevens—inventor of the word "Gevolution." Lou Silver, my attorney, renewed my hope that a just and fair world is actually possible.

Earlier in my adult life I was fortunate to have truly great mentors and role models who enabled me to accelerate my learning and accomplishments. These five incredibly wise and successful men are: my late uncle, Jozsi Alt; my two Stanford University advisors, Dr. Robert Cannon and Dr. Marty Hellman; and two executives I worked for at Mountain Computer, Inc., Bill Bollinger and Jim Sedin. I consider myself very lucky indeed for all their influences on me.

Peter Russell provided the foundation for many of the ideas in this book. Reading his book, *The Global Brain*, not only changed my life, but allowed me to find my life's meaning. Peter has a brilliant mind, lots of integrity, and a most peaceful, witty, and pleasant demeanor. I consider it an honor to be associated with him as his publisher (in 1995 of *The Global Brain Awakens)* and friend.

Many other people helped with the motivation for this book. I owe great thanks to Ron Kmetowicz for giving me the final jumpstart I needed to actually write and publish. Further motivation and research material came abundantly from the Foundation for Global

Community, including its co-founder, Amelia Rathbun, her son, Richard Rathbun, and Karen Harwell, Joe Krese, and Jackie Mathes. The late astrologer Robert Cole also gave me much insight into my mission.

Many people helped with the project of writing this book, and I consider them part of Global Brain, Inc.'s (the publisher of the book) extended family. My first content editor, Gloria St. John, not only provided excellent comments, but also served as an intellectual provocateur to make sure my ideas were well developed. Nancy Capelle did a superb job of copy editing, not only drastically improving the quality of the writing, but also catching many finer points that most people would have missed. Ellen Roddick gave useful advice on how to broaden the book's appeal. Joel Friedlander corrected logical inconsistencies and removed obstacles that could have kept readers from grokking the material.

Danielle LaPorte and Patti Rice have been like right-hand assistants, doing whatever was required for the mission, often making above-and-beyond efforts when it was necessary. Borrowing from the TV series *Star Trek*, I call them "Number One" and "Number One-and-a-half," and we always joke that we're not sure which is higher up in the chain of command. Ray Solnik wrote a superb, thorough, five-year business plan for Global Brain, Inc., and has helped define the mission and suggest solid strategies and tactics to execute it.

Dan Poynter lent his incredible expertise in many facets of the project as a valued member of Global Brain™'s Board of Directors. His book, *The Self-Publishing Manual,* provided invaluable insight into how to actually pull off this venture.

Many reviewers contributed a myriad of suggestions, from many different points of view. It all counted. I would like to thank a reading group at Abbott Labs, Inc., which included Michael Kropft and Bonnie Setzer; and also Barry Katz, Barbara Such, and Gary Zukav.

We received chapter reviews from Yogi Bhajan, Dr. Mihaly Csikszentmihalyi, Dr. Richard E. Cytowic, Willis Harman, Barbara Marx Hubbard, Terence McKenna, and Peter Russell, which helped us make sure we were pointing to the right information. Several people reread the entire manuscript prior to our last marathon editing sessions on Maui, which helped us make some final decisions. My sister Shirli Kopelman proved incredibly helpful with her numerous margin comments and suggestions for the clarification of a number of issues. Konrad Knell was instrumental in persuading us to add "what you can't live with and can't live without" to Commandment No. 18. We also thank Robert Ludlow, Sylvia Previtali, and Don Wright for their supportive and useful dialogues and written comments. A special recognition goes to Pattie Gall and Sheri Short for helping not only with their minds, but also with their hearts.

And finally, I thank Gev and the universe for the fortunate opportunities afforded me in my life, including this writing; and for what I now see to be our worlds of perfect creation of mind and matter.

GLOSSARY

Appropriate *Technology.* Technology developed for accelerating the formation of the Global Brain. It includes freeing us from survival-oriented concerns, and subsequently liberating us to engage in learning, personal-growth, and pleasure activities.

Boundaries. Psychological semipermeable membranes, limits that you set and use to define and communicate the terms under which you will or will not participate with others.

Consciousness. Knowing what we're all about individually and collectively.

Consciousness Age. An era in which personal-growth, learning, and pleasurable enjoyment supplant individual survival as the primary reason for existence.

Gaia. The living organism Mother Earth, including all of its geophysical components and life forms.

Gev. Global EVolution's intelligent life-force purposefully propelling all matter and energy forward.

Gevolution. The process now occurring which will effect a transition from the current, survival-oriented world to the new Consciousness Age. A peaceful, nonviolent form of revolution, that will result in Motofs creating Lokelani and functioning as the Global Brain.

Global Brain. A superorganism consisting of all the people on Earth, functioning as a *noosphere*, or single, inter-thinking group consciousness, and Gaia's nervous and control system.

Global Spirituality. A supra-religion that provides a common ground for all inhabitants of planet Earth to participate in and become a part of the Global Brain.

Grok. The simultaneous comprehension of fully knowing with the head or rational brain, feeling with the heart, and clearly and completely experiencing through all our senses and physical instincts. Really "getting it," not just intellectually knowing it. Coined by Robert Heinlein in his classic science fiction book of the 1960s, *Stranger in a Strange Land.*

Ikorgant. Having knowledge without yet grokking.

Lev. UNCONDITIONAL LOVE. The unconditional emotional acceptance of all humankind, ourselves included, as part of the same whole. The Greeks called this *agape.* Appropriately based on the Hebrew word for heart, *lev,* it is a feeling of acceptance, caring, compassion, and warmth toward all our fellow human beings. It is the most pure form of love.

Lokelani. Heaven-on-Earth. From Hawaiian, meaning "heavenly rose." A state of mind of living to play and enjoy life to the utmost right here and now, while learning and growing.

Meme. A self-replicating thought pattern that competes selfishly for available mental resources. Similar to *gene,* which is a self-replicating molecular pattern which competes selfishly for available physical or materials resources.

Motof. Member Of the Tribe Of the Future. A conscious human who chooses to live by the principles of the 2nd Ten Commandments—whether named such or not—and thereby participates in evolution's creation of a Global Brain in the Consciousness Age.

Psychospiritual Personality Typing (PSPT). A method of describing and evaluating basic personality types, with a continuum of subtypes, aspiring to encompass the spectrum of humanity. Based on psychological personality models, and spiritual teachings of individual "gifts" and "sins."

Soul or *Spirit.* The higher consciousness that transcends our animal nature and bodies, is eternal in some way, and is connected to Gev.

Spirituality. Being able to discern in each moment the enduring from the ephemeral or fleeting, and aligning with the lasting rather than the temporary.

Spiritual Faith. An unprovable belief in the "perfection" of all things—that everything happens for a reason, often unknown to us, and is exactly as it's supposed to be.

Spiritual Principles. Fundamental underlying laws that govern human nature, that we can use our free will to choose to follow.

Success. Exercising our free will to choose to spiritually evolve toward higher consciousness and eventually enlightenment, by increasingly following spiritual principles.

Supra-religion. A set of spiritual beliefs and practices that encompasses, and allows continuing practice of, all others, so that all citizens of the planet can participate in it.

Win-win. Strategies for how to interact with others in a way that is mutually satisfactory—no one loses and everyone gains.

NOTES AND REFERENCES

PART I: EVOLUTION TO A GLOBAL BRAIN AND THE
      CONSCIOUSNESS AGE

1. An Invitation to the Global Promised Land

1. "Timeline," Issue No. 4, July/August 1992, bimonthly publication of the Foundation for Global Community, 222 High Street, Palo Alto, California, 94301, p. 9.
2. I finally now understand why my little brother Leeron Kopelman has been repeating this phrase for as long as I can remember. Thank you.
3. I'm indebted to Mark Lorentzen, my best friend of 25 years, for a conversation we had that led to the emergence of the prison or playground concept. The "Earth school" term came from Gary Zukav, *The Seat of the Soul*, Simon and Schuster, 1990.
4. Richard E. Cytowic, M.D., *The Man Who Tasted Shapes: A Bizarre Medical Mystery Offers Revolutionary Insights into Emotions, Reasoning, and Consciousness*, Warner Books, 1993, p. 207.

2. Your Flight Plan Summary

3. The Map for Success as a Motof

1. Peter F. Drucker, "The New Society of Organizations," in *Harvard Business Review*, September-October, 1992, p. 100.
2. Stephen R. Covey, *The 7 Habits of Highly Effective People, Powerful Lessons in Personal Change,* Fireside, 1990, p. 49.
3. Ed. Jack Canfield, Mark Victor Hansen, *Chicken Soup for the Soul*, Health Communications, Inc., pp. 55–58, 1993. Many thanks to Art and Rainya Dann for providing the source. Adapted from a story by Terry Dobson, "Another Way."

4. From Moses to Motofs: From Slavery to Freedom

1. Encyclopedia Judaica and King James Bible. Notice that the correct interpretation from Hebrew of the Sixth Commandment is "Thou shall not murder," rather than " Thou shall not kill."
2. Hobbes, 16th-century English philosopher. Burns, Lerner, Meacham, *Western Civilizations*, W.W. Norton & Company, Inc., 9th ed., 1980.
3. David Daiches, *Moses*, Weidenfeld and Nicolson Ltd, 1975, p. 235.
4. Yogi Bhajan (Siri Singh Sahib), lecture notes "The Ten Commandments and Ten Promises," August 6, 1991, graciously given to the authors by Yogi Bhajan, in Beverly Hills, California, on January 14, 1993.

5. The idea came from Stuart Wilde, "*Thirty-Three Steps Beyond The Earth Plane*," an eight-tape audio series, White Dove International, Inc., 1985.
6. Cytowic, *The Man Who Tasted Shapes*, pp. 19–22.
7. Cytowic, *The Man Who Tasted Shapes*, p. 191.
8. Covey, *The 7 Habits of Highly Effective People*, p. 52.
9. Covey, *The 7 Habits of Highly Effective People*, p. 33.

5. The Impact of Accelerating Change
1. Alvin Tofler, *Future Shock*, Bantam Books, 1970, p. 9.
2. Erik H. Erikson (ed.), *The Challenge of Youth*, Anchor Books, 1963, p. 197.
3. Tofler, *Future Shock*, Chapter 1.
4. Pamphlet "The S-Shaped Curve: Emerging Values in a New Reality," 1990, Beyond War (now Foundation for Global Community), 222 High Street, Palo Alto, California, 94301.
5. Ibid.
6. From the TV show *Star Trek*.
7. *The World Almanac and Book of Facts 1995*, Funk & Wagnalls Corporation, 1995.
8. Sources for data in the table: Georges Anderla, Organization for Economic Cooperation and Development, 1973; from Peter Russell's *The White Hole In Time: Our Future Evolution and the Meaning of Now*, HarperSanFrancisco, 1992, p. 28, quoted in *Prometheus Rising* and elsewhere by Robert Anton Wilson. Also French astrophysicist Dr. Jacques Vallee, and mathematical extrapolation.
9. Russell, *The White Hole in Time*. This date is derived from a mathematical model in which an infinite number of turns converge to a finite length, using the Taylor series addition of terms: $1 + 1/2 + 1/4 + 1/8 + 1/16 + \ldots$
10. Russell, *The White Hole in Time*.
11. From a source at the Foundation for Global Community, Palo Alto, California.
12. Joseph Williams and Jon D. Clark, *The Information Explosion: Fact or Myth?*, in *"IEEE Transactions on Engineering Management, Vol. 39, No. 1, February 1992."*
13. International Civil Aviation Organization, in *"USA Today"* newspaper, January 1993.
14. "San Francisco Chronicle," 8/11/93, "NASA Getting Closer to Earth."
15. "New US spy plane 'can fly at Mach-8'," in *"International Herald Tribune"* newspaper, December 1992. Articles used *"Jane's Defense Weekly"* as source.
16. *The 1993 Information Please Almanac Access to Facts*, Houghton Mifflin Company, 1992.
17. *US News and World Report*, July 26, 1993.
18. Rene Van De Carr and Marc Lehrer, *The Prenatal Classroom*, Humanics Press, 1992.
19. "Spinal injuries due to leading with head, according to doctor," "International Herald Tribune," December 1992, p. 10.

6. Humanity and Technology Form the Global Brain

1. Peter Russell, *The Global Brain Awakens, Our Next Evolutionary Leap*, Global Brain, Inc., 1995.
2. *The International Thesaurus of Quotations*, Rhoda Thomas Tripp, ed., Harper & Row, 1970.
3. James E. Lovelock, *Gaia: A New Look at Life on Earth*, Oxford University Press, 1979. Pioneer in this new concept. Seemed ridiculous at the time, but now almost obvious.
4. Russell, *The Global Brain Awakens,* p. 60.
5. Russell, *The Global Brain Awakens,* pp. 61-62.
6. Russell, *The Global Brain Awakens,* p. 145.
7. Russell, *The Global Brain Awakens,* p.147.
8. Russell, *The Global Brain Awakens,* p. 92.
9. Russell, *The Global Brain Awakens,* p. 143.
10. Russell, *The Global Brain Awakens,* p. 149.
11. Russell, *The Global Brain Awakens,* p. 210.
12. Marvin L. Patterson, *Accelerating Innovation*, Van Nostrand Reinhold, 1993, p. 55.
13. Russell, *The Global Brain Awakens,* p. 57.
14. Elliot Miller, *A Crash Course on the New Age Movement: Describing an Evolving and Growing Social Force*, Baker Book House, 1989, p. 100.

7.Does 2012 A.D. Equal 0 G.B. (Global Brain)?

1. *The International Thesaurus of Quotations*, 296-18, p. 187.
2. Peter Russell, *The Global Brain Awakens,* on front cover.
3. Sylvanus G. Morley, George W. Brainerd, Robert J. Sharer, *The Ancient Maya*, Stanford, 4 ed., 1983, pp. 548–563, 595–603.
4. McKenna is quoted in Russell, *The White Hole in Time.*
5. Sociologists at U.C. Santa Barbara, "*The Quest for a New Age,*" Marilyn Ferguson, in the "Los Angeles Times/Book Review," Feb. 16, 1992.
6. Russell, *The Global Brain Awakens,* p. 239-240.

8. Gev: An Updated, Universal Concept of God

1. *The International Thesaurus of Quotations*, 844-1, p. 564.
2. *The International Thesaurus of Quotations*, 385-8, p. 248.
3. M. Scott Peck, *The Road Less Traveled: A New Psychology of Love, Traditional Values and Spiritual Growth*, Touchstone, 1978.
4. Robert K. Barnhart, ed., *The Barnhart Dictionary of Etymology*, The HW Wilson Co., 1988, p. 440.
5. David Daiches, *Moses*, pp. 49, 103.
6. Barry M. Katz, *Technology and Culture: A Historical Romance*, Stanford Alumni Association, 1990, p. 85.
7. *The International Thesaurus of Quotations*, 844-12, p. 564.
8. *The International Thesaurus of Quotations*, 844-7, p. 564.

9. Willis Harman, "Reconciling Science and Metaphysics: The Union Whose Time Has Come," Institute of Noetic Sciences, Sausalito, California, January 1991, p. 9.

10. Willis Harman, Ph.D., *Global Mind Change, The New Age Revolution in the Way We Think*, Warner Books, 1988. Solid analysis of consciousness and science merging to synergize a new science.

9. Global Spirituality Creates a Heaven-on-Earth

1. *The International Thesaurus of Quotations*, 844-4, p. 564.

2. Dean Halverson, "Transformation Celebration," SCP Magazine, Jan. 1984, p. 4.

3. My sister Shirli Kopelman clarified these concepts for me in conversations.

4. *Reincarnation Anthology*, ed. Joseph Head and S. L. Cranston (New York: Julian Press, Inc.), quoted in Joseph Gaer, *What the Great Religions Believe*, Signet, 1963, p. 28.

5. Gaer, *What the Great Religions Believe*, p. 23.

6. Zukav, *The Seat of the Soul*, p. 127-131.

7. Zukav, *The Seat of the Soul*, p. 131.

8. Abraham Maslow, *Toward a Psychology of Being*, D. Van Nostrand Inc., 1962.

9. Harville Hendrix, Ph.D., *Getting The Love You Want: The Guide for Couples*, Harper Perennial, 1988.

10. Aldous Huxley, *The Perennial Philosophy*, Harper Brothers, 1945.

10. The Rewards of Truth and Freedom

1. *The International Thesaurus of Quotations*, 361-25, p. 230, from introduction to *Philosophy of History* (1832), tr. John Sibree.

2. Reprinted with permission from *The Power of Unconditional Love: 21 Guidelines for Beginning, Improving, and Changing Your Most Meaningful Relationships*, by Ken Keyes, Jr., copyright 1990 by Love Line Books, p. 45.

PART II: THE COMMANDMENTS

11. Commandment No. 11: FLOW

1. Friedrich Nietzsche, *Beyond Good and Evil*, translated by Kaufman, Walter, Vintage Books, 1966 (original in 1886), p. 83.

2. Mihaly Csikszentmihalyi, *Flow: The Psychology of Optimal Experience,* Harper Perennial, 1990, p. 20.

3. Dan Millman, *Way of the Peaceful Warrior: A Book that Changes Lives*, H.J. Kramer, Inc., 1980, p. 151.

4. Csikszentmihalyi, *Flow*, p. 24.

12. Commandment No. 12: WHOLENESS

1. Thank you Michael Kropft for providing this quote.

2. *The International Thesaurus of Quotations*, 677-13, p. 464.

3. Connie Zweig and Jeremiah Abrams, *Meeting the Shadow, The Hidden Power of the Dark Side of Human Nature*, Jeremy P. Tarcher, Inc., 1991, p. 12.

4. Zweig, *Meeting the Shadow*, p. 3.

5. Zweig, *Meeting the Shadow*, p. 4.
6. A. H. Maslow, *The Farther Reaches of Human Nature*, Penguin Group, 1971, p. 49.
7. Also: Martin Buber, *On Judaism*, Schocken Books, 1967. The purpose of life as transformation from dualism to individual and humanitarian unity ("einheit").
8. Also: Louise Hay, *You Can Heal Your Life*, Hay House, 1987.

13. Commandment No. 13: SELF-ACCEPTANCE
1. Thank you Michael Kropft for providing this quote.
2. *The International Thesaurus of Quotations*, 870-16, p. 579.
3. Francine Klagsbrun, *Voices of Wisdom, Jewish Ideals & Ethics for Everyday Living*, Nonpareil Books, 1990, p. 5.

14. Commandment No. 14: BALANCE
1. *The International Thesaurus of Quotations*, 711-4, p. 491.
2. *The International Thesaurus of Quotations*, 742-2, p. 513.
3. Covey, *The 7 Habits*, pp. 145-182.
4. Covey, *The 7 Habits*, p. 146.
5. Covey, *The 7 Habits*, p. 149.
6. Burns, Lerner, Meacham, *Western Civilizations*, W.W. Norton & Company, Inc., 9th ed., 1980, p. 131.
7. Burns, *Western Civilizations*, p. 131.
8. Covey, *The 7 Habits*, p. 71.
9. Don Richard Riso, *Personality Types: Using the Enneagram for Self-Discovery*, Houghton Mifflin Company, 1987, p. 5.
10. Solomon Schimmel, *The Seven Deadly Sins: Jewish, Christian, and Classical Reflections on Human Nature*, Free Books, 1992.
11. Adin Steinsaltz, *The Thirteen Petalled Rose*, translated by Yehuda Hanegbi, Basic Books, 1980, pp. 62-63.
12. Riso, *Personality Types*, pp. 321–343.
13. Don Richard Riso, *Discovering Your Personality Type: The New Enneagram Questionnaire*, Houghton Mifflin Company, 1995.
14. Riso, *Personality Types*, pp. 218–219.

15. Commandment No. 15: INNER VOICE-MISSION
1. Thank you Danielle LaPorte for providing this quote.
2. *The International Thesaurus of Quotations*.
3. Aldous Huxley, *The Perennial Philosophy*.
4. Peggy Anderson, *Great Quotes from Great Leaders*, Celebrating Excellence Publishing, 1990.
5. For some ideas refer to the catalog "Tools For Exploration," San Rafael, CA, 1-800-456-9887.
6. Ken Keyes, Jr., *The Power of Unconditional Love: 21 Guidelines for Beginning, Improving, and Changing Your Most Meaningful Relationships*, p. 78.
7. Victor Frankl, *The Will to Meaning*, A Meridian Book, 1970.

8. Anderson, *Great Quotes*, p. 51.
9. Campbell, *The Hero's Journey*, HarperSanFrancisco, 1990, p. 214.
10. From a videotape by Anthony DeMello, a twentieth-century minister.
11. Yogi Bhajan (Siri Singh Sahib), lecture notes "The Ten Commandments and Ten Promises."

16. **Commandment No. 16:** SURRENDER-COURAGE
   1. *The International Thesaurus of Quotations*, 239-19, p. 152.
   2. Alcoholics Anonymous World Services, Inc.
   3. Anderson, *Great Quotes From Great Leaders*.
   4. "I Can Surrender," "*Living Love Songs*," Live Love Publications, 790 Commercial Ave., Coos Bay, Oregon 97420, p. 97.

17. **Commandment No. 17:** UNCONDITIONAL LOVE
   1. *The International Thesaurus of Quotations*, 282-34, p. 178.
   2. *The International Thesaurus of Quotations*, 548-236, p. 373.
   3. Keyes, *The Power of Unconditional Love*.
   4. Paraphrased from a lecture on videotape by the late minister Anthony DeMello.
   5. Franklin D. Roosevelt, President of the United States, 1932-1945.
   6. Also: Ken Keyes, Jr., *Handbook to Higher Consciousness*, Love Line Books, 1975.

18. **Commandment No. 18:** BOTTOM LINES
   1. *The International Thesaurus of Quotations*, 787-1, p. 535.
   2. Harville Hendrix, Ph.D., *Getting the Love You Want*, pp. 35-46.
   3. Keyes, *Handbook to Higher Consciousness*, p. 39.

19. **Commandment No. 19:** SYNERGY
   1. *The International Thesaurus of Quotations*, 187-4, p. 114.
   2. Russell, *The Global Brain Awakens*, p. 147.
   3. Covey, *The 7 Habits*.
   4. Roger Fisher and William Ury with Bruce Patton, ed., *Getting to Yes: Negotiating Agreement Without Giving In*, Penguin Books, 1983.
   5. Also: Covey, *The 7 Habits,* 4th and 5th habits: win-win and synergy, pp. 204-234, 261-284.

20. **Commandment No. 20:** REPAIR
   1. *The International Thesaurus of Quotations*, 225-40, p. 143.
   2. Barbara Marx Hubbard, *The Revelation: Our Crisis is a Birth*, Foundation For Conscious Evolution, 1993.
   3. Ayn Rand, *The Virtue of Selfishness*, Signet New American Library, 1961.
   4. Steinsaltz, *The Thirteen Petalled Rose*, pp. 62-63.
   5. Seneca clan mother Hazel Dean-John.
   6. "Timeline," July/August, 1994, p. 12.
   7. Said by a wise man and quoted by the Simon Wiesenthal Center's letter of Robert Clary, a holocaust survivor.

PART III: GETTING ON THE PATH TO THE GLOBAL
PROMISED LAND

21. Accepting the Responsibility of Being a Motof

1. Thank you Danielle LaPorte for providing this quote.
2. Thank you Danielle LaPorte for providing this quote.
3. Anderson, *Great Quotes from Great Leaders,* pp. 2-3.
4. Beyond War (now the Foundation for Global Community), 222 High Street, Palo Alto, California, 94301, published a book called *Breakthrough: Emerging New Thinking* which was co-edited by United States Professor Martin Hellman and past Soviet Foreign Minister Gromyko. The Soviet Union's top scientists upon reading it became convinced that a nuclear holocaust between the two superpowers loomed inevitable. As a result, ex-Prime Minister Gorbachev decided to bring the Cold War to an end.
5. Foundation for Global Community, 222 High Street, Palo Alto, California, 94301.
6. Millman, *Way of the Peaceful Warrior,* pp. 37, 133.
7. Don Richard Riso, *Understanding the Enneagram: The Practical Guide to Personality Types,* Houghton Mifflin Company, 1990, p. 3.
8. Millman, *Way of the Peaceful Warrior,* p. 63.
9. Russell, *The White Hole In Time.*
10. Zukav, *The Seat of the Soul,* p. 137.
11. Joseph Campbell, *The Hero with 1000 Faces, Vol. I, The Adventure of the Hero,* on audiotape, Audio Renaissance Tapes, Inc., 1981.
12. "University of California at Berkeley Wellness Letter," Vol. 10, Issue 3, December 1993, p.1.

22. Nine Great Ideas for Becoming a Motof

1. Anderson, *Great Quotes from Great Leaders.*
2. Anderson, *Great Quotes from Great Leaders.*
3. Foundation for Inner Peace, *A Course in Miracles,* Foundation for Inner Peace, 1975, 2nd edition.
4. Riso, *Personality Types,* p. 30.
5. Norman Katz, Ph.D., and Marc Lehrer, Ph.D., Esalen Institute, "Living Hypnotically" Programs, 1984-1991.
6. Covey Leadership Center, P.O. Box 19008, Provo, UT 84605-9925, tel. (800) 553-8889, provides an excellent weekly worksheet and planner to do this, and even further to schedule each individual day (not everyone finds the daily part useful). You can also find a similar version of this in Covey's book *The 7 Habits.*

23. Motofs: The Adapters Survive and Succeed

1. Alvin Tofler, *Future Shock,* p. 35.
2. Everett M. Rogers, *Diffusion of Innovations,* The Free Press, 1983.
3. Stephen W. Hawking, *"A Brief History Of Time,"* Volume I of audiotape, Dove Books on Tape Inc., 1988.

4. *Investors Business Daily*, 7/21/93.
5. CNN Headline News, 10/21/93.
6. "Machinery Strikes Fear," *San Francisco Examiner*, 8/8/93, p. E-16.
7. "Just Say Yes," *San Francisco Chronicle*, 11/21/93, quoting a Family Circle poll.
8. Robert A. Heinlein, *Stranger in a Strange Land*, Berkeley Books, 1961.
9. Francis Bacon, 17th-century English philosopher.
10. Pamphlet "The S-Shaped Curve."
11. Covey, *The 7 Habits*, pp. 81-90.
12. "Maui Man" CD and cassette by Patricia Watson and Spiritual Warrior. Available from Global Brain, Inc., at 555 Bryant St., #369, Palo Alto, CA 94301-1704, tel. 1-800-U-GO-GLOBAL.
13. Ken Carey, *The Third Millennium: Living in the Posthistoric World*, HarperSanFrancisco, 1995, p. 7.
14. Universal Star Alliance Foundation, *Declaration for Universal Alliance through Sharing our Highest Common Ideals*, April 23, 1993. You can get one by calling 1-800-DECLARE! or 510/540-8887, or writing to P.O. Box 2856, San Francisco, CA 94126, or 2375 Shattuck Avenue, Berkeley, CA 94704.
15. Millman, *Way of the Peaceful Warrior*, p. 211.

24. One Is All, and All Are One

1. Laurel Murphy, "One Is All, and All Are One," *Maui News*, p. C-1, 10/24/93.
2. Janina Lamb, On a postcard, Lamb and Lion Studio, Box 298, Tamworth, NH 03886.
3. Foundation for Inner Peace, *A Course in Miracles*, p. 483.
4. Chart developed by the World Game Institute for the World Game Workshop, 1995. For more information: WGI, 3215 Race Street, Philadelphia, PA 19104.
5. George Smoot and Keay Davidson, *Wrinkles in Time*, William Morrow and Company, Inc., 1993.
6. Murphy, "One Is All, and All Are One."
7. Murphy, "One Is All, and All Are One."
8. Joseph Chilton Pearce, *Magical Child*, Penguin, 1991, p.6.
9. Russell, *The Global Brain Awakens*, p. 319.
10. Murphy, "One Is All, and All Are One."

Afterword: Do You Want To Save Changes? [YES, NO, CANCEL, HELP]

1. "Week in Review," Vol. V, No. 29, April 2, 1994. Based on an address by Rebbe Shlita, Jan. 15, 1962.
2. "Week in Review," Vol. V, No. 29, April 2, 1994.

INDEX

Abrams, Jeremiah, *Meeting the Shadow,
The Hidden Power of the Dark Side of
Human Nature,* 299
Acceptance.
  See also SELF-ACCEPTANCE
  and SURRENDER, 38
  and UNCONDITIONAL LOVE,
    39, 187–89
Actions
  "golden rule" of, 216
  and habits. *See* Habits
  of Motofs, 254
  out of Lev, 180, 188–89, 257
  plan of, 242
  and REPAIR, 216–17
  right, 51, 170, 237, 254
  unselfish, 181–82
Adopters, 249–50
Adoption of innovations/ideas, 249*fig.*
Aeronautics, technology of, 80–81
Agape, love, 186
Ages of humanity, 63*fig.,* 101–4
  Agricultural Age, 62–63
  Consciousness Age, 7, 65–66, 269,
    305
  Industrial Age, 62–63
  Information Age, 62–63, 65, 182
  New Age, dawning of, 59, 105–8
  Stone Age, 62–63
Agricultural Age, 62–63
American dream, 98, 228–30, 275
Anthromorphization, 111
Appropriate technology. *See* Technology
Aristotle, 11, 163
Asexual reproduction, xiv
Atheism, 110
At-one-ment, 146, 189
Attitude, 33, 140, 142, 258
Auden, W. H., 193
Awareness. *See also* Consciousness
  of self, 198–99
  and WHOLENESS, 34, 150–53
BALANCE, 15, 161–66
  and COURAGE, 164
  as experienced by Motofs, 28
  and INNER VOICE, 164
  and MISSION, 241
  and personality types, 165–66
  and priorities, 162–63

proportion in, 164
and REPAIR, 218
summary of, 36
and SURRENDER, 164
and SYNERGY, 163
and WHOLENESS, 153, 166
Baron, Renee, *The Enneagram Made
Easy: Discover the 9 Types of People,*
296
Begin, Menachem, 257
Beyond-individual-survival-oriented
  living, 93
Beyond War
  *Breakthrough: Emerging New
    Thinking,* 316*n.*21:4
  movement, 224
Bhajan, Yogi, 177
Bible, references to
  Genesis, 176
  Hebrews' exodus, 46–48, 50, 252,
    257, 270
  Ten Commandments, 5–7, 46–47.
    See also Ten Commandments
Big bang theory, 102, 110, 264–65
Bonhoeffer, Dietrich, 109
BOTTOM LINES, 16, 193–201
  and boundaries, 29, 196, 198, 204
  as experienced by Motofs, 29
  features of, 196–97
  in relationships, 194–96, 206–7
  in romantic love, 199–201
  summary of, 40
  and SURRENDER, 194, 198
  and SYNERGY, 41, 198, 204, 206
  types of, 195
  and WHOLENESS, 194
Boundaries, 305
  and BOTTOM LINES, 29, 196,
    198, 204
  setting, 206
  and SYNERGY, 16, 41, 204–5, 207
Bradshaw, John, 3
  *Bradshaw On: The Family: A
    Revolutionary Way of Self-
    Discovery,* 297
Brain. *See also* Consciousness; Mind
  evolution of development of, 55–59,
    61
  function of, xv

hologram concept of, 265–66
utilization of, 171–72
Breakthrough: Emerging New Thinking
(Beyond War, Hellman, Gromyko),
316*n*.21:4
Buck, Pearl, 109

"Calendar Round", 102–3
Campbell, Joseph, 177, 228, 284
Carey, Ken, 257
Cellular phones, current use of, 79
Changes. *See also* Evolution
acceleration of, 69–71, 246–47
permanence of, 85–86
recent global, 21
resistance to
and adaptation, 249–50
of new technology, 93–94
of "old ways", 50, 226, 252–53
of rationalist movement, 106
summary of major, 71–85. *See also*
specific changes
Chemistry, human, 198–99
Christ, Jesus, messages of
"golden rule", 214–15
immortality of soul, 123
love thy neighbor, 39, 187–88
togetherness, 203
unity among souls, 107–8
Churchill, Winston, 181
Circle, WHOLENESS, 147–48, 194
*Closer to the Light, Learning from the
Near-Death Experiences of Children*
(Morse), 298
Code of values, 5–9. *See also* Values
Columbus, Christopher, 22
Commitment. *See* Relationships
Communication networks, 71, 78–80,
82–83
Compassion, 15, 39, 189–90. *See also*
UNCONDITIONAL LOVE
Computers, current use of, 72, 81–83
Confucius, 175
Connectivity, international, 82–83
Conscience, 223
Consciousness. *See also* Brain; Grok;
Mind; Wisdom
of choice in death, 255
definition of, 66, 305
development of higher

by following the 2nd Ten
Commandments, 54–55
pyramid of, 127
through discipline, 233–35
through INNER VOICE, 37,
57–58, 170–72
through REPAIR, 218–19
through spiritual evolution, 61
through UNCONDITIONAL
LOVE, 189
as future goal, 65–66
group, 59
raising corporate, 98
and reasoning ability, 56–57
shift to collective, 94, 104–8
and society, 48–49
and subconsciousness, 56, 58,
233–34
and technology, 21. *See also*
Technology
and UNCONDITIONAL LOVE,
39
and WHOLENESS, 34
Consciousness Age, 7, 65–66, 305
Constitution, personal, 239–41
Contraception, current use of, 84
Copernicus, 93–94, 110
Cortex region of brain, 56–57, 91, 128.
See also Brain
COURAGE, 15, 179–82
and BALANCE, 164
as experienced by Motofs, 29
and fear, 179
and FLOW, 142
and INNER VOICE, 38, 182
and MISSION, 176
and REPAIR, 218
summary of, 38
and SURRENDER, 180–82
unselfish, 182
and WHOLENESS, 146
Cousins, Norman, 223
Covey, Stephen R.
basis of doctrines of, 123
on effectiveness, 60
on habits, 238
maturity level defined by, 27
on priorities, 162

The 7 Habits of Highly Effective People, Powerful Lessons in Personal Change, 207, 240, 295
Covey Leadership Center, 316*n.*22:6
Creation myth, 126
Csikszentmihalyi, Mihaly, 140
   Flow: The Psychology of Optimal Experience, 297
Cytowic, Richard E., *The Man Who Tasted Shapes: A Bizarre Medical Mystery . . . ,* 297

Darwin, Charles, 250
Dawkins, Richard, 95
De Chardin, Pierre Teilhard, 92–93
Declaration for Universal Alliance through Sharing our Highest Common Ideals (Universal Star Alliance Foundation), 317*n.*23:14
DeMille, Cecil B., 60
Democratic governments, 71, 80
Dependent level of maturity, 27, 135
Descartes, Rene, 115, 123
Discipline, 141
Discovering Your Personality Type: The NEW Enneagram Questionnaire (Riso), 295
Divine guidance, 58, 179. *See also* God
DNA (deoxyribonucleic acid), xiv
Do What You Love, the Money Will Follow: Discovering Your Right Livelihood (Sinetar), 299
Dreams
   American dream, 98, 228–30, 275
   world dream, 98, 228, 230
Drucker, Peter F., 23

Earth. *See also* Evolution; Gaia
   destruction of. *See* Environment
   "school", concept of, 9, 49–50, 309*n.*1:3
   as superorganism, 56, 88–90, 266
Edison, Thomas A., 145
Education, importance of, 151, 242–43. *See also* Learning
Effectiveness, definition of, 60
Einstein, Albert
   belief in God of, 116, 119, 123
   theory of relativity of, 103, 110

Emerson, Ralph Waldo, 13
Emotions
   and INNER VOICE, 170
   source of, 57
   and UNCONDITIONAL LOVE, 187–89
Empowerment, 228. *See also* Power
Enlightenment, 150. *See also* Consciousness; Spirituality
Enneagram, 165, 235–37. *See also* PSPT
   Discovering Your Personality Type: The NEW Enneagram Questionnaire (Riso), 295
   The Enneagram in Love and Work: Understanding Your Intimate and Business Relationships (Palmer), 298
   The Enneagram Made Easy: Discover the 9 Types of People (Baron, Wagele), 296
Environment. *See also* Earth
   caretaking of, 42, 267
   destruction of, xvii–xviii, 5, 16–17, 91
   new rules of, 21
Erikson, Erik, 69
Eros, love, 186
"Evil" versus "good", 103, 216–19
Evolution. *See also* Changes; Earth; Humanity
   adaptation in, 246
   basic understanding of, 114
   global. *See* Gevolution
   of human brain, 55–59, 61. *See also* Brain
   of life, xiv–xvii, 4–5
   motive power of, 169
   pace of, 63–64
   of universe, 102, 110, 264–65
Existentialism, 110

"Faces of God" of the Kabbalah, 165
Fairness, 42, 215–16
Faith. *See also* Spirituality
   placement of, 111, 117
   spiritual, 125, 259–60, 307
Faxes sent, 79, 86
Fears
   of change, 251

and COURAGE, 179
freedom from, 134–35
immature, 182
influence of, on personality, 149
versus love, 55
reactions to, 187
survival, 4
techniques for controlling, 172
transcendence of, 67–68, 93–94,
128–29
and WHOLENESS, 180
Feldenkrais therapy, 278
Fiddler on the Roof, issue of tradition in,
226–27
Fight-or-flight response, 56
FLOW, 14, 139–42
and attitude, 33, 140, 142, 258
and BALANCE, 142
as experienced by Motofs, 28
learning in, 141
and MISSION, 141
summary of, 33
and SURRENDER-COURAGE,
142
and SYNERGY, 207
*Flow: The Psychology of Optimal
Experience* (Csikszemtmihalyi), 297
Forgiveness, 15, 39, 189–90
"Formation for Global Community"
movement, 224
Fractals, 264–65
Free choice
and BALANCE, 163–64
and becoming a Motof, 268–71
and COURAGE, 38
and habits, 238. *See also* Habits
and MISSION, 130–31, 174
and responsibility, 225
and spiritual principles, 60
and SURRENDER-COURAGE,
180–81
and SYNERGY, 204
and UNCONDITIONAL LOVE,
188
and WHOLENESS, 34, 146
Freedom
from fear, 134–35
and MISSION, 130–31, 174, 239
and WHOLENESS, 146–47
Freud, Sigmund, 149, 165

Frost, Robert, 177
Future Shock (Tofler), 70, 245, 299

Gaia. *See also* Earth
definition of, 305
effect of betrayal on, 173
experiences of, 132*fig.*
global brain of, 16–18, 93, 96. *See
also* Global brain
health of. *See* Health
and humankind, 90–93
hypothesis of, 88–90
oneness of, 258, 261, 263. *See also*
WHOLENESS
parts of, 131
Gaia: A New Look at Life on Earth
(Lovelock), 88
Genes
concept of, 110
definition of, 95
and learning, 148
Genetic information, xiv–xv
*Getting the Love you Want: The Guide for
Couples* (Hendrix), 296
Gev. *See also* God
concept of, 129
connection to, of higher mind,
170–71
definition of, 305
etymology of word, 114–15
placement of faith in, 117, 125,
259–60. *See also* Spirituality
purpose of name of, 116
as source of MISSION, 174–77,
264
Gevolution, 17, 258, 270, 305
Ghandi, Mahatma, 123, 171
Gilbert, W. S., 155
Global brain. *See also* Global society
definition of, 93, 305
formation of
estimated date for, 102–4, 108,
246–47, 250
through spirituality, 120–21
through SYNERGY, 204–5
through technology, xvi–xvii, 21,
92–93
function of, 96–97, 132
individual's role in. *See also* Motofs
accelerate evolution, 41, 59

acceptance of all others, 39, 187
finding personal MISSION, 37
maintain sanity, 162–63
management of Gaia, 16, 90–93
insanity of, risk of, 11
as last frontier, 58–59
laws of interaction in, 198
Motofs' belief in, 254
participation in, 248*fig.*
principles for development of,
xviii–xix
Global Brain, Inc., 271, 287
*The Global Brain Awakens: Our Next
Evolutionary Leap* (Russell), 101,
295
Global citizen. *See* Motofs
Global competition, 95
Global evolution. *See* Gevolution
Global language. *See* Language
*Global Mind Change, The New Age
Revolution in the Way We Think*
(Harman), 297
Global Promised Land, 22, 30–31, 131,
262–63. *See also* Lokelani
Global society. *See also* Global brain
adaptation of, 48–49, 94, 245
new age of, 59, 105–8
survival codes for, 5–9
Goals
and BALANCE, 15
prioritizing, 162, 241–42
God. *See also* Gev; Religions;
Spirituality
concept of, 109–13, 115–16
divine guidance of, 58, 179
etymology of word, 113
parable of God and Moses, 35
Golden mean, ethics of, 163
"Golden rule", 42, 214–16
Good deeds. *See* REPAIR
"Good" versus "evil", 103, 216–19
Gorbachev, Mikhail, 166, 316*n*.21:4
Governments, democratic, 71, 80
Gray, John, *Men are from Mars, Women
are from Venus,* 297
Green, Barth, 85
Grok. *See also* Consciousness
definition of, 31, 306
and higher wisdom, 58, 129
Growthologist, 269

Habits
versus conscious actions, 232–33
developing better, 237–38
giving up old, 251–53
Handbook to Higher Consciousness
(Keyes), 296
Happiness. *See also* Success; Win-win
definition of, 19
influence of Commandments on, 52
Harman, Willis, 94
*Global Mind Change, The New Age
Revolution in the Way We Think,*
297
Harmony
and SYNERGY, 41
and WHOLENESS, 146
Hate, 187
Hay, Louise, 213
You Can Heal Your Life, 296
Health. *See also* HIGH
BALANCE as key to, 164
in Consciousness Age, 269
discipline of, 234–35
effect of betrayal on, 173
and INNER VOICE, 174
and malignant behavior, 218–19
Hegel, Georg Wilhelm Friedrich, 133
Heinlein, Robert A., 31, 254
Stranger in a Strange Land, 70, 297
Hendrix, Harville, 199
*Getting the Love You Want: The
Guide for Couples,* 296
Herzl, Theodore, 273
Higher mind. *See* Consciousness
HIGH (Happy, Inwardly peaceful,
Growing, and Healthy), 128
High Speed Civil Transport Program,
81
Hillel (the Elder), 157–58, 215–16
Hologram concept of brain, 265–66.
See also Brain
Homeostatic condition, 88
Homo sapiens, 4, 103, 246. *See also*
Humanity
Honesty, 37, 173–74
Horney, Karen, 165
Humanity. *See also* Society
chemistry among, 198–99
duality of, 152–53

evolution of brain of, 55–59, 61. *See also* Brain
and freedom, 134–35
history of. *See also* Evolution
destruction, xvii–xviii, 5, 16–17
significance of, xiv
survival behavior in, 48, 56
time periods in, 62–63, 101–4. *See also* Consciousness Age; Information Age; New Age
interactions of, 198. *See also* Relationships
knowledge of. *See* Knowledge
language of. *See* Language
life-span of, 71, 74–75, 84–85, 252
nature of, 165–66
ongoing desires of, 262–63
relationship with Gaia, 90–93. *See also* Gaia; Global brain, individual's role in
spirit of. *See* Spirit; Spirituality
as system-level organisms, 173
trinity of makeup of, 152
values of. *See* Values
Hurry sickness, 279–80
Huxley, Aldous, 124, 171

Ideals, religious, 6
Ideas, adoption of, 249 *fig.*
Ikorgant, meaning of, 31, 306
"Imago Match", 199–200
Immortality, 255
Income, American, 228–30
Independent level of maturity, 27, 135
Industrial Age, 62–63
Information. *See also* Knowledge; Technology; Wisdom
evolution of processing, xiv–xvii
exchange of, 78–80
genetic, xiv–xv
influence of, on mind-sets, 64–65
management of, 8
prioritizing use of, 162–63
qualitatively significant, 57
Information Age, 62–63, 65, 182
Ingestor subsystem, 89
Ingression of novelty spiral, 77 *fig.*, 102
Inner child, 54, 152
Inner parent, 54, 152
INNER VOICE, 15, 169–77

and BALANCE, 164
and COURAGE, 38, 182
as experienced by Motofs, 28
and higher mind, 57–58, 170–72
and MISSION, 174–77, 240
and psychotechnology, 234
and REPAIR, 214–15
and reverence, 216
and self-esteem, 172–74
summary of, 37
and SURRENDER, 38, 173
and SYNERGY, 205
and WHOLENESS, 152, 216
and win-win, 208
Innovations
adoption of, 249 *fig.*
technological, 94. *See also* Technology
Integrity
and INNER VOICE, 37, 172, 174
in WHOLENESS circle, 147
Intelligence, 37. *See also* Consciousness; Knowledge; Wisdom
Intention, clear, 207–10
Interconnectedness. *See* WHOLENESS
Interdependent level of maturity, 27, 136, 255
Internet, 82
Intuition, 37, 58. *See also* INNER VOICE
Iroquois, Great Law of, 219
Israelite empire, 47–48

Jampolsky, Gerald G., *Love Is Letting Go of Fear,* 298
Jesus Christ. *See* Christ
JKLM (Joy, Knowledge, Lev, Mission), 126–32
Joy, 128, 131–32, 174
Jung, Carl, 149–50, 165, 169

Karma, 42, 172, 217–18
Katz, Barry M., 115
Technology and Culture: A Historical Romance, 298
Keller, Helen, 45
Keyes, Ken, Jr., 173, 186, 282
Handbook to Higher Consciousness, 296

The Power of Unconditional Love: 21 Guidelines . . . , 298
Your Life Is a Gift, So Make the Most of It, 295
Keyser, Svetlana, 278–79
King, Martin Luther, Jr., 10, 117, 166, 223
Knowledge, human. *See also* Information; Technology
  and faith, 110–11
  and Global brain, 131–32
  versus grok, 129. *See also* Grok
  rapid increases in, 75–76, 77 *fig.,* 310*n.*5:9
Kopelman, Orion Moshe
  on assembly of *2nd Ten Commandments,* 8–11
  Personal Constitution of, 290–91
  personal journey of, 274–88
  philosophy of, 267

Ladder of spiritual success, 209 *fig.*
Laggards, 250
Lamb, Janina, 261
Language, human
  complications of, 186–87
  global, 72, 81, 96, 255
  new terminology in, 23–26
Leadership
  and BALANCE, 166
  and COURAGE, 15
  of Motofs, 256–58. *See also* Motofs, as leaders of gevolution
Learning. *See also* Education
  in FLOW, 141
  and genes, 148
  as means toward WHOLENESS, 151
Lehrer, Marc, 279, 283, 286, 288–89
Lev. *See also* JKLM; UNCONDITIONAL LOVE
  actions taken out of, 180, 188–89, 257
  definition of, 129–30, 306
  experience of, 131–32
  and oneness, 129, 189–90. *See also* WHOLENESS
  and REPAIR, 218
  and WHOLENESS, 129, 148, 189–90

Life
  Bradshaw on, 3
  Hay on, 213
  Keller on, 3
  respect for, 146
  systems and subsystems of, 89–90
  Wilde on, 213
Life-span, human, 71, 74–75, 84–85, 252
Limbic region of brain, 56–57. *See also* Brain
Litvak, Rabbi Rick, 282
Logic, development of, 171–72. *See also* Mind
Lokelani, 126, 258–60, 306. *See also* Global Promised Land
Lombardi, Vincent J., 231
Love. *See also* Lev; UNCONDITIONAL LOVE
  versus fear, 55
  romantic, 199–201
  of self, 155
  Tillich on, 185
  types of, 186–87
Love Is Letting Go of Fear (Jampolsky), 298
Lovelock, James, *Gaia: A New Look at Life on Earth,* 88
Loyalty
  and INNER VOICE, 37, 173–74
  King on, 223
  in WHOLENESS circle, 147–48

MacLean, Paul, 56
Magical Child (Pearce), 265–66
Majorities, 249–50
Male myths, 286
Mandelbrot, Benoit, 264–65
The Man Who Tasted Shapes: A Bizarre Medical Mystery . . . (Cytowic), 297
Margolin, Marcia, 279
Marriage, 75
Martiain, Jacques, 101
Maslow, Abraham, 29, 127–28, 152
  Toward a Psychology of Being, 298
Materialism, 17, 48, 68, 149
Maturity
  continuum of, 27
  dependent level of, 27, 135
  independent level of, 27, 135

interdependent level of, 27, 136
Nietzsche on, 139
McKenna, 102
Mead, Margaret, 267
Medicine, advances in, 72, 84–85
Meditation, 234
Medulla region of brain, 56. *See also*
Brain
*Meeting the Shadow, The Hidden Power
of the Dark Side of Human Nature*
(Abrams, Zweig), 299
Memes
conflicts surrounding, 94–95
definition of, 306
*Men are from Mars, Women are from
Venus* (Gray), 297
Metaphors, educational use of, 11
Miller, James, 89
Millman, Dan, 225
*Way of the Peaceful Warrior: A Book
that Changes Lives,* 298
Mind. *See also* Brain; Consciousness
rational, 57–58, 171
states of, 57
subconscious, 56, 58, 233–34
"wars", 95
MISSION, 15, 169–77
definition of, 129
as experienced by Motofs, 28
and FLOW, 141
freedom of, 130–31, 174, 239
and INNER VOICE, 174, 177, 240
summary of, 37
and SURRENDER-COURAGE,
176
understanding personal, 129–32,
174–77, 240–41
and WHOLENESS, 152
Moderation, 36
Monotheism, 110
Moral codes, 105, 214–16. *See also*
Values
Morse, Melvin, *Closer to the Light,
Learning from the Near-Death
Experiences of Children,* 298
Moses. *See* Bible
Motofs. *See also* Global brain, individual's role in
adaptability of, 249–53

coping with societal changes,
225–28
definition of, 11, 25, 306
estimate of number of, 246–50,
248 *fig.*
facing fear, 134–35
as leaders of gevolution, 17–18, 98,
132, 166, 224–25, 256–58
level of maturity of, 27
path to becoming, 30–31, 68, 136,
232–43
agreement with Global concepts,
254–56
English as language of, 255
exemplary, 28–29
interdependent values, 255
kinship, 66–68
leadership of Gevolution, 256–58
live by 2nd Ten Commandments,
254
new approach to survival, 255
openness, 253–54
respect for appropriate technology,
254–55
right actions, 254
world dream of, 98, 228, 230
Mountain Computer, Inc., 275–76,
287
Muller, Robert, 119
*New Genesis: Shaping a Global
Spirituality,* 296–97
Mumford, Lewis, 161
Myers-Briggs personality tests, 165

Namasté, definition of, 189
NASA (National Aeronautics and Space
Administration), 81
Natural selection, 250
Needs
hierarchy of, 127–28
physical versus psychological, xviii
survival, 4, 56, 71, 78
Neomammalian brain, 56. *See also*
Brain
New Age, dawning of, 59, 105–8
*New Genesis: Shaping a Global
Spirituality* (Muller), 296–97
"New World", 22
Nietzsche, Friedrich, 139
"No-deal" option, 208

Non-locality principle, 265
Noosphere, 93

Objectives, 241–42. *See also* MISSION
Oneness. *See also* WHOLENESS
  with Gaia, 258, 261, 263
  and Lev, 129, 189–90
  science's search for, 264–66
  of spirit, 121, 125, 129, 258
  and spirituality, 263
Openness
  as characteristic of Motofs, 253–54
  and UNCONDITIONAL LOVE,
    187–89

Pacesetters, 249
Paleomammalian region of brain, 56.
  See also Brain
Palmer, Helen, *The Enneagram in Love
  and Work: Understanding Your
  Intimate and Business Relationships,*
  298
Parables, 31–32
  of Brah Harris, 39
  of God and Moses, 35
  of King Solomon, 36
  of Outasync and Samaritan, 42
  of Plato, 37
  of Prince Profitus, 40
  of Shela, 34
  of the sparrow and the mountain, 41
  of Sufi Dervish, 33
  of Wei-Chei Ho, 38
Peace agreement
  Israel-Egypt, 257
  Israel-PLO, 80
Pearce, Joseph Chilton, *Magical Child,*
  265–66
Peck, M. Scott, *The Road Less Traveled:
  A New Psychology of Love, Traditional
  Values and Spiritual Growth,* 296
Perfection
  quest for, 148–50
  and SELF-ACCEPTANCE, 35,
    156–57
Perseverance, 141
Personal constitution, 239–41
Personality
  formation of, 149
  and SELF-ACCEPTANCE, 157

testing. *See* PSPT
  types, 165–66, 235–37
Perspective, 15, 36
Philia, love, 186
Philosophy
  of golden mean, 163
  perennial, 124
  of soul, 123
Planetary clan, 246
Pollard, John K., III, *Self-Parenting: The
  Complete Guide to Your Inner
  Conversations,* 296
Polytheism, 110
Pope, Alexander, 87
Population. *See also* Society
  adapting, concept of, 249–50
  aging of, 252
  growth of Earth's, 71–72, 73*fig.,* 74
  production of sustenance by, 71, 78
Postal Service, U. S., 79
Power, assuming, 176, 180–81, 228
*The Power of Unconditional Love: 21
  Guidelines . . .* (Keyes), 298
Prayer, function of, 177. *See also*
  Religions; Spirituality
Principle-centered behavior, 237–38
Principles, spiritual, 307
Priorities, 15, 162–63
Proactive, meaning of, 164
Proportion, concept of, 164
PSPT (Psychospiritual Personality
  Typing), 165–66, 235, 237, 306
Psychologist, spiritual, 269
Psychotechnology, 234

QRPD (quality rapid product development), 10
Quantum physics, 264–65

Rand, Ann, *The Virtue of Selfishness,*
  298
Rationalist movement, 106, 115
Rational mind. *See* Mind
Reasoning ability, 56–57
Relationships
  and BOTTOM LINES, 16, 40,
    194–201, 206–7
  as experienced by Motofs, 29
  exploitation in, 193
  and INNER VOICE, 173–74

and REPAIR, 218
romantic, 199–201
and SYNERGY, 206, 209–10
types of love in, 186–87
Relativity, theory of, 110
Religions. *See also* God; Spirituality
basis of monotheistic, 6, 55
definition of, 107
doctrine of respect for life, 146
need for unity among, 112–13,
119–22
as parental guiding force, 54
versus science, 109, 115–17, 119
truth, concept of, in, 171
world membership in, 293
Religious persons, 169, 171
REPAIR, 16, 213–20
as experienced by Motofs, 29
and the "golden rule", 214–16
and good deeds, 16, 215–19
and success, 242
summary of, 42
and SURRENDER-COURAGE,
218
Reproduction, xiv
Responsibility
and BALANCE, 164
and MISSION, 176
of Motofs, 224–25. *See also* Motofs
and REPAIR, 219
and SELF-ACCEPTANCE, 35, 156
of society, 49–50
and SURRENDER-COURAGE,
180
in technology, 93–98
and win-win, 208
Reverence, 42, 215–16
*RHETI (Riso-Hudson Enneagram Type
Indicator)*, 165
Riso, Don Richard, 227
*Discovering Your Personality Type: The
NEW Enneagram Questionnaire*,
295
Robbins, Anthony, 231
Rogers, Everett, 249–50
Roles, identifying, 240–42
Roosevelt, Franklin D., 166, 189
Ruskin, John, 145
Russell, Peter
on current times, xiii–xiv, 8

on destruction of environment,
xvii–xviii
on evolution of life, xiv–xvii
*The Global Brain Awakens: Our Nex
Evolutionary Leap*, 101, 295
on high-synergy society, 87
on humankind's function, 90–91
on Kopelman's work, xviii–xix
*The White Hole in Time, Our Future
Evolution and the Meaning of
Now*, 298–99

Sadat, Anwar, 10, 257
Saint-Exupéry, Antoine de, 185, 203
St. John, Gloria, 287
Satir, Virginia, 135
Satori, concept of, 140
Science's search for oneness, 264–66
Scientific knowledge, 75–76, 77*fig.*,
110–11. *See also* Knowledge;
Technology
S-curves
of adoption of ideas, 249
growth of Motofs, 248*fig.*
population changes, 72, 73*fig.*
shift in consciousness, 104*fig.*
The Seat of the Soul (Zukav), 296
Seattle, Chief, 245
2nd Ten Commandments. *See also indi-
vidual Commandments*
cohesiveness of, 135–36
compared to original Ten
Commandments, 50–55, 156
as guidelines for success, 20, 26–27,
60–62, 266, 269
Motofs' belief in, 254
overview of, 14–16
BALANCE, 161–66
BOTTOM LINES, 193–201
FLOW, 139–42
INNER VOICE-MISSION,
169–77
REPAIR, 213–20
SELF-ACCEPTANCE, 155–59
SURRENDER-COURAGE,
179–82
SYNERGY, 203–10
UNCONDITIONAL LOVE,
185–90
WHOLENESS, 145–53

purpose of, 11, 16–18
terminology used in, 23–26
Security, concept of, 45
"Sefirot", 165
Selection, natural, 250
SELF-ACCEPTANCE, 15, 155–59
  as experienced by Motofs, 28
  for the greater whole, 157–59
  and perfection, 156–57
  summary of, 35
  and WHOLENESS, 148
Self-actualization, 29
  definition of, 128
  pyramid of, 127
  and WHOLENESS, 146, 148, 152
Self-destructive behavior, 251
Self-esteem
  and INNER VOICE, 37, 172–74
  and MISSION, 174
  in WHOLENESS circle, 147–48
Self-evaluation, 165–66, 236
Self-expression, 175
Selfishness, 17
Self-knowledge, 198–99
Self-love, 155
*Self-Parenting: The Complete Guide to
  Your Inner Conversations* (Pollard),
  296
Self-sufficiency, 216
"Serenity Prayer", 180
"Seven Deadly Sins", 165
*The 7 Habits of Highly Effective People,
  Powerful Lessons in Personal Change*
  (Covey), 240, 295
Sexual reproduction, xiv
Shakespeare, William, 161, 179
Shaw, George Bernard, 169
Shedd, William, 45
Sinetar, Marsha, *Do What You Love the
  Money Will Follow: Discovering Your
  Right Livelihood,* 299
Slave-mentality, 5–7, 47–48, 252
Smoots, George, 264
Society. *See also* Global society;
  Humanity; Population
  acceptance of new paradigm of,
    252–53
  adaptation of, 246
  adaptation to, 269
  and consciousness, 48–49

high-SYNERGY, 204–6, 215–16
  responsibility of, 49–50
  Russell on, 87
Socrates, 225, 227, 273
Soul. *See also* Spirit; Spirituality
  definition of, 307
  existence of, 123–24
  as higher consciousness, 122, 170
  and Lev, 131–32
Speech, function of, xv–xvi
Spirit. *See also* Soul; Spirituality
  belief in human, 120
  definition of, 307
  as higher consciousness, 122, 170
  oneness of, 121, 125, 129, 258. *See
    also* WHOLENESS
Spirituality. *See also* Religions
  definition of, 120–21, 307
  as doctrine, 123–24
  and faith, 117. *See also* Faith
  global. *See also* Gev
  as characteristic of Motofs, 254
  cornerstones of, 124–25, 190
  definition of, 306
  and development of Global brain,
    120–22
  supra-religion of, 107–8, 113, 120,
    307
  guidelines for, 26
  and Karma, 217–18
  ladder of success, 209*fig.*
  and oneness, 263. *See also* WHOLE-
    NESS
  practical, 21–22
  and prayer, 177
  principles of, 59–60
  psychologist of, 269
  rules of, 214–16
  as value, 17
Steinsaltz, Adin, *The Thirteen Petaled
  Rose,* 299
Stone Age, 62–63
Stranger In A Strange Land (Heinlein),
  70, 297
Subconscious mind, 56, 58, 233–34
Substance abuse, 251
Success. *See also* Happiness; Win-win
  and American income, 228–30
  in Consciousness Age, 59–66
  definition of, 19, 60, 307

Emerson on, 13
following spiritual principles, 60–61
and INNER VOICE-MISSION, 37
ladder of spiritual, 209 *fig.*
and levels of maturity, 27
Lombardi on, 231
new rules for, 21
personal constitution for, 239–41
and REPAIR, 242
Robbins on, 231
2nd Ten Commandments as guidelines for, 20, 26–27, 60–62, 266,
269
through personal evolution, 242
through SYNERGY, 207–10
Superorganism, 56, 91–93. *See also*
Gaia
Supra-culture, 255–56
Supra-religion. *See* Spirituality, global
SURRENDER, 15, 179–82
and BALANCE, 164
and BOTTOM LINES, 194, 198
and COURAGE, 180–82
as experienced by Motofs, 28–29
and FLOW, 142
and INNER VOICE, 38, 173, 182
mature, 181–82
and MISSION, 176
and REPAIR, 218
summary of, 38
Survival
beyond-individual-survival-oriented
living, 93
codes for global, 5–9
fears, 4
history of human, 48, 56
needs, 4, 56, 71, 78
new approach to, 255
Sustenance, production of, 71, 78
Synchronicity, 284
SYNERGY, 16, 203–10
and BOTTOM LINES, 41, 198,
204, 206
as experienced by Motofs, 29
and INNER VOICE, 205
natural law of, 204
and reverence, 215–16
in society, 87, 204–6, 215–16
summary of, 41
through common vision, 207–10

and UNCONDITIONAL LOVE,
188
and WHOLENESS, 152
System-level organism, 173

Technology. *See also* Information;
Knowledge
of aeronautics, 80–81
appropriate, 9, 93–98, 254–55, 305
collaborative links through, 205–6
of communication networks, 71,
78–80, 82
and consciousness, 21
fear of, 251
innovations in, 94
for provision of sustenance, 71, 78
psychotechnology, 234
rapid advances in, xiii–xiv, xvi, 7,
64, 71–72, 75–76, 77 *fig.*
and values, 5, 11, 17
*Technology and Culture: A Historical
Romance* (Katz), 298
Telephones, current use of, 79
Television, cable, 79
Ten Commandments, original
acceptance of, in U.S., 254
as code of values, 5–7, 46–47
compared to 2nd Ten
Commandments, 50–55, 156
interpretation of 6th of, 309 *n.*4:1
as spiritual guidelines, 26
Theory
of relativity, 110
unified field, xiii
*The Road Less Traveled: A New
Psychology of Love, Traditional Values
and Spiritual Growth* (Pec), 296
The Thirteen Petaled Rose (Steinsaltz),
299
Tikkun, 218
Tillich, Paul, 185
Time, 33
Tofler, Alvin, 69, 245
Future Shock, 70, 299
Tomlin, Lily, 19
Toward a Psychology of Being (Maslow),
298
Tradition
issue of, 226–27, 253
wisdom behind, xviii

Travel, worldwide, 71, 80–81
Tribe, concept of, 66–67
Trinity, human, 152
Triune model of brain, 56. *See also* Brain
Trust
    and INNER VOICE, 37, 174
    mutual, 254
    and WHOLENESS, 148
Truth
    of the heart, 286
    and INNER VOICE, 171, 173
Turner, Ted, 13, 101

UNCONDITIONAL LOVE, 15, 185–90. *See also* Lev; Love
    complications in understanding of, 186–87
    as experienced by Motofs, 29
    and openness, 187–89
    and REPAIR, 214
    summary of, 39
    and SYNERGY, 188
Unified field theory, xiii
Universal Star Alliance Foundation, *Declaration for Universal Alliance through Sharing our Highest Common Ideals,* 317 n.23:14
Universe, science of, 102, 110, 264–65

Values
    core of human, xvii–xix
    and moral codes, 104–5
    of Motofs, 255
    needed changes in system of, 179
    personal statement of, 239–41
    and technology, 5, 11, 17
    Ten Commandments as code of, 5–7, 46–47
    universal code of, 5–9
Virtual reality systems, 82
The Virtue of Selfishness (Rand), 298
Vision, common, 207–10
Voltaire, François, 155
Von Goethe, Johann Wolfgang, 162

Wagele, Elizabeth, *The Enneagram Made Easy: Discover the 9 Types of People,* 296
Watson, Patricia, 257

Way of the Peaceful Warrior: A Book that Changes Lives (Millman), 298
The White Hole in Time, Our Future Evolution and the Meaning of Now (Russell), 298–99
WHOLENESS, 14–15, 145–53. *See also* Oneness
    awareness as means toward, 150–53
    and BALANCE, 153, 166
    and BOTTOM LINES, 194
    circle, 147–48, 194
    and COURAGE, 146
    as experienced by Motofs, 28
    and fears, 180
    and free choice, 146
    and INNER VOICE, 152, 216
    and learning, 151
    and Lev, 129, 148, 189–90
    and perfection, 148–50
    and reverence, 216
    and romantic love, 199
    summary of, 34
Wilde, Oscar, 116, 213
Win-win
    definition of, 204, 307
    for success, 207–10. *See also* Success
    and SYNERGY, 16, 29, 41, 205–6
Wisdom, perennial, xviii, 24, 117, 129. *See also* Consciousness
Witt-Miller, Harriet, 264–65
World dream, 98, 228, 230
Wounded healers, 274
"Wrinkles in time" theory, 264

Yeltsin, Boris, 65
Yom Kippur War, 257
You Can Heal Your Life (Hay), 296
Your Life Is a Gift, So Make the Most of It (Keyes), 295

Zukav, Gary, 126, 228
    The Seat of the Soul, 296
Zweig, Connie, *Meeting the Shadow, The Hidden Power of the Dark Side of Human Nature,* 299

NOTES

NOTES

Available from
Global Brain™, Inc...
Synergizing Technology & Consciousness

	Quantity	Total
The 2nd Ten Commandments, book Orion Kopelman with Marc Lehrer, Ph.D., Hard cover, $19.95		
The Global Brain Awakens, book Peter Russell Hard cover, $22		
The Global Brain, Video Peter Russell 35 minutes, $30		
The Prenatal Classroom, book Rene Van de Carr, M.D. & Marc Lehrer, Ph.D. Soft cover, $16.95		
The White Hole In Time, book Peter Russell Soft cover, $11		
The White Hole In Time Video Peter Russell 27 minutes, $30		
Q*R*PD: The Guidebook to Quality *Rapid* Product Development Orion Kopelman binder, $49		
Quality *Rapid* Product Development, Video, A one hour short course Orion Kopelman $89		
Five hour Quality *Rapid* Product Development Video course, $395		
Sub Total =		

Order Here...

☎ **Fax orders: (415) 327-2028**

✆ **Telephone orders and more information:**
Toll free 1-800-U-GO-GLOBAL (1-800- 846-4562).
Outside of the USA, call (415) 327-2012

✆ **On-Line orders: GloblBrain@aol.com or**
http://www.globalbrain.com/global/2ndten

✉ **Mail orders: Global Brain, Inc., 555 Bryant St, #369,**
Palo Alto, California, USA 94301-1704

Name: _____

Company: _____

Address: _____

City:_____ State:_____Zip: _____

Tel#:_____ Fax#: _____

E-mail: _____

Sales Tax, California residents only: please add 7.75% sales tax.

Domestic Shipping & Handling: $4.50 + $1 for each additional item. Please call for international and overnight rates.

Green Tax* Add 5%. Paper costs the planet...Green Tax is a contribution that you **_voluntarily_** make and Global Brain, Inc. dispenses it to environmentally restorative projects.

Payment

Sub Total:	$ _____
CA tax, 7.75%:	$ _____
Ship & Handling:	$ _____
Green tax*:	$_____
TOTAL DUE:	$_____

Please check off appropriate box....

☐ Check enclosed ☐ Money Order enclosed

Credit card:

☐ Visa ☐ MasterCard ☐ American Express ☐ Discover

card number: _____exp. date:_____

name on card: _____